D0442084

# Piaget
# and
# Knowledge

*Der Primat des Intellekts liegt gewiss in weiter, weiter, aber wahrscheinlich nicht in unendlicher Ferne.*

FREUD

*PRENTICE-HALL, INC.,* Englewood Cliffs, New Jersey

# Piaget
# and
# Knowledge

THEORETICAL FOUNDATIONS

## HANS G. FURTH

Department of Psychology
Catholic University of America

Library of Congress Catalog No. 68-31732

Printed in the United States of America

Current printing (last digit):

10  9  8  7  6  5  4  3


PRENTICE-HALL INTERNATIONAL, INC., *London*

PRENTICE-HALL OF AUSTRALIA, PTY. LTD., *Sydney*

PRENTICE-HALL OF CANADA, LTD., *Toronto*

PRENTICE-HALL OF INDIA PRIVATE LTD., *New Delhi*

PRENTICE-HALL OF JAPAN, INC., *Tokyo*

# *foreword*

JEAN PIAGET

This excellent book by Professor Furth answers a real need and therefore in no way duplicates the conscientious summaries that have previously appeared in Italian and German under the authorship of G. Petter or in English under the authorship of J. Flavell. These latter introductions to our Genevan work were principally meant for a large audience which was more interested in factual than in theoretical questions. This audience was apparently satisfied with a psychology in the strict (or narrow) sense and felt no concern with those fundamental relations which a theory of development, if it is at all comprehensive, must necessarily establish with biological and epistemological perspectives. In this connection I do not forget other works, such as the scholarly study of P. Wolff, relating my ideas and Freudian theory, or the fine surveys contained in the works of J. McV. Hunt, R. Brown and A. Baldwin. But here, too, we are still confined to psychology in the limited sense of the term.

In contrast, the present study goes beyond that limit, without of course neglecting the genuine requirements or interests of a psychological science. On the contrary, Furth dwells on my basic theoretical positions the better to clarify psychological problems. In fact, I have never been able to imagine, much less to do, psychological research without constantly keeping in mind the interdisciplinary relations which more and more (and now more than ever) all contemporary natural sciences must establish between themselves and towards other sciences. In the particular case of a psychology of development and of the cognitive functions, there are links with biology on the one hand and, on the other hand, with all other disciplines that can teach us something about the nature and the evolution of reason—in particular, links with epistemology, including its inherent connection to the history of sciences and logic.

To begin with biology, Furth has admirably understood my position which I did not spell out in great detail until my recent book *Biologie et connaissance.* (It has always seemed to me that a valid interpretation of cognitive functions and their development must take into account biological considerations.) Biology imposes profound modifications upon a stimulus-response model, notwithstanding the great number of psychologists who do not see the relevance of these points. In fact, a response is a biological reaction, and contemporary biology has demonstrated that the reaction cannot be determined merely by outside factors but depends on "reaction norms" which are characteristic for each genotype or each genetic pool. This fact implies an indissociable interaction between interior structures and the stimulations of the external environment. (A stimulus cannot be active unless it is assimilated to schemes of reactions which provoke the response. This assimilation, and not associations to which one so often limits the analysis, constitutes the primary process insofar as assimilation makes associations possible.)

In short, biological considerations lead to the three following fundamental notions: (1) the organization or internal structures to which the environment is assimilated; (2) the epigenetic constructions (proper to the development of the phenotypes) which come about through indissociable interactions between the structure and the environment; and (3) the progressive self-regulation or equilibration which assures the mechanism of these constructions. It would seem that one cannot explain the development of intelligence without recourse to these three kinds of notions. Thus it remains a mystery to me that the typical theories of learning are so little concerned with these notions.

Throughout the book Furth shows very clearly how these notions form the basis of our theory. His chapters 2 and 14 in particular provide appropriate overviews for the reader. The structures with which to start are the general coordinations of actions as the source of the future logical and operational structures. However, there is in these coordinations no preformation or predetermination of logic, since a long period of construction is required that leads from the limited source to the richness of the final structures. The continuity of this construction is based on an indefinite sequence of "reflecting abstractions." Moreover, this construction is regulated according to a partially intrinsic determination. The "operations" constitute the final term of these self-regulations. Hence there is a central factor of equilibration which is necessary to explain development. This alone suffices to show why development can never be reduced to a mere succession of empirical acquisitions.

The biological dimension, indispensable for our interpretation of development, has thus been well propounded by the author of the present work. But Furth has as well understood the necessity of the logical and epistemological dimension which completes the picture. When one sets out to do experimental psychological research with subjects of a given intellectual stage (adults or infants), it is easy to dissociate the purely psychological questions of functioning from the epistemological questions of validity or of the subject-object relation. But if the aim of research, as is ours, is to explain the development of intelligence and to comprehend how from elementary forms of cognition superior levels of intelligence and scientific thinking come about, one faces then the classic problem of epistemology: How is scientific thinking possible? Instead of dealing with this problem in the abstract or by purely speculative or reflective methods, we have attempted to explain knowledge by its very development. Philosophers at times argue that we have here two separate questions; but they forget that no science is complete and that all knowledge is ever in a state of transformation, hence of development. As for psychologists, they should certainly consider epistemological questions as legitimate problems of their interest without, however, attaching themselves in advance to any of the possible solutions. The role of the experimental study of cognitive development is precisely to demonstrate whether a particular solution is or is not appropriate. For example, it is a question of fact, consequently a problem of psychological demonstration, whether logical operations derive primarily from language or from the general coordinations of actions. It is a question of fact whether these coordinations come about independent of all physical experience or are constructed little by little through interaction of subject and object. It is a question of fact whether analytic and synthetic judgments are clearly distinct at all levels of development or whether there are transitions between them; etc., etc.

In a word, the work of Furth insists throughout on the biological and epistemological dimension of the questions that are being asked, over and above their narrow psychological aspects. In this task Furth appears to us to have been remarkably successful. In fact, the reader will find detailed discussions on operative knowing, on assimilation and accommodation, on symbols or figurative representations, particularly also on the relation between development through equilibration and through learning. Thanks to his comprehensive perspective, the author has unquestionably clarified all these important topics.

It is a pleasure in this preface to have insisted with Furth on some of the fundamental notions which he has so well understood. We are very grateful for this effort and are sure that this book will render most valuable service to an understanding of the problems of development which we have investigated.

# *preface*

It seems trivial for an author to say that his book was written because a need existed which the writing of the book was meant to fill. Yet in a way this is my only justification. For a number of years, I have been trying to understand Piaget's thought and employ it both in my research and teaching. As I studied the increasing number of books coming out of Geneva, I kept making mental notes on sundry theoretical points in order to unify my understanding and relate earlier notions to more recent formulations by Piaget. A sabbatical at Piaget's center provided an unusual opportunity for personal contact with Piaget and his associates. I could therefore observe the ongoing research before it was put into print in French publication. Moreover, judging by past precedents, it is uncertain as to which portions of Piaget's present work will finally appear in English translation. Last but not least, I had sufficient time at hand to put my mental notes into writing. While doing so, I could not help but notice that the growing popularity of Piaget was not matched by a proportionate understanding of some of his chief theoretical notions.

Initially, I had set out to write a book at a more popular

level with emphasis on the educational implications of Piaget's theory. I had planned to highlight in two or three introductory chapters those theoretical notions which were most widely misinterpreted. As I proceeded in this endeavor I came to realize that a popular summary —if this is possible—must be preceded by more scholarly research. This book is therefore both a witness to my failure to write a simplified summary and the result of examining Piaget's psychological theory of knowledge in a consistent and exhaustive manner. While I have not discarded my original idea and the application of Piaget's theory to education remains a point of great concern for me, I believe that this present rendering of Piaget's theory should be helpful to the serious student and serve as a motive for deeper study of Piaget's own theoretical writings.

One may ask: In what respect does this book represent Piaget's authentic opinion? Since Piaget has always avoided forming a school in the sense that an official viewpoint is presented and enforced, there can be no question here of setting one interpretation against another or of citing one passage in order to argue against another passage. As a matter of fact, when I state that Piaget's theory is misunderstood, this refers not so much to the fact that too many different opinions of his theory have been expounded, rather to the opposite that unhappily too little serious thought is given to his theory. If this introduction to Piaget's theory should become the occasion for a lively critical discussion on the points mentioned in the book as well as on other theoretical questions raised by his work, this would be a most desirable outcome indeed.

Take a sample of questions like these: In what manner are sensory-motor acts interiorized to become operations? What happens to accommodation on the operational level? Can there be physical abstraction without reflecting abstraction? Does every symbol have a figurative and an operative aspect, or just one of these aspects, or neither? Why is intelligence the structural aspect of behavior? In what way is a logical model arbitrary or necessary? What are the differences among equilibration, development, and maturation? What exactly is internalized in image formation? Is accommodation synonymous with learning? Such questions—and there are many others like it—are not a matter of splitting hairs. Rather they seem to be central problems for anyone who would give Piaget's theory more than a passing nod of acquaintance. Yet would anyone know where to turn for a ready answer to these questions, either in Piaget's own books or in the writings of other scholars who have summarized his work?

Piaget himself has discussed all the elements which enter into our questions, but he has written about them in different contexts and from different viewpoints. Can a theorist with a progressively developing theory be blamed for not saying everything in his theory from every angle? Is not Piaget's time and effort well taken up by opening up new vistas and constructing new approaches? Thus it is up to the student to extract answers from an overall understanding of his theory. In going about this task, I have made a constant effort to rephrase the ideas in my own terms rather than repeating the words of Piaget. Thus in the main body of the text I have avoided quotations altogether. If this is considered a blameworthy omission, the reading sections together with the footnotes should in part make up for this deficiency.

While I am obviously sympathetic to Piaget's general theory, I trust I have not been a blind or uncritical follower. The reader should have no difficulty in distinguishing those passages where I am just summarizing Piaget's explicit teaching from others where I am interpreting him and from those where I state my opinion in projecting or in opposing Piaget's formulations. Nevertheless, it may be opportune to list here the main notions in which my personal interpretations go beyond Piaget's explicit writings. 1) The process of operational *interiorization* is differentiated from symbolic *internalization*. 2) The figurative aspect in language, as in other symbolic instruments, is given emphasis. 3) Accommodation is defined as the application of a knowing structure to a particular instance regardless of whether it issues in a new structure. 4) Insofar as "reflecting" abstraction is considered to be the primary source of growth in general knowledge at all stages it is here not limited to the operational period of intellectual development. Mainly for this reason I term it "formal" abstraction, the word *formal* referring to a general *form* that is progressively dissociated from particular *content*. 5) An attempt is made to relate Piaget's theory to the growth of knowledge in evolution, interpreted in terms of the writings of K. Lorenz. In addition it will be noted that I have discontinued the usual practice of translating Piaget's *schème* as "schema" for the simple reason that Piaget himself distinguishes *schème* from *schéma*; these two words are here rendered as "scheme" and "schema" respectively.

The manuscript was critically read by my colleagues in Washington, D.C. at the Catholic University Center for Research in Thinking and Language—J. Youniss, B. Ross, and H. Hoemann—as well as by B. Inhelder and H. Sinclair from Geneva. This is an appropriate place to thank them for their encouragement and critical comments, the benefits of which are handed to the reader. Some points were also discussed with J. Piaget as well as with other members working at the International Center of Genetic Epistemology in Geneva. I mention these names with a certain degree of uneasiness because I may thereby give the impression of making them responsible for the authenticity of interpretations. This is of course not the case at all, as anybody knows who is acquainted with the ordinary process of critical writing. Nevertheless, the ready acceptance of my general approach to Piaget's theory on the part of persons closely associated with him should be of some assurance to the reader that Piaget would recognize his thinking in the pages that follow.

This book is therefore a general introduction to Piaget's theory, or more precisely, to those general theoretical questions that are of primary concern to the psychological investigator. Not only does it leave out whole content areas or mention them only in passing—e.g. space, time, number, causality—it also limits itself to those theoretical questions that have general implications and are in need of clarification from an overall viewpoint. Thus very little is said about Piaget's specific statistical theory of perception, but the relation of field effects to operativity is gone into in considerable detail. Piaget's formal logical systems are given less space than the general factors of equilibration and reflective abstraction from which natural logico-mathematical thinking derives. Since I was writing as a psychologist and for psychologists, I have only barely mentioned strictly epistemological and philosophical questions.

Finally, I should explicitly state two tendencies of mine which naturally color my way of seeing and interpreting Piaget's work. One is a consistent attempt on my part to present Piaget's theory as having the widest possible application to all areas of human behavior and not only as something that is suitable for an explanation of logico-mathematical thinking in the narrow sense of the term. All behavior implies some structuring that manifests the same internal biological organization which, according to Piaget, also underlies logical thinking. My manner of somewhat enlarging Piaget's symbol theory and my suggestions for a change in terminology are inspired by this same concern for a wider application of his theory.

My second preoccupation is expressed by the fact that nearly one-third of the text is devoted to general biological problems. It has long impressed me that Piaget deals with biological intelligence and not with the intelligence referred to in the studies of individual differences or learning theories to which most of us are accustomed. I am unable to see how one can feel at home with his model of intelligence unless one sees intelligence as a prolongation of organic development. Without a biological basis, Piaget's formal logical model becomes what to many it unfortunately appears: a cold, artificial system of ratiocination that has no relevance to full blooded real life. In like manner, a notion like equilibration must remain incomprehensible if one's gaze extends no further than the external factors that influence the growth of intelligence. And if equilibration is an internal factor, as Piaget stresses, it surely does not start with the birth of the human baby. With his recent publication of *Biologie et connaissance*, Piaget provides an explicit biological framework within which his theory becomes unified. In fact, when I mentioned to Piaget the purpose of my writing and some current misunderstandings due to an inadequate comprehension of his overall theory, he asked how I liked his book on biology and then added for those who find his theory difficult to understand: "Let them read it." This advice, applied to the entire range of Piaget's works, sums up the purpose of my endeavor.

H.G.F.
International Center of
Genetic Epistemology
Geneva / March, 1967

*for*
*Sonia,*
*Peter,*
*Julia,*
*Daniel,*
*David,*
*Paul,*
*Catherine,*

*and for*
*Madeleine and Oma*

# contents

## *I*

### *INTRODUCTION*

1  On Asking the Right Question  3
2  Preliminary Theoretical Perspective  12

*READING  1*
*Some aspects of Piaget's genetic approach*
*to cognition*   INHELDER   22

## *II*

### *OPERATIVE KNOWING*

3  Sensory-Motor Intelligence  43

*READING  2*
*Assimilation and sensory-motor knowledge*
PIAGET   52

4   Operational Intelligence   55

*READING   3*

*Piaget's theory of knowledge: the nature
of representation and interiorization*
FURTH   *68*

# III

## SYMBOLIC KNOWING

5   Symbolic Behavior   85

*READING   4*

*Concerning Piaget's view on thinking
and symbol formation*       FURTH   *99*

6   Language and Verbal Behavior   107

*READING   5*

*Language and intellectual operations*
PIAGET   *121*

# IV

## FIGURATIVE KNOWING

7   Perception and Image   133

*READING   6*

*Assimilation and perception*
PIAGET   *144*

8   Memory   148

*READING   7*

*Memory and intelligence*
PIAGET   *155*

# V

## BIOLOGY AND KNOWLEDGE

9   A Biological Approach to Intelligence   167
10   Adaptation and Knowledge   175
11   Knowledge in Evolution   182

READING   8
Biology and knowledge
PIAGET   193

# VI

## DEVELOPMENT AND LEARNING

12   Equilibration and Development   205
13   Learning and Intelligence   220

READING   9
Learning and knowledge   PIAGET   235

# VII

## SUMMARY

14   An Overview of Seven Themes   243

Autobiography   PIAGET   253
Bibliography   257
Glossary   259
Index   267

# I
# *Introduction*

# 1

## on asking the right question

"What is intelligence?" is a question that has been asked throughout the ages ever since individuals began to reflect on their own existence. It has been asked in many different forms and from many different viewpoints. Some philosophers directed their attention to intelligence as the one major faculty of a rational soul, the other being the will, others focused on the nature of knowledge. Take a sample of questions such as these: "From where do general ideas or universally valid concepts derive?" "Is human knowledge something different from animal knowledge?" "Is intelligence a fixed disposition transmitted through heredity that largely determines our capacity to behave intelligently?" "Do we acquire the general knowledge implied in intelligence in the same manner in which we learn any particular skill or fact?" "Is intelligence mainly a matter of memory?" All of us by the fact that we use our intelligence have given some partial answers to these and similar questions.

If we turn to persons who are professionally concerned with intelligence, as for instance, educators or psychologists, their view on intelligence is frequently linked to intelligence tests. However, intelligence tests were not intended to answer the questions of the first paragraph. They supply a statistical instrument through which an individual's performance on a variety of skills can be classified in relation to a standardized sample. These skills are related to our common sense notion of intelligent behavior and correlate highly with school performance and chronological age.

Perhaps empirical science cannot provide an answer to these questions. Are they then philosophical questions which only philosophers are capable of scrutinizing? And are our own implicitly given answers to these questions merely a reflection of our own philosophical views? To a large extent the answer to this last question is undoubtedly "yes." Some of us may protest against the imputation of a philosophical view. We may assert that our view of intelligence has nothing to do with philosophy and, moreover, that we consider philosophical questions meaningless. In any case, as we look at these questions again they do not seem to be in themselves philosophical questions. They are theoretical questions, no doubt, but so are many important problems that belong to empirical science. We might ask ourselves why these questions about human knowledge are considered to belong to philosophy at all.

This is not the place for a historical perspective that would explain why philosophy has claimed the nature of intelligence, and indeed all psychology, as falling within its purview. It is a historical fact which we cannot gainsay. It is a fact which is ingrained into our way of thinking, our language, our customs. Consider the stubborn belief in a stationary, flat earth around which the sun circled. For many generations not only theoretical speculations but sound mathematical arguments were available about the roundness of the earth before a man actually dared to observe whether a western passage to India could be found.

For some generations old philosophical speculations about human nature have lost their hold on man's imagination and have slowly slipped into textbooks on the history of philosophy. About 100 years ago, Darwin published his discovery of the marvelous unity or continuity manifest in the great variety of living species. By patient collection of relevant data, he had laid the groundwork for a scientific theory of biological evolution. Evolutionary theory gave a lasting impetus to view man in relation to his biological roots. More recently,

Freud's impact in many different areas of human life bears witness to a readiness for a decisive change in our way of thinking about psychological phenomena.

Freud, too, discovered hitherto unsuspected continuities, this time between apparently disparate behavior patterns within one person. He came to see that adult behavior had deep roots in the life of early childhood or infancy. He observed that values, motives, and aspirations of an adult can often be traced in a living continuity to early reactions within the infant's personal environment. In particular, the salient cause or occasion for many strange types of emotional suffering or disequilibrium was found in early emotional reactions of which the adult was completely oblivious. Actions that took place long before the "rational" mind could be active were found to shape the manifestation of so-called intelligent adult behavior.

This view has led to far-reaching changes in modern man's attitude towards the infant's or adult's personality. Naturally, Freud's insights were not the only cause, and at the same time changes were not always as dramatic as one could wish. Above all, Freud's teaching was often misunderstood, misinterpreted, or merely superficially and partially accepted. Nevertheless, the crucial importance of the early years in the development of the human personality is now everywhere recognized. Our schools, our prisons, our clinics, to mention only a few more obvious cases, have realized the beneficial impact of Freud's view. Serious attempts are made to treat children as something other than misformed adults whose natural reactions have to be crushed by adult discipline; prisons are thought of as places of rehabilitation rather than mere punishment; emotional suffering finds an enlightened understanding even though it cannot invariably be relieved.

In the light of these revolutionary changes in man's emotional and motivational life, views on human intelligence seem strangely exempt from any need for modification. We may grant that the motivational aspect of human life, in some respects, is more important. Motivation deals directly with the dynamic sources of action and behavior. We also agree that this dynamic aspect of human life is more obscure, hence in greater need of light based on new critical observations. Yet merely because Freudian psychology has found the rational intellect frequently wanting or led astray by unconscious emotional forces, or because intelligence is only a limited aspect of human life, there is no reason to neglect its tremendous role or consider a fresh look at its functioning unnecessary. There is an obvious danger that one accept too readily traditional beliefs and superficial introspective experience as incontrovertible evidence. While one may see the need for Freud's innovation in the necessarily impalpable and obscure area of human motivation and emotion, is not intelligence apparent, conscious, and visible to any observing person? (The fruit of intelligence is clear knowledge or understanding, and all of us have some measure of these.) Hence, it may appear that we can easily see what intelligence is and how it functions. Perhaps, after all, the questions posed in the beginning about the nature of intelligence need not be asked since the answers lie so readily at hand.

Nearly fifty years ago, Jean Piaget asked these questions about intelligence and knowledge. He recognized that they were legitimate questions, unlike other investigators who discarded them as not befitting an empirical science. He was a biologist concerned with the problem of the adaptation of a species to its environment. Like Columbus he did what some day no doubt will appear to be the most obvious and natural thing to do. "The idea of a genius, such simplicity," remarked Einstein with reference to Piaget's developmental method. Piaget treated questions concerning knowledge as any other biological problem that needed an answer. He decided to observe for himself in a systematic and critical manner how general knowledge comes about. To this preliminary empirical work he planned to devote a limited number of years and then continue with what he considered more fruitful theoretical problems of knowlege and biology. It did not quite turn out the way he had planned. Today Piaget is still working on the same questions. Together with his associates and students he continues to make literally thousands of observations to build up the body of empirical data on which his theory of the developing intelligence rests.

Piaget's view of intelligence is no less revolutionary than Freud's on motivation. It is revolutionary because it cuts through age-old distinctions and definitions that have beset our assumptions about intelligence and obscured a critical view of its biological nature. Many of these assumptions are so firmly part of our general cultural heritage that a quick assimilation of Piaget's ideas is out of the question. It takes time to get used to a new outlook on intelligence, and there really is no short cut.

How could one best highlight the intelligence revolution which constitutes Piaget's work? One can point to three modern revolutions that have changed the outlook of modern man. They are associated with the names of Copernicus, Darwin, and Freud respectively. The first placed the earth and the sun within the greater totality of the universe and the second did the same with respect to man and the greater biological totality. Freud finally took away the unquestioned prerogative of conscious reason as the principal motive force of behavior. Have these views—revolutionary for their contemporaries—made us less worthy or less human? On the contrary, they have resulted in a tremendous upsurge of human energy and in freedom for scientific discoveries. Man recognized that his place in the universe, in life and in reason, had to be worked out and achieved through individual effort.

I would propose that Piaget's revolution removes knowledge and intelligence from philosophical assumptions and speculations and puts them into the totality of natural, biological life. Such attempts have been made before, but always in a manner that preempted certain vital questions which were simply taken for granted. For example, when Piaget investigated the development of spatial concepts, he had to reject the tacit assumption that spatial relations are merely objectively determined or the alternative assumption that spatial categories are innate. Piaget discovered that it is through the development of intelligence that the individual constructs spatial notions. The "objective" constructs that we are accustomed to place within the environment are for Piaget identical with the structure of intelligence. In fact, everything that we commonly connect with objective, stable reality, e.g., perception, identity, spatial coordinates, objective time, causality, Piaget regards as constructions and as active, living operations.

In his view, the more differentiated and the more decisive the subjective contribution of operational intelligence is, the more differentiated and the more objective the resulting knowledge becomes. The implications of Piaget's theory of operational intelligence are not limited to psychological science but apply to science and philosophy in general insofar as they are concerned with theoretical questions of knowledge. More importantly, really revolutionary changes in the whole field of education and human relations seem to be a direct consequence of a deeper understanding of Piaget's theory. Who dares to guess how our primary education would change if teachers really took seriously Piaget's proposition that knowledge is an operation that constructs its objects?

The contrary assumption that a stable object is objectively given and that our knowledge merely takes in what is out there is apparently confirmed by, if not founded on, introspective evidence. Piaget's position on this, as on most other points, does not conform to traditional assumptions. But to understand the evidence for this uncommon view requires a considerable effort of study and rethinking. We can take heart in the fact that the notion of a moving earth was also based on complicated reasoning and went contrary to direct, obvious experience.

As a further difficulty, Piaget's writings present an unusual feature. On the one hand he has a multitude of empirical observations and experiments which are readily comprehended and easily hold the interest of a person concerned with human development. On the other hand, the bulk of his writing is on a theoretical level. Misunderstandings are common with any creative, challenging writer, and, as Piaget himself admits, his theoretical work is not easy reading. Moreover Piaget, like Freud before him, is a prolific writer whose books witness the gradual unfolding of a living theory that can have no definitive or final outline as long as the probing, the observing, and the thinking continue. Consequently it is not surprising that even among the group of psychological scientists who consider him a towering figure, Piaget is frequently praised more out of respect for the sheer volume of his output and the ingenuity of his observations and experiments than out of a sympathetic understanding of his theoretical views.

Piaget himself has never taken the time to present his overall theoretical position in a complete and unified manner. Explicit presentations of his theory that have appeared in public are often embedded in a much more detailed description of his experimental work. A reader could easily get the impression that Piaget merely uses difficult words and an unnecessary philosophical overlay to say what most enlightened experts are saying all over the world.

In this essay an attempt is made to go to the core of the theoretical problems in as explicit a fashion as possible and to confront Piaget's position on key issues with the weight of traditional theoretical assumptions about the nature of the intellectual process. Such a confrontation is unavoidable and will serve to highlight the nature of Piaget's revolution. It is a revolution against philosophical views, whether in the explicit form of philosophical wisdom or in the more implicit guise of a mechanistically conceived science. While in the name of scientific purity some behavioral scientists have discarded questions about the nature of intelligence altogether and while others have been content to stay on a necessarily superficial level of measuring performance, Piaget dared to treat such questions as empirical problems to be investigated in the manner of biological phenomena.

What is the nature of intelligence? What is the source of knowledge? These are indeed the right questions, and even though they sound theoretical they are by no means philosophical in themselves. On the contrary, they must be asked and answered in an explicit manner if our knowledge about intellectual processes would claim to be scientifically acceptable. I believe that Piaget has asked these questions in a manner that should claim our critical attention. Whether he succeeded in answering them satisfactorily or not is a matter which each one has to judge for himself. But Piaget's theory has a right to be heard if only because everything that Piaget did, every observation, experiment, analysis and theoretical discussion, was dominated by a search for a critical answer to these theoretical questions.

The chief aim of this essay is therefore to bring together in the following chapters some of the main themes of Piaget's theory in a unified manner. To reach this goal, the next as well as the last chapter contains a summary description of what I consider to be the main aspects of Piaget's theory of intelligence. These summary chapters should serve to unify the contents of the other chapters. Since a chief aim of the book is to help attain an overall view, the next chapter previews in rough strokes a unitary approach to Piaget's theory. The final chapter can be used as a quick overall reference whenever the need for a summary is felt by a reader.

The chapters that follow are divided into six sections. After the introductory Section I, Section II on Operative Knowing follows; it includes two chapters, both dealing with the essential, operative aspect of intelligent functioning. Section III is concerned with Symbolic Knowing in relation to general intelligence. One chapter is devoted to symbolic behavior in general, the other to Language and Verbal Behavior. Section IV emphasizes Figurative Knowing with one chapter on Perception and Mental Image and another on Memory. Section V groups together three chapters on general biological problems related to knowledge. Finally, Section VI, Development and Learning, deals in two chapters with the two main factors contributing to development: equilibration and learning.

Each section also contains one or two pertinent reading selections with some added notes of commentary and summary. Most of the readings are original translations of excerpts from theoretical works of Piaget that are currently unavailable in the English language (the selections on memory were translated from the manuscript before Piaget's book was published in French) and represent some of his more difficult writings. The most important function of the readings is to provide pertinent references to the chief topics discussed in the text.

The introductory section contains as the first reading a reprint from the pen of Piaget's chief collaborator, Bärbel Inhelder. This should serve, together with the first two chapters, as an additional informal outline of the skeleton of Piaget's theory. Readings 3 and 4 are theoretical articles, one of which was prepared as a lecture at the Center for Genetic Epistemology, while the other was written in response to some misunderstandings of Piaget's theory that had appeared in American publications.

A glossary of the more important terms in Piaget's theory is provided at the end of the volume. The index refers to the pages where these and other terms are more fully discussed in the body of the book. The short autobiography, found in the last section of the book, should be of particular interest to students of Piaget since it includes a brief self-evaluation of his entire work.

Piaget frequently presents his views in such a manner as to contrast them with the opinions of other scholars. A reader who does not hold to these often opposed opinions may find these comparisons distracting, if not irritating. On this point two remarks are in order. Piaget has been criticized for holding a distorted view of the aims and nature of association psychology. While such criticism may at times be justified, no attempt is made here to "reconcile" Piaget to modern learning theories or vice versa. Certain aspects of the association position are here presented from Piaget's point of view in order to clarify his formulations. The question of whether or not Piaget has been "fair" to learning theory or gives credit where due for its accomplishments does not concern us here.

A second related consideration has to do with the place of Piaget's theory within the spectrum of philosophy. Here too it must be remembered that Piaget is writing for French-speaking Europe; he finds himself surrounded by a long tradition of philosophically tinged writings on psychology. One who is not familiar with philosophical traditions may find it hard to see the relevance of some of Piaget's arguments. Nevertheless the reader is urged to keep in mind that Piaget's positions, although theoretical, are not philosophical; on the contrary, Piaget is opposed to investigating psychological problems by the introspective-speculative methods of philosophy as much as any tough-minded behaviorist could wish.

If one takes any one part of Piaget's theory and attempts to study it more than superficially, one is necessarily led to consider it in the light of the whole theory. This fact creates a problem for the person who summarizes the theory. Where should a writer start, and how can he proceed without too many repetitions, omissions, or merely anticipated points which find a fuller explanation at a later place? Fortunately, a relatively small number of central and interrelated ideas pervades the entire theory and can be discussed in connection with each major topic.

Such repetitions can possibly serve a useful purpose in presenting the same theoretical point in different contexts. On the other hand, the reader may frequently feel the need for further elaborations, greater detail, and more concrete illustrations. With regard to these various possibilities I have aimed at a reasonable compromise, keeping in mind that the unitary view could not be conveyed if any single content area were treated in anything like a full or exhaustive manner. For this reason I have introduced empirical examples only for the purpose of clarifying theoretical points. Moreover, I did not see the need for replicating existing excellent summaries. This work should be regarded as nothing more than an introduction to Piaget's psychological theory and an invitation to a deeper study of his writings.

# 2
# *preliminary*
# *theoretical*
# *perspective*

The purpose of this chapter is to provide a perspective on the unity and comprehensiveness of Piaget's theory of intelligence before going into more detailed discussions. The reader is asked not to expect from the present "preview" more than its stated aim. Piaget's theoretical perspective is unusual because it goes well beyond what is commonly considered to fall within the legitimate sphere of psychological science. Perhaps it is instructive to show in this one chapter how basic psychological notions of his theory are closely linked to questions concerning biology on the one hand and the theory of knowledge on the other hand.

In fact, a relatively small number of key notions are variously employed throughout the different aspects of Piaget's theory. I propose here to enlarge on one of these notions, namely that of "living organization," in order to indicate its broad interrelatedness with other notions within his theory. The first aim will be to show that biological growth, including the development of intelligence, is not something added to some given organism, coming from outside, but corre-

12

sponds to the nature of the organism. In other words, for Piaget the development of intelligence finds its deepest explanation in the structure of intelligence and vice versa. But insofar as change in behavior is more readily observable than an underlying structure, developmental observations have become the main method for Piaget to lay bare the structures of intelligent behavior. What dreams were to Freud, the psychoanalyst, developmental observations are to Piaget, the epistemologist.

A biological organization or organism implies a structure which is responsive to its environment. The structure is constituted and maintains its integrity by factors that are not entirely extrinsic to the organism. When we say that the organism manifests a certain degree of spontaneity we imply some such kind of internal activity. Yet this spontaneity is not something arbitrary, removed from lawful determination. On the contrary, the intrinsic spontaneity is the criterion of the living lawful structure which the organism possesses.

A reaction of an organism is therefore not merely a response to an outside stimulation, but is always and at all levels also the response of the underlying structure within the organism. In order to explain a response in any relatively complete manner, one must investigate the underlying structure that makes that response possible and adaptively appropriate. In fact, it is only after one has discovered the structure that is at the basis of the response that one can describe the nature of the stimulus with any degree of accuracy. In other words, from a biological perspective the stimulus is not something that is constituted ready-made outside the organism.

When a four-, a six- and an eight-year-old look at an ordered series made with sticks of decreasing length, the underlying respective structures of intelligent behavior explain to a great extent what these children psychologically perceive. The stimulus can be said to be that aspect of the environment to which an organism is responding, and the chief determining factor of response is the underlying structure of the organism. Here we are close to the heart of Piaget's "constructivist" theory. For Piaget, a response is always the response of a living organism, always something constructed in part according to determinants that are intrinsic to its own structure. A stimulus, too, is something intrinsically related to the structure or as Piaget says, something that can be "assimilated" by the structure.

Assimilation is a critical concept in Piaget's theory. It is his technical term for the psychological relation of a stimulus to a reacting organism and expresses an inner correspondence or sameness between an environmental phenomenon and the structure within the organism. In later sections we refer to this relation as an inward-directed tendency of a structure to draw environmental events towards itself. Assimilation will be contrasted with accommodation, an organism-outward tendency of the inner structure to adapt itself to a particular environmental event. Suffice it to stress here that these concepts are not free-floating entities or events, but conceptual aspects of an integral knowing process which at all levels is a constructive activity of the biological organism.

To illustrate briefly the concept of <u>assimilation</u>, take a baby who has acquired the ability to grasp things in his environment. Piaget conceptualizes this state of affairs by saying that the baby has a sensory-motor scheme of grasping. This grasping scheme functions by assimilating a great variety of external things to itself; in other words, the baby is observed to grasp and handle many different objects. These things have in common that they are amenable to grasping even though their specific figural outlines may differ one from the other. The grasping scheme corresponds to this common property of the objects or, even better according to Piaget's theory, confers this common property on them.

If the stimulus could not be assimilated, it would not constitute a biological stimulus; it would simply not exist for that particular organism. Thus the ordered arrangement of the sticks, even though present objectively—that is, to a critical adult intelligence—does not exist for the four-year-old who fails to perceive an ordered arrangement different from an unordered arrangement. The four-year-old's intelligence cannot assimilate seriated order.

However, as soon as a stimulus is reacted to by the organism we are justified in asserting that the organism has imparted something of its own to the milieu. Such a contribution according to the organism's own inner structure is for Piaget characteristic of all behavior. The underlying structure of the eight-year-old will most likely assimilate the perceptual data quite readily. He will be able to recall such an arrangement even after a considerable lapse of time. A six-year-old may be close to mastering and perceiving the ordered arrangement of the series; however, through close observation based on having the child draw, reconstruct, or complete the series, one is able to demonstrate important differences in the just emerging structure of the younger child as compared to the completed structure of the eight-year-old.

Piaget holds that behavior at all levels demonstrates aspects of structuring, and he identifies structuring with knowing. Knowing is here taken in a very general sense and as such does not imply any conscious or reflective knowing. It is by definition synonymous with "assimilable to the organism's structure." Such a view simply proposes that an organism cannot respond to a stimulus unless the stimulus is at least in some rudimentary way meaningful or known to the organism. Biologists frequently use a different terminology and prefer to say that an organism has some specific information about its milieu. The main point for Piaget is that behavior at all levels demonstrates aspects of construction which derive at least partly from the behaving organism's intrinsic structure and that this structuring aspect is identical with meaningful, knowing behavior.

To know is therefore an activity of the subject and knowledge is a construction in the true sense of the term. Yet this should not be understood as implying that any specific behavior, human or animal, taken in its concrete situation, is nothing but knowing behavior. Knowing activity is only a partial aspect of the whole, i.e., the organism's concrete behavior, and there are other aspects which always form part of that whole, as, for instance, motivational aspects, affects, and values. Even behavior that may seem to be entirely intellectual, e.g., problem solving or mathematical computing, must necessarily involve some aspects of interest and cooperation. Without some motivation the effort requisite for that behavior would not be made.

Consequently, when Piaget studies knowing behavior he arbitrarily limits his investigation to that aspect of the situation which manifests most readily the structuring activity of the subject. More precisely, when Piaget observes the knowing aspect of a behavior, he aims at uncovering the structuring capacity of the organism, namely, the inner structure that underlies the knowing response at a particular developmental level. One must go even further in specifying what Piaget considers a structure of knowing in relation to some concrete behavior. Not only is knowing revealed as a partial aspect of such a behavior—the structuring aspect—it is at the same time and for similar reasons limited to the generalizable, not the unique aspect of that activity. Piaget's aim in observing seriation behavior is first and foremost to discover the general behavior of relating and ordering that can become manifest in a great variety of different concrete situations. Does this mean that Piaget is not directly concerned with individual differences? If so, this may on the surface appear to be a loss, a neglect of an important dimension.

Actually, Piaget made his first acquaintance with children's intellectual functioning by working with items on Binet's intelligence test, the instrument invented for the specific purpose of standardizing the assessment of individual differences. However, Piaget as a good biologist was profoundly interested in the normative structures of human intelligence. This question is surely more vital than the discovery of a range of variability around a given norm. Piaget was not content with just any behavioral norm of performance that satisfied some statistical criterion. He wanted to get at the inner structures which underlie a broad spectrum of intellectual behavior. These structures of necessity imply the capacity to act in a knowing manner, not only in one, but also in other similar situations.

In this sense, Piaget studied what is general or generalizable in the knowing structure of an individual; his subject of investigation is, as he says, man as a knower in general rather than one particular knower with a unique individuality. This is really the crux of Piaget's argument against those who consider that his constructivist theory does away with objective truth and simply leaves knowledge at the whim of mere subjective invention. On the contrary, Piaget would assert that the subjective structures of which he speaks do not belong to an individualistic fancy—they have nothing to do with the devaluative connotation of a subjective egocentric opinion—but are the normative rules to which a biological organism is subject under pain of ceasing to be what it is. Piaget's subjectivism has therefore an objective quality, but it is opposed to an extrinsic objectivism of a transcendental or physical reality. More on this later.

In the meantime, if this is granted, must one infer that Piaget neglects the social influence which surely is of vital importance in the intellectual life of any person? I do not think so, because Piaget does not study man in a biological vacuum. Man is a living organization which in spite of, or rather because of, his inherent structure and self-regulation is in no way self-sufficient. The environment is not an added luxury or some item dispensable to an essentially autonomous structure. The biological environment is the necessary world in and

through which a biological organization lives and with which it interacts. If—as is the case with humans—social and cultural influences are
part of the common environment, then knowing in humans can never
develop humanly without the social and cultural environment. In
other words, Piaget implies and therefore posits the necessity of a
normal, biologically approporiate environment. The structures of
knowing with which he is concerned belong as much to the individual
in society or to the society of individuals as to the individual alone.

It is evident that behavior shows clear differences in capacity for
structuring the environment. Particularly in humans one observes a
long period of gradual intellectual development from birth to adult
intelligence. Moreover, there are characteristic differences between
animal species in capacity for knowing, learning, and problem solving,
even though it is not an easy matter to observe and measure intellectual
performance in animals in an adequate manner. Piaget is profoundly
convinced that knowing behavior at all levels of evolution or development demonstrates a basic continuity insofar as it manifests the structure of the biological organization. At the same time Piaget recognizes
qualitative differences in the manner of knowing.

These differences relate to his theory of stages of intellectual development. It is important to understand that while Piaget may be
appropriately called a descriptive-developmental psychologist, he did
not merely set out to describe age changes in typical behavior or to
develop norms for the standardized assessment of the intellectual
maturity of individual children. When he describes the typical age
range in which some behavior is observed, he does so for the purpose
of ordering the relative sequence of developmental changes in intelligence, not the absolute level of age norms in the manner of, say, a
physical growth curve. Thus, if some rare eight-year-old children
were found with formal operational reasoning, this would not disturb
the theory according to which the formal stage is reached by the age
of 12 or 13. However, it would be strong evidence against his stage
theory if it could be shown that these children reached the formal
stage without having gone through the period of the preceding concrete operational stage. This example illustrates the essential meaning
of stages in Piaget's theory. By stages Piaget refers to the lawful succession of relatively stable structures of knowing which characterize
the behavior of the organism. Moreover the structures are constituted
such that the later ones incorporate what has been achieved at earlier

stages and enrich the earlier structures by their reconstruction and extension on a higher plane.

When asked to name the chief determinant of change, why and how a structure changes, Piaget answers that the fact and the process of change still find their ultimate explanation in the basic notion of a living organization with which we started. A living organization, as was mentioned before, has some intrinsic properties which can be demonstrated at all levels of biology. The organism tends to conserve its own structure and at the same time extends the application of its structure to include as much of its milieu as it can. The organism is of course not simply at the mercy of these partly opposing tendencies. On the contrary, these aspects merely indicate the presence of the living organization which controls its functioning in accordance with intrinsic regulations or self-regulations. These regulations keep the organism in a state of dynamic equilibration, a state that is not the static equilibrium of an unchanging, rigid balance which needs an outside pull to make it move. The living equilibration of a biological organization is ever in a state of flux, if not growing, at least constantly interacting with new elements of the environment, always exercising previously acquired structures.

There is thus in Piaget's theory an intrinsic relation between the self-regulations which determine a living organism, the knowing behavior which structures and regulates the organism's interaction with the environment, and the individual development of intelligence, particularly as observed in the human child. This development manifests in a progressively more explicit manner the structuring and restructuring of higher equilibrated stages. As would be expected, evolutionary progress is for Piaget a process that follows similar self-regulatory laws.

The conclusion of the preceding paragraphs appears to be this: human adult intelligence is the terminal stage of an evolutionary and developmental process that is inherent in the self-regulation of an equilibrated organism.

In order to understand a system of regulations and a structure of potential actions, human intelligence must apply the standards of critical inquiry to its controlled empirical observations. For this reason Piaget aims at formalizing his findings in the language of logic but not so as to impose an arbitrary logical system on human thinking;

rather he is trying to make explicit the forms of logic that spontaneously and in an initially implicit manner arise in the human child.

Whereas Piaget so far can be said to apply commonly accepted propositions of contemporary biology, he finds himself in critical disagreement on the level of logic and the theory of knowledge with most other theoreticians and frequently also with the thinking of the educated man in today's culture. Piaget's theory has an intrinsic unity. His logical perspective is but the counterpart of his biological perspective, and his psychological investigations can be understood only in the light of both. His biological notion of an organism in constant interaction with its milieu is a rather commonplace notion, one would think; but this view has for Piaget the special implication that development and evolution are seen as intrinsic characteristics of the biological knowing process and not as events outside of the process. On the level of the theory of knowledge, this notion corresponds with the thesis that knowledge is neither solely in the subject, nor in a supposedly independent object, but is constructed by the subject as an indissociable subject-object relation.

The notion that knowledge is not a static quality but a dynamic relation appears again to be rather trivial until one follows it through—as does Piaget—to its ultimate consequences. One of the results of Piaget's "radical constructivism" is his resolute refusal to take objectivity in any but a constructivist sense. A thing in the world is not an object of knowledge until the knowing organism interacts with it and constitutes it as an object. As a corollary Piaget rejects the twin alternatives of nativism and empiricism. Nativism endows the human organism with ready-made categories of knowing into which sensory stimulation is channelled. But then development is merely innate maturational activation; knowledge itself has no intrinsic explanation in previous behavior and is not constructed by the developing organism. Empiricism considers the organism as more or less completely subject to environmental contingencies. Knowledge is then a subjective copy of something that is simply given in the external world. For Piaget, however, knowledge at all levels is a dynamic relation. It is intrinsically related to and dependent on the structures of the organism which possesses the knowledge. In structuring the interaction according to intrinsic laws, the organism builds up objective knowledge which can be observed at various stages.

A further point follows from this view with regard to the familiar percept-concept or concrete-abstract distinction. For some people intelligence begins where concrete perception ends and there is a hard-and-fast line of demarcation that separates one from the other. Such a distinction is quite alien to Piaget's perspective, particularly because it implies a qualitative difference between perception and intelligence based on the presence or absence of an external stimulus. Perceptual knowledge would be a more or less passive taking-in of external configurations, while conceptual knowledge would be actively abstracted from the data gained through perception. Piaget does not accept this distinction. On the contrary he goes to great lengths to demonstrate that even the most elementary type of perceptual knowledge is the result of a constructive activity of the organism in interaction with sensory data.

Another consideration in connection with Piaget's theory of knowledge refers to the nature and role of representation and the function of the symbol in human intelligent behavior. These terms have been frequently accepted within a static perspective as if an internalized representation or symbol provided by itself the link between the subject and the known object. For Piaget representation and symbol are consequences of knowing, not explanatory antecedents or intermediaries. For instance, an external or internalized representation of an event—the movement of a football player—cannot be considered as the basis for the knowledge about football in the child. Once the child has become capable of assimilating the perceived movement to underlying structures that are beginning to become permanent even in the absence of the perceived object, only then is he able to deal symbolically with this event. As we shall show later, symbol formation follows from object formation. To comprehend or reproduce a symbol such as a verbal utterance is, according to Piaget, the result of the organism's constructive activity of knowing. The "meaning" of a representation is found in its relation to such knowing activity, and the vital factor of knowledge resides in that relation between knowing and the symbol and not in the symbol or representation as such.

To summarize the second part of this chapter, knowledge is in Piaget's theory never a state, whether subjective, representative, or objective. It is an activity. It can be viewed as a structuring of the environment according to underlying subjective structures or as a structuring of the subject in living interaction with the environment.

In any case the laws of structuring are seen as intrinsically related to the self-regulations which are found at all levels of a developing biological organization.

It is characteristic of Piaget that he can encompass the many different aspects of his theory under a unitary perspective. All the points of this chapter will of course be treated in great detail in later sections. The purpose of this preliminary survey is achieved if we can get a glimpse of how psychological, biological, theoretical, and philosophical questions are intimately related, in fact how each major notion in Piaget's theory implies the others. Piaget's theory is a whole. When this is grasped, the comprehension of specific details falls almost necessarily into place. Yet Piaget himself is the first to point out that his theory is not something that even now could be called finished. Nothing is finally achieved as long as it is living. One likes to think that his theory—like any worthwhile scientific endeavor—develops and is constructed by constant incorporation of new data and new interpretations in a manner similar to the development of general human intelligence.

# Reading 1

## Some Aspects of Piaget's Genetic Approach to Cognition[1]

### BÄRBEL INHELDER

This paper was written by Inhelder expressly to acquaint an English-speaking audience with Piaget's psychology. The first section clarifies briefly the underlying theoretical orientation of Piaget's work, the general method of obtaining empirical data, and the use of logical models in the interpretation of these data. The second section is devoted to the theory of stages. Besides describing the structures characteristic of each of the three chief stages of intellectual development, Inhelder refers here to her own longitudinal studies. Through these studies she is able to suggest a more subtle theory of the construction, establishment, and elaboration of general structures which takes account both of the continuities and discontinuities observed in development. In the last section, Inhelder illustrates her discussion by observational data on spatial notions and classificatory behavior. On both topics she draws from material that was recently collected under her guidance, and she interprets the data within the overall developmental theory of Piaget.

## Point of view, methods, and models

Jean Piaget's work must be both baffling and intriguing to Anglo-Saxon psychologists, particularly to those of the younger generation who have been brought up in S-R theory and in logical empiricism. In fact, it goes beyond experimental psychology. Piaget poses his questions from the point

[1] Reprinted with permission of the publishers from W. Kessen and C. Kuhlman (eds.), *Thought in the Young Child. Monographs of the Society for Research in Child Development*, 27 (1962), No. 2, Serial No. 83, pp. 19-34. The author wishes gratefully to acknowledge the kind help of Mr. G. Seagrim and Mrs. M. J. Aschner in the translating and editing of this chapter.

of view of psycho-epistemology; his methods, in the realm of cognition, are exploratory and flexible; and his methods of analysis are those of logical symbolism. But the experts in each of these disciplines tend to consider him as too eclectic and as something of an interloper. And yet the interest which has been shown in the Genevan researches seems to suggest that the facts brought out by this particular approach shed a new light on the intellectual development of the child.

By way of introduction I would like to outline briefly first, the point of view of genetic epistemology which orients our researches, second, the methods, and third, the models used.

THE POINT OF VIEW OF GENETIC
EPISTEMOLOGY

Piaget has, from the very beginning of his career, constantly posed questions of genetic epistemology. It is true that, in their most general terms, such questions as: "What is knowledge?" can give rise only to speculative controversy; but, if formulated in more restricted terms and in terms of genesis, questions such as "Under what laws does knowledge develop and change?" can be dealt with scientifically. Research work in genetic epistemology seeks to analyze the mechanisms of the growth of knowledge insofar as it pertains to scientific thought and to discover the passage from states of least knowledge to those of the most advanced knowledge. To this end the categories and concepts of established science, such as those of space, time, causality, number, and logical classes, have been studied as they develop in the life of the child.

Before undergoing formal tuition, the young child progressively elaborates his first logical and mathematical constants, such as logical classes and the principles of conservation of numerical correspondences, of spatial dimensions, and of physical matter. These constants allow him to handle the transformations of the physical world in reality and in thought. The laws of this elaboration, while allowing us on the one hand to throw light on epistemological problems, allow us at the same time to analyze more appropriately the active part played by the child in the development of his knowledge of the world. For it does not seem—and I am here anticipating the interpretation of the facts—as if the growth of knowledge in the child were due exclusively to a cumulative stockpiling of information received or exclusively to the emergence of a sudden "insight" independent of preliminary preparation. Rather the development of knowledge seems to be the result of a process of elaboration that is based essentially on the activity of the child. In effect, two types of activity can be distinguished: firstly, a logico-mathematical type of activity, the activity of bringing together, of dissociating, of ordering, of counting, and so on—any activity for which objects are no more than a support; and secondly, an activity of a physical type, an activity of exploration aimed at extracting information from objects themselves, such as their colors, form, weight, and so on. It is thus in acting on the external world that, according to Piaget, the child elaborates a more and more adequate knowledge of reality. It is precisely the successive forms of his activity in the course of his development that determine his modes of knowledge.

One is often puzzled about where to place such an epistemological interpretation in the theory of ideas. Konrad Lorenz, with whom Piaget and I had the privilege of partaking for several years in succession in a seminar on the psychobiological development of the child, expressed, at the end of the third year, his astonished recognition of Piaget's place in the epistemological spectrum: "All along I have thought that Piaget was one of those tiresome empiricists and only now, after studying Piaget's work on the genesis of the categories of thought, I have come to realize that he is really not so far removed from Kant." On the other hand, some Russian colleagues, who believed Piaget to be an idealist because he did not admit that knowledge of the external world is simply a reflection of the objects in it, posed to him the following leading question: "Do you think an object exists prior to any knowledge of it?" Piaget replied: "As a psychologist, I have no idea; I only know an object to the extent that I act upon it; I can affirm nothing about it prior to such an action." Then someone offered a more conciliatory formulation: "For us an object is part of the world. Can the *external world* exist independently of and prior to our knowledge of it?" To this, Piaget replied: "The instruments of our knowledge form part of our organism, which forms part of the external world." Later Piaget overheard a conversation between these colleagues in which he was able to distinguish the following statement: "Piaget is not an idealist." In effect, Piaget is quite willing to label himself a "relativist," in the non-skeptical sense of the term, because, for him, that which is knowable and that which changes during the genesis of knowledge is the relation between the knowing subject and the object known. Some commentators go further and refer to him as an "activist," reflecting Goethe's assertion that "In the beginning was the deed."

### THE METHOD

In studying the formation of concepts and of intellectual operations, we have made use of experimental materials and methods which differ somewhat from the classical ones of child psychology. In associationist or

Gestalt-inspired investigations, the child is presented with elements or configurations; in our investigations designed to lay bare the operational mechanisms of thought, he is brought to grips with physical or spatial transformation of the materials. For instance, he deals with problems related to the pouring of liquids from one container to another or with the spatial displacement of rods. We then observe the manner in which, throughout the course of his development, the child overcomes the conflict presented by the variations and constancies involved.

Since we wish to avoid imposing any preconceived notions on our data, our investigations of the child's thought are always initiated by an exploratory method that is adapted to the child's level of comprehension, both in respect to the nature of the questions and to the order of their presentation. The experimenter does not merely take account of the child's responses but asks also for the child's explanation of them. And, by modifying the questions and the experimental conditions, the investigator seeks to test the genuineness and the consistency of the child's responses. Proceeding cautiously, one attempts to avoid two evils—one, of imposing on the child a point of view which is foreign to him, and the other, of accepting as pure currency each of his responses. By means of this exploratory method—one which calls for both imagination and critical sense—we believe we obtain a truer picture of the child's thought than we would by the use of standardized tests which involve the risk of missing unexpected and often essential aspects of his thought.

It goes without saying that results obtained by such a flexible procedure do not lend themselves to statistical treatment. Because of this we have undertaken, with M. Bang, the standardization of some of our procedures, adapting them to the diagnosis of the reasoning process. When we have once explored the whole range of reasoning exhibited by children of different ages, we then standardize the procedure of investigation. While standardized procedures increase precision, this method loses, of course, some of the plasticity of the exploratory technique. The analysis of our observations then proceeds by the following steps: (a) a qualitative classification of the different types of reasoning; (b) an analysis in terms of logical models; (c) an analysis of frequencies of responses and dispersions by ages; (d) an hierarchical analysis by means of ordinal scales.

It is noteworthy and reassuring that this hierarchical and statistical analysis lends broad confirmation to the succession of stages of reasoning which had been established in a preliminary form by qualitative and logical methods.

THE MODELS

For the analysis of the operations of thought processes, Piaget has borrowed models from modern mathematics, such as Klein's "four group" (*Vierergruppe*) and the lattices and structures of Bourbaki (algebraic structures, structures of order, and topological structures). He has himself constructed weaker structures, called *groupements*, which are comparable to semilattices. The use of such models in no way implies that the psychologist has succumbed to logicism, that is, has decided in advance that the real thought of the child should conform to the laws which govern logical and mathematical structures. Only the facts can decide whether or not it does so conform, in exactly the same way that facts decide whether a statistical distribution obeys one law or another. These models represent the ideal system of all possible operations, while actual thought makes but one choice amongst them. More than 20 years of research have shown that cognitive development approximates these models without attaining them completely.

The effective operations of the child's concrete thinking and of the formal thinking of the adolescent constitute among themselves closed systems of which the most important characteristic is their reversibility. An operation can be defined psychologically as an action which can be internalized and which is reversible—capable of taking place in both directions. Piaget distinguishes two forms of reversibility: inversion (negation) and reciprocity. At the level of concrete logical thought, negation applies to the classificatory operations, and reciprocity to those involving relations. While the thinking of a child of less than 6 years (in Switzerland at least) is still characterized by the absence of the reversibility, from 6 to 11 years the child can already achieve, in given situations, one or the other, but not both, of these forms of reversibility. Those more able adolescents who come to handle formal and propositional operations use the two forms of reversibility simultaneously. These two sets of operations form a unitary system which corresponds to the model of the four transformations (IRNC) described by Piaget.[2] This double reversibility confers a higher degree of mobility and coherence upon formal thought.

[2] I = Identity; R = Reciprocity; N = Negation; C = Correlate; NR = C; CR = N; CN = R; NRC = I.

*Cognitive development*

### DEFINITIONS, CRITERIA OF STAGES, AND WORKING HYPOTHESIS

Like many other authors, Piaget describes cognitive development in terms of stages. Whereas somatic and perceptual development seem to be continuous, intellectual development seems to take place in stages, the criteria of which can be defined as follows:

1. Each stage involves a period of formation (genesis) and a period of attainment. Attainment is characterized by the progressive organization of a composite structure of mental operations.

2. Each structure constitutes at the same time the attainment of one stage and the starting point of the next stage, of a new evolutionary process.

3. The order of succession of the stages is constant. Ages of attainment can vary within certain limits as a function of factors of motivation, exercise, cultural milieu, and so forth.

4. The transition from an earlier to a later stage follows a law of implication analogous to the process of integration, preceding structures becoming a part of later structures.

Some of these hypotheses, advanced in connection with our previous research, have already found confirmation in the two-year longitudinal study which we have conducted. As we have outlined earlier, on the basis of having seen each child on only one occasion and at a definite moment of his development, the different types of reasoning seem to recur in a stable order of developmental stages.

In other respects we have noted certain differences between the "longitudinal" results now obtained and those obtained by former methods. The elaboration of certain notions and of methods of reasoning was found to be slightly accelerated in the subjects of the longitudinal study as compared to those of the control (cross-sectional) groups. This acceleration, probably resulting from practice, does not seem the same at all levels. When the child is given a series of reasoning procedures, we notice a tendency to homogeneity and generalization in his reasoning behavior which, though slight in the course of the formation of a structure, manifests itself more clearly once the structure has been achieved.

In certain areas, it now seems possible to separate some relatively constant evolutionary processes. For example, at regular intervals, the experimenter confronts the child with the problem of the conservation of a given physical quantity. A liquid is poured from one container into another of a different size. In early trials the child is impressed by the change in one of the dimensions of the liquid, neglecting others. With naive commitment to his position, he refuses to admit any conservation of the liquid quantity. Some months later, however, the same child is beginning to doubt his earlier stand. He tries to put the different changes into perspective, without, however, attaining an understanding of their compensation or inversion. One frequently observes a whole series of attempts to establish relationships, from the simplest to the most complex. Still later, the child finally affirms the constancy of the liquid quantity: "There is the same amount of liquid to drink." His justifications become more and more coherent; they indicate that he is beginning to comprehend the changes in the liquid as a reversible system of operations in which the modifications compensate each other. Strangely enough, not only does the child seem to have forgotten his own trials and errors, but he considers their possibility quite absurd. The events seem to suggest that a mental structure is prepared by a continuous series of trials, but that once it is established it becomes relatively independent of the processs involved in its formation.

A theory of stages remains incomplete, however, as long as it does not clarify the contradiction between two concepts of development—the one stressing the complete continuity, and the other the absolute discontinuity, of stages. It seems to us, however, that this contradiction is more apparent than real. Our first longitudinal investigations led us to a third notion (as a hypothesis); namely, that in the development of intellectual operations, phases of continuity alternate with phases of discontinuity. Continuity and discontinuity would have to be defined by the relative dependence or independence of new behavior with respect to previously established behavior. Indeed, it seems as if during the formation of a structure of reasoning (characteristic of stage A) each new procedure depends on those the child has just acquired. Once achieved, this structure serves as a starting point for new acquisitions (characteristic of stage B). The latter will then be relatively independent of the formative process of the former structure. It is only in this sense that there would be discontinuity in passing from one stage to another.

If this working hypothesis were confirmed, the theory of developmental stages would take on a new meaning. We would then be inclined to regard it as more than a methodological tool. Rather, it would seem to offer a true picture of the formation of the child's intellectual processes.

### STAGES OF COGNITIVE DEVELOPMENT
### IN TERMS OF THEIR GENESIS
### AND STRUCTURES

Three operational structures can be distinguished in the cognitive development of the child; each one characterizes the attainment of a major stage of development and, within each one, substages can be distinguished.

STAGE I. SENSORY-MOTOR OPERATIONS. The first major stage occupies approximately the first 18 months. It is characterized by the progressive formation of the scheme of the permanent object and by the sensory-motor structuration of one's immediate spatial surroundings. The observations and longitudinal studies carried out by Piaget on his own children indicate that this progression originates in the functional exercising of mechanisms that are reflexive in origin, and leads gradually to a system of movements and of displacements. In this way the child's conception of the permanence of objects is brought about. This sensory-motor system is made up of displacements which, although they are not reversible in the mathematical sense, they are nonetheless amenable to inversion (*renversables*). The displacements made in one direction can be made in the inverse direction; the child can return to his starting point; he can attain the same goal by different routes. In the coordination of these movements into a system, the child comes to realize that objects have permanence; they can be found again, whatever their displacements (even if these be out of the field of vision). Piaget has compared this system, which has the characteristics of a group structure, to the structure of Poincaré's model of the geometric "group of displacements."

One can distinguish six substages in the course of this first major stage of development; their continuity is assured by "schemes" of action. The schemes are transposable or generalizable actions. The child establishes relations between similar objects or between objects which are increasingly dissimilar, including relations between those objects and his own body (for instance the extension of the scheme of graspable objects to that of invisible objects). Thus, a scheme can be defined as the structure common to all those acts which—from the subject's point of view—are equivalent.

The development of sensory-motor schemes is distinguished from habit-family hierarchies by the fact that a new acquisition does not consist merely in the association of a new stimulus or a new movement-response to already existing stimuli or movements. Instead, each fresh acquisition consists in the assimilation of a new object or situation to an existing scheme, thus enlarging the latter and coordinating it with other schemes.

On the other hand, a scheme is more than a Gestalt in that it results simultaneously from the action of the subject and from his prior experience of accommodation to the object. The scheme is thus the result of a process of assimilation which, at the level of psychological behavior, is a continuation of biological assimilation.

STAGE II. CONCRETE THINKING OPERATIONS. The second developmental stage extends from the middle of the second year until the eleventh or twelfth year. It is characterized by a long process of elaboration of mental operations. The process is completed by about the age of 7 and is then followed by an equally long process of structuration. During their elaboration, concrete thought processes are irreversible. We observe how they gradually become reversible. With reversibility, they form a system of concrete operations. For example, we can establish that although a 5-year-old has long since grasped the permanence of objects, he has by no means yet any notion of the elementary physical principle of the conservation of matter.

Let us consider one of the many possible examples. Given two equal balls of plasticene, the child is asked to roll one of them into a long sausage form, to flatten it into a pancake, or to break it into small pieces. He is then asked, in terms adapted to his understanding, whether the quantity of matter has increased, decreased, or remained the same. This experiment and others similar to it have shown that most 5- or 6-year-olds assert without hesitation that each change in form involves a change in the amount of matter. Influenced sometimes by the increase in one dimension, sometimes by the decrease in the other, the child seems uncritically to accept the dictates of whatever aspect of change he happens to perceive. Errors decrease gradually, as the older child becomes more and more inclined to relate different aspects or dimensions to one another, until we finally come to a principle of invariance, which may be formulated somewhat as follows: "There must be the same amount of plasticene all the time. You only have to make the sausage into a ball again and you can see right away that nothing is added and nothing is taken away."

After a period of gradual construction, and at about 7 years of age, a thought structure is formed; as a structure, it is not yet separated from its concrete content. In contrast with the sensory-motor actions of the first stage—which were executed only in succession—the various thought operations of the second stage are carried out simultaneously, thus forming systems of operations. These systems, however, are still incomplete. They are characterized by two forms of reversibility: (a) negation, as expressed in the plasticene experiment, in which a perceived change in form is canceled by its corresponding negative thought operation; and (b) reciprocity, as expressed in the child's discovery that "being a foreigner" is a reciprocal relationship, or that left-right, before-behind spatial relationships are relative. At the concrete level, these forms of reversibility are used independently of one another; in formal thought, they will form one unified system of operations.

The gradual formation of this system of reciprocal relations can be observed most easily in an experiment concerning the relativity of points of view in a system of perspectives. The material for such an experiment—conducted by Piaget and Meyer-Taylor—consists of a landscape of three cardboard mountains, and a series of pictures of landscapes drawn from different points of view. The child remains at a given position, while the experimenter moves from one to another. For each position taken by the experimenter, the child is asked to select the picture which represents what the experimenter sees. It is difficult for 5-year-olds to realize that another person may see something different from what he (the child) sees. However, during the following years, the increasingly operational character of the child's thought leads to a definite progress in his choice of pictures, until finally he solves the problem.

Thus, during the course of this second period of development, we can follow the genesis of thought processes which—at about 7 years of age—issues in the elementary logico-mathematical thought structures. Nevertheless, it still requires years before these structures are brought to bear on all possible concrete contents. It can be shown, for example, that the principle of invariance (constancy, conservation) is applied to the quantity of matter earlier than to weight, and to volume still later. In every case, as earlier schemes are integrated into later ones, they are altered in the process. Thus, the process seems indeed to be one of genetic construction—a gradual process of equilibration within a limited system of concrete operations. Equilibrium within this system is attained at about 11 or 12 years of age. This operational structure, in turn, forms the basis of the development of the formal thinking operations.

STAGE III. FORMAL THINKING OPERATIONS. The third stage of intellectual development begins, on the average, at about 11 or 12 years of age and is characterized by the development of formal, abstract thought operations. In a rich cultural environment, these operations come to form a stable system of thought structures at about 14 or 15 years of age.

In contrast to the child in stage II, whose thought is still bound to the concrete here and now, the adolescent is capable of forming hypotheses and of deducing possible consequences from them. This hypothetico-deductive level of thought expresses itself in linguistic formulations containing propositions and logical constructions (implication, disjunction, etc.). It is also evident in the manner in which experiments are carried out, and proofs provided. The adolescent organizes his experimental procedure in a way that indicates a new sort of thought structure.

The following are two of many possible examples of formal thinking, one concerning combinatorial or formal logic, and the other, proportionality. In the experiment on combinatorial logic, the child is presented with five bottles of colorless liquid. The first, third, and fifth bottles, combined together, will produce a brownish color; the fourth contains a color-reducing solution, and the second bottle is neutral. The child's problem is to find out how to produce a colored solution. The adolescent in this third stage of development gradually discovers the combinatorial method. This method consists in the construction of a table of all the possible combinations and of determining the effectiveness or the ineffectiveness of each factor.

In experiments on proportionality the adolescent is given a candle, a projection screen, and a series of rings of different diameters; each ring is on a stick which can be stuck into a board with evenly spaced holes. The instructions are to place all the rings between the candle and the screen in such a way that they will produce only a single "unbroken" shadow on the screen—the shadow of "a ring." Gradually, the adolescent discovers that "there must be some relationship," and he tries to find out what relationship it is by systematic attempts, until finally he becomes aware that it is a matter of proportionality. As one bright 15-year-old said, "The thing is to keep the same proportion between the size of the ring and the distance from the candle; the absolute distance doesn't matter."

These experimental methods of procedure were not "taught" in our Geneva schools when our subjects were at this age level. Our subjects, at the point of departure for the formal thought structures, discovered these procedures without specific tuition.

In analyzing these thought structures, Piaget found that they come more and more to approximate formal models as the subject's experimental procedures become more and more effective. The combinatorial method, for example, corresponds to a lattice structure and the method of proportionality to the structure of a group. Above all, the formal thought structure, as compared to the concrete, is marked by a higher degree of reversibility. And, in this case, the two forms of reversibility already constituted—negation and reciprocity—are now united in a completely operational system. We can say that the new operational abilities formed during this third period are the abilities that open up unlimited possibilities for the youth to participate constructively in the development of scientific knowledge—provided that his setting offers him a suitable practice-ground and a favorable intellectual atmosphere.

AN HYPOTHESIS CONCERNING FACTORS
OF COGNITIVE DEVELOPMENT

According to Piaget the genesis of the mechanisms of knowledge cannot be explained by any of the classical factors of developmental theory; it is not due solely to maturation (we observe only phenotypes, never genotypes); it does not result solely from learning on the basis of experience (the capacity to learn is itself tied to development); and it does not result solely from social transmissions (a child transforms the elements received while assimilating them). Piaget advances the hypothesis that another factor must be put into play with those above. This is the factor of equilibration. It operates in the sense which von Bertalanffy (see Tanner and Inhelder, 1960) speaks of in referring to "a steady state of an open system."

Piaget postulates that each organism is an open, active, self-regulating system. Mental development would then be characterized by progressive changes in the processes of active adaptation. The fact that, in healthy children and adolescents in our civilization, this continual mental transformation tends nonetheless toward order and not toward chaos would indicate—according to this hypothesis—the influence of self-regulating processes such as those involved in a principle of equilibrium. Operational structures—both concrete and formal—are a special case of this principle of equilibrium. A change in perception, for instance, can be seen as a disturbance of the equilibrium; operations can restore by compensating or canceling the change.

The states of intellectual development thus represent a constant progression from a less to a more complete equilibrium and manifest therein the organism's steady tendency toward a dynamic integration. This equilibrium is not a static state, but an active system of compensations—not a final conclusion, but a new starting point to higher forms of mental development.

## Additional experimental examples

THE FORMATION OF SPATIAL OPERATIONS
IN THE CHILD

According to a current opinion, spatial notions—particularly the constants of Euclidean metrics (the conservation of dimensions, of distances, and of systems of coordinates)—are a direct extension of perception. It is as if the representation of space (which is commonly called geometric intuition) were no more than a mere "cognition" of perceptual data. But a series of investigations on the child's representation of space and on his spontaneous geometry have indicated to us that spatial notions do not derive directly from perception. On the contrary, they imply a truly operational construction. However, the genetic order of this construction does not follow the historical order of discoveries in geometry; it appears to be more closely related to the system of axioms ordered in terms of complexity. Whereas Euclidean geometry was developed several centuries before projective geometry, and topology (*analysis situs*) has more recently become an independent mathematical discipline, the child's conception of spatial relations begins with the abstraction of certain topological relations, such as homeomorphs, which are then integrated into more specific operations and notions of both Euclidean and projective geometry.

By way of example, here are some illustrations of the transition from topological to Euclidean "space":

1. HOMEOMORPHS. When the child has passed the scribbling stage (at about 3½), he is able, both in his drawings and by haptic recognition, to establish the distinction between open and closed figures. A cross and a semicircle are represented as open figures while, at the same ages, squares, triangles, and diamonds are still drawn as closed and not clearly distinguishable figures. Before the child is able, in his copies, to distinguish between different geometrical forms he is able to draw a figure that is connected with or separated from another closed figure.

2. THE FORMATION OF EUCLIDEAN INVARIANTS. One of the most striking characteristics of the stage of topological representation (from about 3 to about 7 years) is the absence of principles of invariance, or constancies, regarding the dimensions of objects when the latter are displaced, for distances between fixed objects, and for the employment of systems of coordinates. For the child at the preoperational stage, it is as if empty space as well as occupied space possessed elastic dimensions. And it is as a result of the development of his operational activity that he gradually comes to endow his conception of space with an Euclidean structure.

a. For a young child, dimensions or objects change with their displacement. If two equal-length rods are placed congruently and one of them is then displaced in a direction parallel to the other so that their extremities are out of line, we found that 75 per cent of our 5-year-old subjects maintained that the one which "has moved" or which "passes" the other has changed in length relative to the other. From the age of 8, however, 85 per cent of the children maintained with conviction that the dimensions have not changed in spite of the displacement, thus annulling this displacement by means of the reversibility of their thoughts. Their arguments are more or less as follows: "The rods are still the same length, we have only moved them; what a rod has gained at one end, it has lost at the other—which leaves it the same." But it is interesting to note that this phenomenon of nonconservation or of conservation of length in face of displacement appears to be independent of a perceptual estimation of length. According to Piaget and Taponier (1956), the perceptual estimation of the length of two equal-length but offset lines is clearly better at the age of five than eight, showing that different mechanisms seem to be involved in perceptual estimates and in conceptual judgments.

b. For a young child, the distance between two fixed objects appears to alter when a third object is inserted between them. In contrast to the well-known perceptual illusion, two dolls are estimated as being closer together when a screen is inserted between them because "the screen takes up some of the room; if there was an opening in it, the distance between the two dolls would be the same as it was before." Thus, the notion of distance seems to be applied at first only to empty space and the preoperational child appears to experience difficulty in combining partly filled and partly empty spaces into one overall space.

At first, the represented dimensions of space exhibit "privileged" aspects; they are not isotropic. The preoperational child readily asserts that the distance to be traversed by an elevator is greater when it is ascending than when it is descending: "It takes more effort to look or to climb up than down." Spatial representations seem thus to be formed more on the basis of subjective motor experience than of perception, with the result that there is initial nonequivalence in the relation of distances. From the age of 7, in contrast, spatial relations are gradually transformed into a system of symmetrical and reversible relations which insure the invariance of distance, an invariance which the child expresses as follows: "The dolls have not moved, they are always the same distance apart," or again: "The room taken up by the screen counts just as much as the empty space does."

c. The use of a coordinate system is initially blocked by the child's inability to abstract horizontal and vertical coordinates when they are at variance with other indices—this in spite of the fact that the very young child possesses an adequate kinesthetic knowledge of the orientation of his own body in space (*Lagebewusstsein*). If the child of from 4 to 7 years of age is asked to represent and to draw the level of water hidden in a container which is tipped at different angles, he at first represents it as parallel to the base of the container, whatever its position, or even in one corner of the container. It is only after the age of 8 that the child discovers the constant horizontality of the water level. He does so by the use of a system of coordinates which permit him to place objects and their inclinations into mutual relationships. Once spatial representation meets these Euclidean (and Cartesian) requirements the operation of measurement becomes possible.

### THE OPERATIONS OF CLASSIFICATION IN
### THE FORMATION OF CONCEPTS

Contrary to the generally accepted hypothesis that sociolinguistic transmission is the primary mechanism of concept formation, the facts disclosed through our research compel us to conclude that language plays a necessary but not sufficient part in concept formation. It is clear, of course, that language is essential to the subject's attainment of conceptual systems that involve the manipulation of symbols. Nevertheless, language still seems insufficient. This seems due to the fact that the component operations constituting logical classes—as a conceptual system—show evidence of being linked by a markedly continuous progression through such elementary behaviors as "to bring together," "to take apart," to anticipatory and retrospective processes that precede and go beyond the use of linguistic associations or connections.

The children whose classification behaviors we studied ranged from 3 to 11 years in age. Employing a wide variety of techniques, we engaged them in tasks requiring them to classify objects and pictures. After analyzing the protocols of over 2000 children, we are led to the following conclusions:

1. The operations of classification originate in essentially active behavior. In their primitive stages they are framed in the sensory-motor schemes concerned with noting and acting upon resemblances and differences. Long before they are able to handle the verbal counterparts of these concepts, children of 2 or 3 years succeed in bringing objects together in terms of their resemblances—sometimes shouting with the glee of the true classifier, "Oh—the same! The same!" When small children attempt to classify objects, they tend to construct spatial or figural collections. These figural collections seem to show the child's thinking to lie midway between his notion of the object and that of the class.

2. At first, children are unable to distinguish between the two criteria of all logical "classes"—comprehension and extension. *Comprehension* can be defined in the following way: all those essential and distinguishing properties which must be possessed by *any* item to be counted as a member of a given class or genus. The comprehension, thus, consists in general and specific properties. *Extension* can be defined as the sum total of all those items which are members of a given class. In other words, the extension is "the population" of the class. The earliest glimmers of the

child's grasp of "comprehension" are seen in his progressive tendency to assimilate—put together—elements (objects, pictures, etc.) on the basis of their resemblances and differences. The child's first notion of "extension" appears in the way he begins to make particular spatial arrangements among objects.

Here is an example. When the child of 3 or 4 years is required to classify counters or tokens of different forms, colors, and sizes—to put together those which are alike—he tends to put them together, one after the other, on the basis of their resemblances. He seems to have no immediate recognition of the whole set of those tokens or objects which are alike, say in form or color or size. And his successive assimilations of objects into a group seem to be effected on the basis of their spatial proximity and *in terms* of this proximity. Similar objects are placed next to each other in either linear or two-dimensional arrangements. These resemblance relationships, however, are still extremely unstable. At the earliest level of classification procedure, the child loses sight of his criterion—the one with which he began—and ends up, instead, with a complex kind of "object"; he might call it a "train" or a "house." However, it is the composition of elements —chosen by successive assimilation—into a spatial whole which seems to foreshadow the child's eventual grasp of the notion of the extension of a class.

3.  The child's ability to coordinate "comprehension" and "extension"— hence truly to classify—depends upon his control of the logical quantifiers "one," "some," and "all." Such control depends in its own turn upon a progressive elaboration of logical activities of the type: All A's are B's but only some B's are A's. To put this in formal terms: $A + A' = B$, provided that $A'$ is not an empty class.

An illustration of how this behavior progresses is seen in the following example. A row of counters is placed in front of the child. The counters consist of a series of blue and red squares, with a few blue circles among them. The child is asked questions phrased carefully so as to omit the ambiguous word "some." We ask him to consider a proposition coming from some other child—say, Tony: "Tony said all the circles were blue. Now, what do you think? Was Tony right?" A mistaken reply typical among our 5-year-olds would be like this: "No, Tony was wrong, because there are also blue squares." In fact, the child reasons as if the question has been: "Are all the A's also all the B's?" Among the correct answers,[3] arguments appear which show the child's understanding of the fact that the A's are some of the B's. "Yes, Tony is right—all the circles are blue, but not all the blue ones are circles; there are blue squares, too."

[3] Twenty per cent of the responses among 6-year-olds were correct, 50 per cent at 7 years, 50 per cent at 8 years, and 80 per cent at the age of 9.

4. The quantitative aspect of the logical concept of class inclusion, in which, if all A is B, then B includes A (B > A), depends upon the prior formation—full of snares and pitfalls—of a hierarchical system of classes. And the logic of inclusion arises, moreover, out of the psychological elaboration of two types of operations: (a) the inverse relationship of logical addition and subtraction (different from our conventional arithmetical notions of these operations) is represented as follows: If (A + A′ = B), then (A = B − A′); and (b) the complementarity of A and A′ with respect to B is expressed in this way: All A's are B's, and all A″s included all those B's which are not A's.

Although the notion of the inclusion of members in a class is foreshadowed in the child's early semantic frame of reference and is learned along with his learning of language, something more is needed before the child masters the operation of logical inclusion. In our experiments with children around 6 years of age, it has often happened that children who already understand that all ducks are birds will yet maintain that you could take all the birds away and still there would be ducks. Moreover, while some children maintain that not all birds are ducks, they may still go on to say something like this: "You can't tell which kind there are more of in the world. There are too many to count."

Some children show signs of transition to a higher level, during which the classes A and B are thought to have the same extension: "Ducks are birds; it's the same thing," says the child, "so there are the same number of both." Everything seems to show that a young child can compare A and A′ only while neglecting B. Or else he can only compare A and B while neglecting the complementarity of A and A′. In the end—some years later—the child finally understands that B > A. And he expresses his logical reasoning in such statements as: "There must be more birds than ducks. All those which aren't ducks are birds, and they have to be counted along with them." The above experiments and many others confirm our hypothesis that operational behavior and activity make possible and extend beyond the eventual use of linguistic and other forms of symbolic manipulation.

5. The psychological development of such conceptual systems as those of logical addition and multiplication of classes is synchronized and proceeds all of a piece. It is during the same period that two other signs of progress appear. On the one hand, the child overcomes the obstacles which block his understanding of the fact that classes can be ordered into a system of hierarchies. On the other hand, he gradually learns to classify elements according to two or three criteria at once. And he can be observed to do this in experiments dealing with matrices or class inter-

section—in which the common element in a given row and a given column must be found.

6. The ability to "shift" criteria, once achieved, allows the subject to consider a collection of objects from several points of view—either in succession or simultaneously. This is a characteristically conceptual activity rather than a perceptual one. The early interplay of the processes of anticipation and retrospection lays the groundwork for this later ability to "shift." When the child is able to predict several possible ways in which objects might be classified (at about 7 to 8 years or older), his mode of expressing anticipation gives evidence of his retrospective processes. For example, he will say: "Must I first classify them by color and then by shape or size?" This indicates the child's inclination to reconsider—to look back—and choose a criterion which he had earlier considered only as a possibility. And, as we have pointed out before, this process of anticipation and retrospection has its roots in sensory-motor activity and leads up to operational activity. And it is the essential mobility of operational behavior—both mental and physical—which allows for every transformation to be canceled or compensated for by its inverse. And this latter characteristic we believe to be one of the main underlying mechanisms forming the systems of logical classification.

## REFERENCES [1]

Piaget, Jean, 1936, *La naissance de l'intelligence chez l'enfant*, Neuchâtel and Paris: Delachaux and Niestlé; 1952, *The Origins of Intelligence in the Child*, New York: Internat. Universities Press.

Piaget, Jean, 1937, *La construction du réel chez l'enfant*, Neuchâtel and Paris: Delachaux and Niestlé; 1954, *The Construction of Reality in the Child*, New York: Basic Books.

Piaget, Jean, and Szeminska, Alina, 1941, *La genèse du nombre chez l'enfant*, Neuchâtel and Paris: Delachaux and Niestlé; 1952, *The Child's Conception of Number*, London: Routledge and Kegan Paul.

Piaget, Jean, and Inhelder, Bärbel, 1941, *La développement des quantités chez l'enfant*, Neuchâtel and Paris: Delachaux and Niestlé; (1962, 2nd edition).

Piaget, Jean, 1945, *La fonction du symbole chez l'enfant*, Neuchâtel and Paris: Delachaux and Niestlé; 1951, *Play, Dreams, and Imitation*, New York: Norton.

Piaget, Jean, 1946, *Le développement de la notion de temps chez l'enfant*, Paris: Presses Universitaires de France.

[1] These entries, arranged in chronological order, were supplied by the author as general background references for the article.

Piaget, Jean, 1946, *Les notions de mouvements et de vitesse chez l'enfant*, Paris: Presses Universitaires de France.

Piaget, Jean, and Inhelder, Bärbel, 1948, *La représentation de l'espace chez l'enfant*, Paris: Presses Universitaires de France; 1956, *The Child's Conception of Space*, London: Routledge and Kegan Paul.

Piaget, Jean, Inhelder, Bärbel, and Szeminska, Alina, 1948, *La géométrie spontanée chez l'enfant*, Paris: Presses Universitaires de France; 1960, *The Child's Conception of Geometry*, New York: Basic Books.

Piaget, Jean, 1949, *Traité de Logique*, Paris: Collin.

Piaget, Jean, and Inhelder, Bärbel, 1951, *La genèse de l'idée de hasard chez l'enfant*, Paris: Presses Universitaires de France.

Piaget, Jean, 1952, *Essai sur les transformations des opérations logiques*, Paris: Presses Universitaires de France.

Inhelder, Bärbel, and Piaget, Jean, 1955, *De la logique de l'enfant à la logique de l'adolescent*, Paris: Presses Universitaires de France; 1958, *The Growth of Logical Thinking from Childhood to Adolescence*, New York: Basic Books.

Tanner, James M., and Inhelder, Bärbel, 1956, *Discussion on Child Development*, London: Tavistock.

Piaget, Jean, 1956, "Les stades du développement intellectuel de l'enfant et de l'adolescent.' In P. Osterrieth et al., *Le Problème des stades en psychologie de l'enfant*. Paris: Presses Universitaires de France.

Piaget, Jean, and Taponier, Suzanne, 1956, 'L'estimation des longueurs de deux droites-horizontales et parallèles à extrémités decalées', *Arch. Psychol.*, No. 32.

Inhelder, Bärbel, and Piaget, Jean, 1959, *La genèse des structures logiques élémentaires, Classification et sériations*, Neuchâtel and Paris: Delachaux and Niestlé; 1964, *The Early Growth of Logic in the Child*, New York: Harper and Row.

# II

# Operative Knowing

# 3
# *sensory-motor intelligence*

The human child at birth is an extremely helpless creature, totally unable to live without constant motherly help. Apart from a few reflex movements and some vital self-regulated physiological activities, there is not much that the baby seems to "know." Piaget describes the changes in knowing that take place during the first one and a half years, the period of sensory-motor intelligence, as one continuous growth of adaptation through coordinating actions within the subject-environment unit. From an initial undifferentiation, an almost total lack of knowing, the child emerges at the end of this stage as a person who by his adaptive actions shows that he can master means-end relations, explore new features of objects, understand spatial relations between objects in the milieu, and anticipate proximate events. Most importantly, through interlocking mutual coordinations of actions the child reaches the stage of the first basic invariant of all knowledge, that is, the formation of the object, of a thing "out there," independent in existence from his own action. At this point in development, we witness the be-

*obj permanence*

43

ginning of a clear separation between the known thing, namely the object, and the knowing person. Knowledge, in the full sense of its human meaning, is found right between these two terms; for knowledge is but our way of expressing the mutual relation of the knower to the known.

But at birth there is no indication that the infant knows either self or objects. His first adaptations to the environment are in the form of reflex movements such as sucking, grasping, and eye movements. Piaget points out that it is not in accord with biological thinking to consider these reflexes as isolated responses that somehow work and through association develop into more advanced coordinations. Spontaneous activity of the living organism that reveals itself in rhythmic, global movement is at the source of reflexes; the innate differentiation of a reflex from global activity does not result in a rigid automatic reaction for itself. The biological function of the reflex for the total organism is indicated by the continuing change towards more adaptive functioning of just those reflexes which are particularly important. Within a few days the sucking behavior is stronger, more responsive, more functional than on the first day. In fact, right from the start one can observe an active assimilation towards exercising and reproducing the reflex; this so-called functional or "reproductive" assimilation on the one hand prolongs the global rhythmic activity of the organism and on the other hand provides the intrinsic motor force that assures the consolidation of the reflex as a first sensory-motor scheme. A *scheme* for Piaget is here, as always, the coordination and organization of adaptive action, considered as a behavioral structure within the organism, such that the organism can transfer or generalize the action to similar and analogous circumstances.

The notion of assimilation is as basic to Piaget's theory as S-R connections to learning theory, and Piaget frequently makes this comparison. At the same time he stresses what he considers the essential difference. An S-R connection implies a given stimulus, an organism capable of a specific response and a reward that cements the connection. On the other hand, as Reading 2 further explicates, the concept of assimilation primarily presupposes an organism with biological structures by means of which it interacts with the environment. This interaction takes the form of an assimilation of environmental data into the organism through which three things come about. A biological contact is established between the organism and the environment, a previously neutral environmental event becomes a psychological stimulus, and an adaptive response is made. Moreover, in place of a reward added to the S-R connection, the basic motivation for this interaction is built into the structures. A biological structure implies functioning; it requires no source of motivation external to itself in order to function. Piaget likens the internal scheme to a starving animal looking for food which the scheme finds in its interaction with the environment; the scheme assimilates the environmental stuff that provides the necessary food for its functioning.

Besides the primary form of functional adaptation, Piaget defines as "generalizing" assimilation the tendency of a scheme to draw other than its proper objects to itself. In other words, the sucking reflex is soon applied to any object that happens to touch the baby's mouth. Somewhat later, "recognitory" assimilation reveals the beginnings of finer discriminations within a scheme. Thus, the infant's sucking behavior will vary according to the object in his mouth; in particular he will differentiate between sucking that results in swallowing and other sucking.

When behavior sequences appear that definitely go beyond the exercise of innate reflexes, we pass beyond Stage I, according to Piaget's division of sensory-motor intelligence. The elementary habits of Stage II are founded on schemes that smooth out and coordinate previously established reflex activity into a new totality. While an adult observer can point to actions and objects or to goals and means, such distinctions are unavailable to the infant. The activity of elementary habits is fortuitous as far as its particular manifestation is concerned, except in its own reproducing and generalizing functioning. An illustration is sucking the thumb, which for most children is not present from birth and occurs during Stage II after the thumb once accidentally touches the mouth. At this stage, too, reflex seeing enlarges into attentive looking, and vision itself becomes coordinated with the grasping reflex of the hand or with hearing. Any forms of so-called "conditioned" reflex, behavior patterns imposed from without rather than from the child's own action, also belong in the category of elementary habits.

Piaget emphasizes in Reading 2 that the pairing of an object with an activity, whether in conditioning or in natural acquisition, is not adequately described as due to mere association; for among an infinite number of possible pairings, only those that correspond to the given adaptive structure of the organism lead to a structured scheme and hence to a functional habit. Moreover, we must be constantly on guard against projecting our way of speaking into the mind of the child. Where there is coordination between two activities, say between vision and grasping, we are inclined to say that the child, seeing a thing, wants to touch it or vice versa. In reality, Piaget suggests, the infant at this stage has not yet learned to recognize a thing as being the object of seeing; consequently it is misleading to say that a thing is associated to vision and to grasping. As far as the child is concerned, the thing does not exist as a known object at this stage in development; rather, there is reciprocal assimilation of the respective sensory-motor schemes of seeing and grasping. Eventually, a network of reciprocal coordinations involving a variety of schemes leads to the constructing of a thing in the environment as a known object "out there."

A gradual opening up towards the environment is characteristic of Stage III and is primarily accomplished by means of the hand and the eye and their mutual coordination. At earlier levels, vision would unilaterally follow the hand, first as a functional prolongation of a fortuitous vision-hand encounter, then as an intentional activity, and finally as reciprocal assimilation of the schemes of looking and grasping, provided that the hand was close to the object of vision. Now, even if the hand is further away, it is brought into play in order to grasp the object which the infant is exploring visually.

Together with this active exploration of things the child appears to take an active interest in the result of his actions insofar as they have a distinct environmental consequence. Piaget adopts here the term "circular reaction," first coined by the psychologist James Baldwin. This refers to the infant's repeated attempts to prolong an act that produces a fortuitous effect, such as swinging a bell or shaking a rattle that emits a peculiar sound, pulling a string that makes a doll appear, or pressing a button that turns a light on and off. While there is no evidence that the child differentiates the end from the means, Piaget at this stage notes the gradual emergence of a behavioral intentionality that is fully formed only at the next stage.

In fact, Stage IV, insofar as it manifests a clear coordination of means and goals, is considered by Piaget as a first level of structured achievement on the way from reflex to intelligence. Further stages within this period elaborate on this most typical structure of practical intelligence, which is reached in the second half of the first year of life. The child is no longer at the mercy of chance encounters but begins to follow a "logic of action" according to the method of trial and error. The infant will now eagerly explore new things by means of the numerous action schemes with which he is familiar. If he cannot reach a desired object by himself, he will pull his mother's apron to make her bring it to him. Schemes are active and mutually coordinated to serve as means to an end. Piaget illustrates this by numerous observations of the child's removing an obstacle in order to reach a desired, but inaccessible object.

At this stage, too, Piaget marks the beginnings of behavior types that will take on increasing significance in future development. The infant of Stage IV enjoys novelty; having mastered the coordination of basic sensory and motor activities, he is beginning to imitate events not merely in an automatic fashion, but in an exploratory fashion that shows an interest in figural reproduction. (Note that "figural" and "configuration" throughout the book refer to the external outlines of an object or a movement. In contrast, the term "figurative" is reserved for the aspect of knowing which focuses on the figural aspect of an event, as will be explicated in later sections.) Of considerable interest is the *schematic* imitation of movements, as Piaget observed when his child imitated his closing and opening the *eyes* by closing and opening its *hands*. Here the child appears to perform a primitive "abstraction" by imitating the interesting movement while disregarding the particular part of the body that made it.

Moreover, because of the free use of different schemes to explore an identical object there comes about an increased objectivation of the world, a step toward the realization that things exist apart from one's subjective actions on them. Now, for the first time, two objects are established in relation to each other, rather than being undifferentiated prolongations of the child's own actions. Likewise, anticipatory reactions of the child are no longer tied to his own action, as with the knock at the door that heralds the sight of a familiar person. Rather the child can now anticipate the objective consequence of a perceived event, so that the father's getting up from the breakfast table becomes a signal for running ahead to the bathroom to watch him shave.

The Stage III infant will pursue an action to reach a goal, such as pulling a string to make some interesting sight appear, without any comprehension of the connecting link between pulling and the appearance, and he will show this ignorance by continuing the action even if the string is quite obviously disconnected from the object of interest. His actions betray the child's belief that his own activity by itself causes a given event even at a distance, and that, moreover, anything could be causally connected with another thing in any way. Piaget characterizes such causal behavior as magic-phenomenalistic in accordance with the two described tendencies. At Stage IV, due to increased objectivation, causal thinking becomes more realistic so that physical-spatial contact is now seen as a prerequisite for a causal connection.

The infant's spatial relations begin to take on a degree of externalization by partial coordinating of initially disconnected separate spaces. At the earliest stages, Piaget argues, one is justified in speaking of different spaces each centered on a bodily focus of activity such as the oral, tactile, visual, auditory and postural space, without any objective coordination between them. If a bottle is handed to a young baby with the nipple away from his face he would not know what to do with that object. By the time of Stage IV, however, the child appears to know that things have a reverse side. Thus, at this and particularly at the two subsequent stages, the various body-centered spaces become progressively coordinated into larger groups of spatial relations. The final elaboration of one objective external space is, however, intimately linked with the formation of the permanent object towards which the development continues in Stages V and VI.

According to Piaget's sensory-motor sequence, during Stage IV only already familiar schemes are used as means, while at Stage V the child actively seeks new means through differentiation of old schemes. There is still trial and error but with greater freedom of means and a better eye for what things are really good for. This is the stage of discovery of means, for the parent a much more troublesome achievement than the former stage with its mere discovery of novel things. Now the child who is familiar with using one box to stand on for reaching something high will discover that with two boxes he can reach something even higher. In like manner the child shows his new initiative in pulling things to him, in opening things, etc.

Stage VI, which is reached around the middle of the second year, continues the foregoing evolution in the direction that points to a quicker and more functional adaptation. This child is now able to elaborate new means not merely by external differentiation and combination with trial and error, but by internal coordination that manifests itself in new and sudden insights. Here, then, is the beginning of a process of interiorization that in the next period will take more than a dozen years to complete. Significantly, this achievement is contemporaneous with and dependent on the formation of the invariant external object within a coordinated space. As a final consequence of these accomplishments the child is in a position to form and comprehend symbols, and the first manifestations of symbolic behavior can be observed at this stage. Thus, Stage VI is both the end of the first and the transition to the next great period of intellectual development that is characterized by an ever greater and more complete development along the three lines of interiorized coordination of action, formation of invariants, and utilization of symbols.

As an illustration of an insightful solution of a problem, consider a child in a playpen who wants to pull an iron rod of one-foot length into the pen. He may first try to grasp it in the familiar and more convenient horizontal way only to discover that the rod is too long to pass through the bars of the pen. After a moment's hesitation and without any further trial, he will then turn the rod vertically and thus obtain the intended result. At times, Piaget believes that he can observe imitative movements that are connected with the insightful solution, as when his daughter opened and closed her mouth while engaged in the problem of opening a match box.

Evidence for the beginnings of symbolic imitation is found by Piaget in the above example of employing the imitation of opening and closing one's mouth while manipulating the match box. However it is questionable whether the criterion of a true symbol is really fulfilled in this case. A more convincing example is deferred imitation, that is, imitative behavior occurring in spatial and temporal discontinuity from the original event. At earlier stages, the child imitatively reproduces figural aspects in the presence of the model or even in its absence yet in direct continuation of a preceding imitation of the present model. This sensory-motor imitation can be considered an externalization of the accommodatory phase which focuses on the static and figural aspect of a particular event. When, however, Piaget's 16-month-old daughter reenacted an unusual scene of a temper tantrum which she witnessed the day before, he thinks that there is no room for doubt that this out-of-context imitation is functionally equivalent to an evoked memory image. And an image, as we shall see, is for Piaget one of the products of symbolic activity.

Piaget thinks that the chief obstacle towards a true notion of external space is the integration of movements that are due to physical displacements and movements that are caused by the body's own movements, i.e., postural displacement. As long as all notions are centered on one's own bodily activity the subjective viewpoint is predominant; space is parcelled out among parts of the body, and external space independent from one's body simply does not exist. With increasing objectivation of environmental events and increasing coordinating of schemes of actions, knowledge of physical spatial relations becomes manifest. During Stages V and VI, practical space begins to obey a "logic of action" which Piaget, following the mathematician Poincaré, conceptualizes as a "group of displacements." The child coordinates his own movements in space in a relatively stable manner such that he can reach a certain objective, make detours, and return to his initial place. Later in life this structure of practical localization is interiorized and forms the basis for Euclidean geometry. In the course of mastering physical displacement, the child is led to realize that a moving thing is still always the same thing and that a thing that is moved behind a screen is still existing and can be found in the spot where it was displaced. Here one can see the connection between the spatial acts of localization and the logical notion of the existence of a permanent object.

The experiments on searching for a hidden object can be quickly summarized. At the earliest stages a thing that is hidden ceases to exist for the child. A beginning of some permanence that is still strongly tied to the child's own successful action is noticed at Stage IV. If one hides a toy under one of two pillows and the child finds the toy once under the left one, he will now persist in looking for the toy under the previously successful left, even if he sees that the experimenter hides it under the right one. At Stage V the child will immediately look for the spot where he last saw the hidden object, but he fails when the hiding is a little complicated so that the final displacement is not visible and has to be inferred. Only at Stage VI is the evidence of persistent search strong enough to infer that the child knows that a thing's existence is not affected by displacements nor related to his subjective actions.

If one attempts to picture what the world is like to an infant at birth and compares it to the knowledge of the world at the end of Stage VI, one realizes the immense change and veritable revolution that has taken place. Starting with a completely self-centered viewpoint where neither the self nor the world is recognized, there is a gradual transition from subjective body-centered activity to a practical separation of means and ends to a final stage where we can infer a "logic of action." The child is now able to organize reality on the basis of general schemes of actions. These schemes include the organization of space and time, of causality, and, most importantly, of permanent objects, among which is found the self. Yet, all this development of knowledge is on a practical plane; it concerns in the final analysis external actions only. Not that the schemes—a term which we have frequently used—are simply identical with external actions. They are, it bears repeating, behavioral forms or structures of the organism that correspond to the coordinating and organizing of external action. The word "form" here and in other places is to be understood in a technical sense as distinguished from "content." The link of the schemes with the external and immediately given content is implied by the term "sensory-motor," which Piaget gives to the period as a whole. As knowing becomes more interiorized, the general forms of sensory-motor coordinations in the nature of schemes become gradually dissociated from the sensory-motor content. Sensory-motor schemes are thus slowly incorporated into a structure of what Piaget calls operations. As the future development of intelligence tends towards the equilibration of the operations to be established, we shall call the new type of intelligence that is just beginning to emerge *operational* in the wide sense, as distinguished from the practical intelligence of the preceding sensory-motor period.

# Reading 2

## Assimilation and Sensory-Motor Knowledge[1]

In this article Piaget sets forth his ideas on the nature of the most elementary activities of the child and on the relation of these actions to mature operational, i.e., logical intelligence. The selection deals with the first acquired habits which involve reactions to a signal and establish associative links between originally unconnected events. Piaget argues against the opinion that elements are initially given and that knowledge enters the organism in the manner of a copy of what is outside. He considers that the very fact of an action becoming a generalized habit requires the positing of an assimilating inner organization. The most elementary event is meaningfully given (as a signal or as a perception or as a movement) only through the active coordinations resulting from living adaptations. Note the reference to the "genetic circle": assimilation leading to schemes and schemes to assimilation. When it is said that schemes are products of assimilation, this means that new schemes come about only through generalization and differentiation of former schemes. Note also the use of the words "concept" and "judgment" which are equated with a representational scheme and assimilation respectively. "Concept" and "judgment" have here no linguistic connotation, i.e., they need not be couched in verbal terms. Further, the word "representational" is here taken in the broad sense as distinct from sensory-motor and not as necessarily implying a representation in the narrow sense of image.

[1] Jean Piaget, "Assimilation et connaissance," in *Études d'épistémologie génétique*, V (Paris: Presses Universitaires de France, 1958), pp. 56-58. Translated by Hans G. Furth, by permission of the publishers. Presses Universitaires de France publish the entire series of *Études d'épistémologie génétique* and numerous other books by Piaget.

The viewpoint of assimilation starts from a simple consideration. The meaningfulness inherent in signals and associations always derives from the actions of the subject vis-à-vis the object. Accordingly one describes the phenomena [of signal behavior or associative behavior] in relation to the organization of these actions, i.e., in relation to the subject. In this connection, it appears critical that the majority of actions are repeated as a function of subjective equivalence; such is precisely the case with sucking which implies a "history" characterized by the triple criterion of 1) a functional exercise with coordination, 2) recognition and 3) generalization. In that case, from a functional viewpoint the actions are analogous to a practical or sensory-motor conceptualization, and the organization of the actions implies the presence of "schemes" or structures common to the subjectively equivalent actions. The classes of equivalence can, of course, be more or less broad. Note that other reactions can be repeated without resulting in a subjective equivalence, hence without a "history," as a discontinuous series in manifestations of the eyelid reflex. Assimilation is therefore nothing else but the incorporation of objects into schemes (already established schemes or schemes in the process of becoming), and schemes constitute the product of assimilations (previous or present) insofar as equivalence is founded on assimilation. One can note a genetic circle that has nothing to do with circular reasoning; a similar circle is present at a higher level between concept and judgment: the concept or representational scheme is a product of judgments, while the judgment or representational assimilation is either an incorporation of data into concepts or a relation of concepts to each other.

From this the following can be concluded on the subject's "partitioning" and "copying" of the object:

(1) The unity of the scheme excludes all partitioning, namely, the putting together of a whole from preexisting, disjoint elements, but permits a differentiation, which is something quite different. On the one hand, signals only have meaning relative to the schemes. Similarly, associations in response to signals are formed only as links inherent in the schemes. On the other hand, there is a tendency to expand the scheme, expressing the dynamic aspect of a scheme as opposed to its structural, knowing aspect. This tendency relates to motivating needs and satisfactions. In any case the dynamic-affective aspect and the meaning-knowing aspect of schemes are intrinsically linked without being reducible to each other.

With these first points one notices at once that the hypothesis of assimilation contains nothing in opposition to actual schemas of associative learning—pure associationism probably no longer exists—the hypothesis simply clarifies the unity of the associative process, a unity more or less implicitly admitted by everybody. Contrary to associationism, however, this hypothesis has no doubt a different epistemological significance.

(2) If every action implies assimilation and if assimilation is defined as incorporation of objects or of external links into schemes of actions, every action vis-à-vis an object transforms this object in its properties and in its relations. Thus every act of knowing includes a mixture of elements furnished by the object and by the action. These elements are intrinsically united and linked to each other. This unity can result in a distortion of the attributes of the object under the influence of subjective elements (deforming assimilation), or it can result in an adequate recognition of the attributes by means of the elements that derive from the action of the subject (conserving assimilation). This second alternative comes about when a physical property is noted in an objective fashion due to a mathematico-logical frame that serves as the scheme of assimilation. Such an assimilation can take place at an earlier level, as long as there exists a practical logic of action. The essential epistemological significance of the assimilation hypothesis lies therefore in the proposition that objectivity is constructed by means of coordinations of actions or operations instead of resulting from the mere interplay of perceptions and associations.

# 4
# *operational intelligence*

In response to the question, "What is thinking?" Piaget would point to his definition of operation. An operation for Piaget is first of all an action in the same literal sense in which making a detour to find a desirable object is an action. It is an adaptive, functional piece of behavior and as such is indissociably linked to other functional actions within an at least relatively stable organization. Operations differ from external actions in that they are geared to an internal and not merely an external function. From this functional interiorization flow certain attributes which Piaget stresses as being equally characteristic of operations.

The scope of this rather theoretical chapter is limited to a deeper understanding of Piaget's notion of operation. The main strategy is a consistent view of the operational scheme in relation to the sensory-motor scheme which was used to analyse practical intelligence. After a preliminary comparison of these two constructs, questions are raised about the specific manner of interiorization, as to what it is that is being interiorized. From there the discussion leads to a consideration of operation viewed as a construct or an object of think-ing. After stressing the pivotal role proper to the construct of the permanent object and giving some typical examples of concrete-operational constructs, the chapter ends with Piaget's explanation of the origin of abstract concepts and his notion of reflective abstraction. Reading 3, following this chapter, provides some historical-philosophi-cal background on the concept of interiorization and shows that the understanding of this concept is closely linked to an understanding of representation.

It is unfortunate that the pivotal words "scheme" and "operation" suggest that a scheme is something that one *has* and an operation is something that one *does*. No doubt Piaget would have made things easier if he had retained "scheme" as the superordinate concept and added to it the appropriate adjective, "sensory-motor" or "opera-tional." In fact, in Piaget's terminology, "operation" is just short for "operational scheme."

We recall that a sensory-motor scheme refers to the coordinating of external acts. However, the scheme and the act are not identical. If they were, a separate scheme would be required for virtually every act, since no two external acts are exactly alike. This points up the essential difference between the scheme, which refers to the generaliz-able aspects of the coordinating of external acts, and the external acts themselves, which include a variety of act-specific variables. The specific and unique external act, therefore, is the external manifesta-tion of the sensory-motor scheme. Moreover, reciprocal and higher-order coordinations come about and general schemes of action are constructed, as for instance, schemes of means-end relation and locali-zation. We could, of course, continue to speak of "coordinations of coordinations of coordinations" that characterize a child's adaptive behavior. But for the sake of verbal economy and to stress the differ-ence between the *unique* external act and the *general* form or struc-ture of this external act, Piaget has found it convenient to employ the word "scheme."

With this in mind we can assert that a sensory-motor scheme is related to a coordinated external act in the same way as an operation is related to a thinking act. As a sensory-motor scheme is manifest in an external act, so is an operation in an internal act. To put it suc-cinctly, an active scheme is an external action of coordination while an active operation is an internal action of coordination.

There are four reasons why the foregoing analogous relations are not immediately obvious to a reader of Piaget. First, Piaget frequently uses the word "operation" as identical with the act of thinking, and thus the distinction that was always made between scheme and external act is not applied to operations. In fact he adopted this word from its use in mathematics and logic where it refers to specific activities that have those characteristics which his theory attributes to operational thinking in the strict sense. The need for the distinction is perhaps not so urgent, since the term "operation," in contrast to the term "external action," by definition implies the generalizable logical aspect of the action. In any case it is useful to remind ourselves that Piaget uses "operation" both as the general rule that is manifest in a particular thinking action, and as the thinking action itself.

Second, since "scheme" is always used as referring to an inner form, higher-order schemes are still called "schemes." Since operations can also refer to specific actions, a different word is used for higher-order organization of operations, namely structures or groups.

Third, Piaget primarily uses "operational" in the narrow or strict sense as an adjective descriptive of thinking that conforms to his strict criterion of an operation. The term "preoperational" refers then to thinking behavior that is already interior and tends toward but has not reached the stage of operation. Both terms, "operational" and "preoperational" in the strict sense are here included in and form two parts of the superordinate term, "operational in the wide sense." We shall frequently use the term "operational" in this wide sense to differentiate the subsequent stages of intelligence from sensory-motor intelligence while the term "operation" will always be used in the strict or narrow sense.

Finally, Piaget's recent terms "operative" and "operativity" were derived from the word "operational" and have a meaning that is even wider than what is called here operational in the wide sense. Operativity refers to the active aspect of the internal structure through which reality is assimilated and transformed into objects of practical or theoretical knowledge. It covers thus the whole gamut of functional adaptation from sensory-motor to operational in the strict sense, and it is coined in contrast to the notion of figurative knowing which focuses on the static, figural aspect of a given situation.

The following figure indicates the various uses of the word "operational" in a schematic outline of aspects and stages of knowing. The four entries on the right side of the figure correspond to developmental stages proper to operative knowing. In distinction, the figurative aspect of knowing does not have an intrinsic development but remains ever in close dependence (illustrated by the arrows) on the operative developmental stages. This will be made clear in the following chapters where some further details on the operative stages will also be provided. Suffice it to mention here that according to Piaget's more recent enumeration of stages, Stages I and III are sensory-motor and formal-operational respectively, while the preoperational and concrete-operational period form the total Stage II.

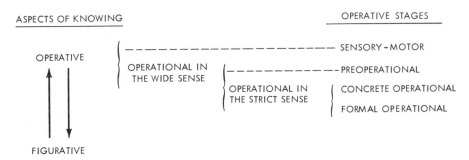

FIGURE 1. Schematic outline of the relation of the term "operational" to other terms in Piaget's theory of knowing.

We are now in a better position to turn to the crucial problem of the meaning of interiorization in Piaget's theory. First there is the question of what it is that is interiorized. When Piaget states that an operation is an interiorized action one must limit the meaning of the word "action" to its generalizable aspect. In fact, Piaget stresses frequently that operations derive not from any kind of action but from the most general actions such as the actions of uniting and ordering. General actions that are said to become interiorized are those which can be found in any coordinating of particular actions.

Consider the continuous compensation for slight deviations from the desired direction that is manifest in the use of tools and the subsequent operational knowledge that can anticipate and comprehend compensatory movements. For Piaget this knowledge is an operation that has its deep roots in sensory-motor behavior, such as making a detour when the normal route is blocked. The practical coordinations of the early stages lead in a continuous interiorization to the logical comprehension of the formal operational stage. According to Piaget no mere repetitions of piling up blocks on top of others or driving nails into planks is a sufficient cause to bring about this interiorized knowledge. In his theory, the coordinations that regulate sensory-motor detours include in a radical manner the coordinating of practical and finally operational compensation and spatial orientation. Sensory-motor schemes including, of course, an ordinary amount of environmental experience, lead with development to the degree of interiorization prerequisite for the appearance of operations.

Perhaps we can frame the question, "What is interiorized?" in a different manner, keeping in mind a comparison of operational with sensory-motor intelligence. What in fact is the biological function of a thinking operation, what is the outcome or the object of thinking? With regard to sensory-motor schemes, the function of some instinctual coordinated movements of lower animals can be seen in the consummatory act, such as the obtaining of food or warding off an intruder. At a more advanced level, the seen branch of a tree serves for the monkey's grasping or avoiding it when jumping. Similarly a baby's seeing a thing carries with it the total organism's tendency to move to it, to touch it. In all these cases we can understand that the biological function of knowing a thing in the environment is to react to the thing in an adaptive manner. In Piaget's terminology, the assimilation of a sensory-motor scheme is always simultaneous with an accommodation to the external aspects of things. In more simple language, a baby can only "think" of a bell when he has the bell in his hands, in his ears, or in his eyes.

Where does an analogous reasoning lead us with regard to operational schemes? The popular reply is at hand. We think in order to act. We plan a trip and subsequently execute it, or we think up appropriate questions for an exam which will be given tomorrow. Such a view prides itself in being activist, for putting thinking in its proper place subordinate to action. Thinking is here regarded as a planning, a prelude to action, such that the consequent action gives it a functional, full-blooded existence.[1]

---

[1] Concerning the view that thinking is *for* acting, see Dewey's "instrumentalist" theory of knowledge or the functional pragmatism stemming from W. James with its motto "Truth is what works." See also G. A. Miller, E. Galanter and K. H. Pribram, *Plans and the Structure of Behavior.* New York: Holt, Rinehart and Winston, 1960.

Yet Piaget insists on the simple statement that thinking *is* action, and not merely *for* action. For him, operational thinking is an interiorized or internal action. But is it internal merely in the sense that it does not take place overtly and is not easily observable? No, because sensory-motor schemes as such are also internal. It is internal in the more revealing sense that the object of thinking is not outside the thinking scheme, as is the case in sensory-motor actions, but remains within and can itself be called a product of thinking. Thinking and its functional object are within the same psychological plane. This is, no doubt, the profound reason why the one word "operation" suffices on the operational plane for the two words "scheme" and "external action" on the sensory-motor plane.

We shall reserve for this type of functional interiorization the word "interiorization," in order to differentiate it from a "real" internalization that is characteristic of internalized partial movements. Reading 3 elaborates upon this distinction between interiorization and internalization and discusses its significance from a theoretical and historical perspective. Insofar as an operation in contrast to a sensory-motor scheme is not tied to an external act, Piaget refers to interiorization aptly as an increasing dissociation of general form from particular content. The sensory-motor scheme of weight in the very young child requires the feeling and sensing of the heaviness of objects, affording him a practical concept of weight. Later interiorization dissociates the concept from the experiential content; the operational concept of weight may be accompanied by the experience of heaviness, but the experience is no longer a necessary condition of the process. However, in internalization, to be discussed in the following chapter, the particular content is not only always there, but, even though it becomes covert, constitutes an essential aspect.

After these preliminary considerations on the meaning of interiorization in connection with sensory-motor schemes and operations, some few remarks on thinking as an action may be in order. These paragraphs may help clarify further the nature of interiorization. For Piaget thinking is an activity that transforms the things in the environment so as to construct them into objects of thinking. The knowing adult person stands in a different relation to the known ball as compared to the infant who identifies a ball. The infant's knowledge of the ball is manifest in his reacting externally to the ball. In distinction from this "practical" knowledge, the "operational" intelligence of the adult responds to the ball as a known object; it transforms the external ball and assimilates it to operational structures such as classifying it as a particular object. While one can say in the one case that sensory-motor knowledge of the ball is the same as reacting to the ball, one can likewise say that operational knowledge of the ball is the same as the ball known as an object. This operational knowing must not be conceived as a totally abstract, nonpractical knowledge because of its basic dissociation from external acts. Sensory-motor schemes are at least implicitly present or subsumed in operational schemes. Thus, ball known as an object carries with it an implicit functional potential, e.g., something that can be rolled, thrown, punctured, kicked, dropped, bounced, hidden, but not poured, eaten, twisted, etc.

Intellectual knowledge is thus an activity in the creative sense of the term. It does not merely act on things. It transforms them and turns them into objects of knowing. However, one must be careful not to externalize this object from the thinking act and consider the object as some thing apart which thinking contemplates. As an illustration, the number system as an object of a person's knowledge is not something that exists apart from his number operations; the two expressions "number operations" and "the known number system" are two sides of the same coin. Yet it will be argued that this number system can be represented in symbols and put into books; it thus appears to be separate from the knowing operation. As will be pointed out in the next chapter, objects of knowledge are in fact frequently symbolized in external ways and as symbols enjoy a borrowed existence of their own. But unless there is somebody knowing who first produces the symbols and somebody knowing who can reproduce them, the numbers and words of the book would remain empty lines and strokes, bereft of any intellectual meaning.

The reader may have noticed that we have been speaking of intellectual operations and even of constructs or objects of thinking without using words like "perception," "representation," "symbol," "language." While the kinds of behavior conveyed by these words play an important and necessary role in the total intellectual life as lived concretely, it is imperative to grasp that in Piaget's theory these things are not essential parts of operational intelligence as such. For this reason the reader's attention is again directed to the largely verbally-caused fallacy that gives the object of an action an independent existence. When our linguistic usage asserts that the infant "recognizes the ball" or that the adult "knows the set of numbers," we are readily inclined to attribute separate existences to the acting persons and to the objects. This tendency of reification was pointed out already in connection with the words "organism" and "environment." While the ball has a physical existence apart from any psychological reaction to it—in distinction from the number system which exists only on the plane of operational constructs—it is still true that the ball is not identified by the infant as having a separate existence apart from his reaction. The scheme of the permanent object must be formed before one can speak of a separate existence from the infant's viewpoint. Nor does the number system exist as a separate entity apart from the knowing activity of the person; it requires a subsequent formation of symbols to give to this knowledge a kind of concrete existence, as, for instance, the numbers written in books.

We turn now to a second notion linked to operation, namely reversibility, before returning again later in this chapter to mental constructs and their genetic derivations. Reversibility is stressed by Piaget as a foremost characteristic of operations. Yet it seems that a better understanding of the necessity of reversibility can be achieved when it is seen as a consequence of interiorization.

According to Piaget, progressive interiorization of a scheme goes hand in hand with an increase in mobility. Mobility refers here to a scheme's range of potential application within the totality of available schemes. A four-year-old child may be able to work out slowly that $5 + 3$ makes 8 by means of a preoperational scheme that cannot by itself be applied to the problem of $3 + 5$; that is, the child's scheme of addition is not mobile enough to disregard the order of the elements and conserve itself as a stable system.

Operational actions according to Piaget derive from sensory-motor actions by the progressive interiorization and structuring of coordinating action schemes. The developmentally final operations form a coherent system, the most characteristic attribute of which is the full reversibility of operations in Piaget's strict sense. Both attributes, belonging to a system and reversibility, follow from functional interiorization. The first construction that is truly interior to the sphere of thinking is the construction of the permanent object. This paves the way and is the beginning of operational thinking. For as the constructs or objects of knowing become more internal to the thinking act, they become also less specific and less immediate along the evolutionary development of knowing. They become increasingly dissociated from a particular content and take on a general and at the same time more tightly organized character. A similar developmental process can be illustrated already on the sensory-motor level: the sensory-motor scheme of hearing, i.e., paying attention to sound, requires a lesser degree of organization than the scheme of looking for the source of the sound which must coordinate the separate schemes of hearing, looking, and moving.

Piaget observes that as long as the thinking organization is incomplete, its actions are not fully reversible. Reversibility of thinking action thus becomes Piaget's observational criterion for differentiating operation in the strict sense from preoperational activity. As was mentioned before, operation is Piaget's technical term for the mature thinking activity towards which earlier forms of thinking tend. In fact, Piaget has no unique term to cover the long period between one and one-half years and six to seven years during which thinking is no longer merely sensory-motor nor yet fully operational. Usually he employs the term "preoperational" to cover this period. As said before, we use the term "operational" in the wide sense to include both preoperational and operational intelligence in the strict sense.

There follow now some typical examples illustrating the transition from preoperational to fully reversible operational thinking. First, in the area of classifying, a three-year-old child may hold that any man can be a father or a postman, but does not understand that one person can simultaneously be a father and a postman. The child's thinking is still too specific, too immediate, and not reversible. His knowledge about fathers and postmen is specifically tied to his own experience and, while he can move in thought from either father or postman to man, he cannot reverse the direction which would make him realize how these two classes relate to the superordinate class of men and to each other. In other words he knows that all fathers and all postmen are men, but not that some men are postmen or fathers and that within this subgroup is a special group of those who are both postmen and fathers. By the time a child is about eight years old, his knowledge of classes is sufficiently organized so that he can coordinate comprehension and extension of a class or subclass. He can then move from an instance to a class, or from a subclass to a higher class and reverse the movement: his system of classification is reversible and thus operational. The general system of classifying things has the logical form of what Piaget calls a "grouping" and constitutes a first fundamental structure of operational intelligence.

Another basic structure that evolves about the same time as classification is the ability to put things in a serial order from least to most, from smallest to biggest, etc. This ability develops slowly from a purely perceptual grasp at age two, when a child succeeds in building a tower in the form of a pyramid. But as soon as the size differences are made less apparent, the child manifests an almost total lack of understanding of serial ordering. When a child of three years is asked to arrange a series of sticks from large to small, he will randomly pair a big and a little stick, with no serial coordination. Later on, some incomplete overall regulations appear which, however, permit serious lacunae or incongruencies within the series. Again it is only by the age of about seven or eight years that the child fully grasps the double principle of seriation which requires that each element must be consistently compared to its neighbor in the one direction and to its neighbor in the reverse direction. When this is mastered and the operation of seriation is reversible and firmly structured, the principle of transitivity follows as a matter of course. If A is bigger than B and B is bigger than C, it is understood through thinking alone that A is bigger than C.

Piaget has shown both by logical analysis and through observations of children's behavior that comprehension of the system of numbers presupposes the operations of classes and of seriation and is a synthesis of these two operations. This is an instance where Piaget's empirical method of genetic psychology has clarified important theoretical questions on the nature and genesis of mathematical concepts. To put it in a few words, it stands to reason that the set of natural numbers 1, 2, 3, 4 . . . to infinity demonstrates properties of seriation where each element $(n)$ is related to its preceding $(n - 1)$ and its succeeding element $(n + 1)$. Moreover, the number system also has characteristics of classification as each lower number is included in the higher number. In fact, number operations begin to appear about the same time as the operations of classes and seriation have been established.

Now that some examples of what Piaget calls concrete operations have been given, we return to the theoretical question that was asked as to the functional status of the objects of thinking. We learned that the objects of thinking are constructs of thinking, in this case, the constructs of class, ordered series, number. They are objects to be known not merely in the vague and misleading sense of "things put before our mind to be known." Such a mode of speaking is more appropriate for representational symbols, as is discussed in Reading 3 and in the following chapter. Nor are they objects that exist as a kind of representation·of reality on which the thinking acts. As general constructs, they are also objects in the more general sense that they provide the logical framework on which our mature knowledge of the world is based. All our understanding of reality is ultimately dependent on these "abstract" categories.

Why is it that these mental constructs are so obviously adapted to the physical world? What is the source of these constructs and what corresponds to them in the physical world? Piaget accepts the notion that they are abstracted from experience but he thinks it necessary to distinguish two kinds of experiences or abstractions: a physical experience that abstracts from the physical things to which knowing is directed and a logico-mathematical experience that abstracts from the knowing activity itself.

Piaget suggests that operational schemes derive principally from the second kind of abstraction. He calls it logico-mathematical abstraction because it leads to the logico-mathematical constructs on which so much of scientific thinking rests. He also uses the term "reflecting" abstraction since he considers this abstraction in the manner of an internal feedback that progressively enriches the internal structure. The organism reflects on its own coordinating activity, not in an introspective, self-reflective sense, but in a self-regulatory and self-expanding sense. The abstraction, as a feedback, is an internal regulatory mechanism; and as an internal enrichment, it becomes the principal source of growth of the operative structure. This growth takes the form of an internal increase where on a higher plane later structures subsume or "reflect" earlier structures. Operative growth is thus not a cumulative addition of externally imported elements.

Since Piaget does not derive general operational constructs from physical experience as such, he has to explain why the constructs of reflecting logico-mathematical abstraction "fit" the physical world. Reflecting abstraction is the source of operational schemes; but, being internal to the schemes, they can be said to have their own source in these schemes. Ultimately all schemes derive from the most primitive organismic-environmental matrix. At this deep level there is no hard and fast line between the physical and the biological; hence it appears reasonable that the biologically derived construct should fit the physical world. Because knowing at all levels implies a meaning-ful, functional relation of a living organization to its environment, "abstractions" work precisely because they express on the level of intelligent knowing, in an explicit fashion, laws of general coordina-tions that are implicit in all living structures and possibly in all organi-zations, whether biological or physical.

These notions are difficult in themselves and in their philosophical implications. We will come back to them frequently, particularly in Section VI of this book. In the meantime, it seems appropriate to suggest the term "formal abstraction" for Piaget's reflective, logico-mathematical abstraction so that we can freely employ the same word for sensory-motor and operational forms. The word "formal" stresses, moreover, the general form which is progressively abstracted from particular content. In this manner the close connection between formal abstraction and operational interiorization becomes evident.

Formal abstraction is then distinguished from "physical or empiri-cal abstraction" in which the organism reflects on the physical result of its action. Examples of constructs of physical abstractions would be all particular physical notions such as height, color, weight, shape, etc. In this case the particular role of the physical object is obviously crucial in contrast to formal abstraction where the role is reduced to providing an opportunity for being acted on. However, Piaget hastens to add that physical abstraction is not a process that can take place without the more general formal abstraction. The scheme to which particular physical experience is assimilated is always a general form, which is itself the product of a formal abstraction.

In fact, it is the group of action schemes, the practical group of localizations together with other intersensory and higher order co-ordinations that bring about the first "abstraction" in the ordinary sense of the term. The construct of identical object stands at the threshold of operational intelligence. This is the most general, the most basic construct that is implied in any type of intelligent knowing. With the creation of the "object," the human person has reached the stage where things are not merely reacted to but where things exist *and* are known to exist, or better, exist *because* they are known to exist, independent from one's own external actions on them.

This fundamentally new relation between the knower and the known has two dramatic consequences. From knowing that things exist, the step to represent things as symbols follows naturally. Thus, symbol formation becomes manifest soon after object formation and has its base and finds its explanation in operational knowing. At the same time the growing knowledge of the physical world must from now on constantly interact with the child's own and other people's symbolic behavior. The equilibrated state of practical sensory-motor organization has been broken. The path of preoperational thinking is described by Piaget as a laborious adapting to the use of symbols and a slow reconstructing on the operational plane of that which was already achieved on the plane of sensory-motor coordination.

# Reading 3

PIAGET'S THEORY OF KNOWLEDGE

# The Nature of Representation and Interiorization

HANS G. FURTH

Since misunderstandings concerning Piaget's theory frequently center around the notion of representation, a short historical survey of this notion in philosophical theories of knowledge is presented. It is pointed out that the manner in which contemporary scientific theorizing typically uses the concept of mediating representation has deep and often unanalyzed philosophical roots. For Piaget, the *operative* process by which we construct reality-as-known and the *symbolic* process by which we re-present known reality are functionally different and possess a different reality status. A corresponding distinction is proposed for Piaget's term *intérioriser:* while symbols derive from a real *internalization* of accommodated external actions, the functional *interiorization* of operations refers to the increasing dissociation between general form and particular content, not to something that was first overt and then becomes covert. In contrast to current representational theories of knowledge, Piaget's model is unique in incorporating the two competing and often confused meanings attached to the word "representation."

For well over 300 years the notion of representation has taken on increasing significance for a theory of knowledge. The emphasis on representation started as a reaction to a theory of intentionality which had derived from Aristotle and the scholastics. During the late Middle Ages this theory had declined into a veritable play on words in which theological preoccupations and an unchecked tendency for formulating end-

[1] Reprinted from *Psychological Review*, 75 (1968), 143-154 by permission of the American Psychological Association. This article is the substance of a paper delivered at the International Center for Genetic Epistemology, Geneva, Switzerland and was written during the author's sabbatical stay at the Center. The author thanks J. Piaget, H. Sinclair and M. Chandler for critical discussion and reading of the manuscript.

less distinctions and reifications were rampant. With the advent of Occam's position that concepts which previously were held to be universal and eternal were nothing but a name, a "flatus vocis," the time was ripe for a reappraisal. Descartes is commonly recognized as being the person who gave philosophy the new direction it needed.

This paper first focuses on different meanings attributed to the word "representation" by examples from Descartes and other philosophers of the idealistic type. Subsequently the interpretation given this term in the English empiricist tradition is discussed. This tradition was taken over into the mechanistic-positivist atmosphere that surrounded the birth of empirical sciences concerned with human knowledge, as linguistics, psychology, anthropology, semiotics. With this as background, the place and meaning of the two words "representation" and "interiorization" in Piaget's theory will be reexamined. Two main conclusions are suggested: (1) Piaget's system is able to incorporate competing and frequently confused meanings of the words by assigning them to clearly different functions and different genetic derivations; (2) in view of the inherent ambiguities of the words and the misunderstandings which ensue, it would be advisable to recognize explicitly the sense in which the words are taken or even limit their use to one specific meaning.

The discussion starts with the word "representation" and brings in "interiorization" later on in connection with specific interpretations of representation. The term "representation" can be understood in either an active or a passive sense; the passive sense can be further divided into a narrow configurative and a wider or general significative sense. The primary meaning of the term is active: "to make something present by means of . . ." ("rem praesentem facere"). In this case the person is the subject of the activity and a mediating instrument is implied. "The deaf person reveals his knowledge about the alleged event by means of natural gestures" is an example of the active sense of representation: a person who knows something about an event communicates this knowledge to others by means of gestural representation. In its passive sense the mediating instrument becomes the subject of the sentence, i.e., "something stands in the place of something else." In the narrow configurative sense we have this example: "A map represents the outlay of the city"; and in the wide significative sense there is: "The letter X represents those children of the city who are between 6 and 10 years of age." Note that in the configurative sense there is an inherent correspondence between the drawing of the map and the real thing or that knowledge of the representation by itself gives or implies a corresponding information about the real thing. In the general significative sense, the X as such has no intrinsic relation to the real thing and knowledge of X by itself provides no information.

One can notice already that in the passive sense of "A thing that represents something else" the word "to signify" can readily be substituted for "to represent." Thus representation seems to take on the added property of signifying and comes to have the same meaning as signification. In this view representation in the wide sense refers to signification generally while representation in the narrow sense means a special kind of signification, namely a signification that is mediated by some configurative correspondence between the representation and the thing. This ambiguity in meanings could only arise once the basic active sense of the notion of representation had been lost sight of.

In the French Cartesian tradition the expression "l'idée représentative" became part of the philosophical vocabulary. For Descartes the idea is that which we know, the direct object of knowing. It has its efficient factual cause in the real thing that enters our senses. Its formal cause, i.e., that which explains the specific nature of the idea, is found in the general idea of the self-as-knowing within which are implicitly all possible ideas.

For Descartes the thing-concept relation is an efficient causality relation which does not imply any intrinsic connection between the two terms. An efficient cause is frequently only a signal of its effect with no inherent relation between the nature of this signal and its effect. A broken window can be the result of a variety of efficient causes and tells us very little about the specific nature of the causal event. Descartes whose philosophy did not envisage knowledge as based on efficient causality alone, realized that his theory provided no intrinsic assurance that the ideas which we knew represented the real thing in any relevant or nontrivial way. Therefore he has recourse to God, to his veracity and his goodness, suggesting that the will of God is the basic ground for our belief that knowledge is trustworthy.

Descartes says in his *Meditationes* (III, 9): "There is in me some faculty ... able to produce these ideas without the help of any exterior thing, as ... when I sleep they produce themselves in me without the help of the objects which they represent, while I remain convinced that they are caused by these objects. ..." Here we see various meanings of the word "representation" intermingled, there is the active faculty to produce, the passive images of dreams that represent external objects and it is intimated that the ideas are similar to images in their ability to represent. Note also Descartes' reference to the efficient causality of things vis-à-vis images, and by analogy, vis-à-vis ideas.

Leibniz continued to use the word "representation" in a passive sense of correspondence. He explains that the monad constitutes "a representation of many things in one only." Wolff, who popularized Leibniz in Germany, translated representation as "Vorstellung" and there was then a mutual influence on the meaning of the word "representation" between German and French philosophers. In both these languages, representation has come to have two meanings, a wide and a narrow one. (1) In the wide sense, it is any kind of knowing, of "putting a thing before one's mind," without the thing being present to the senses; this can involve a sensory representation or take place in a non-sensory manner. (2) In the narrow sense it is limited to the sensory manner of representation, or to the making present of sensory content. Notice that because of the above-mentioned confusion attached to the passive sense of the term "representation" meaning 2 is now a subpart of meaning 1. For the notion 1 minus 2 there is no special word in French or in English but the Germans can speak of *Unanschauliches Denken*. Hence the following semantic muddle: *Vorstellendes Denken* (representational thinking in the wide sense) is divided into *Vorstellendes Denken* (in the narrow sense) and *Unanschauliches=Unvorstellendes Denken!*

While this development was taking place on the continent, English empiricism followed Descartes' lead and began treating concepts like images. Locke still used "idea" in a sense similar to Descartes as referring to any object of knowing, imaginal or non-imaginal; but the empiricist tradition which he founded was soon satisfied with an efficient causality of knowledge. Therefore Locke's followers like Hume considered ideas like superfaint copies of the real thing, with images being faint copies. The difference between an idea or an image became merely a difference in degree of acuity. For 19th-century associationists whose views deeply influenced the founding fathers of scientific psychology, images and concepts were internal representations in the copy sense, caused by internalized perception. In the English language today representational thinking means distinctly thinking in images, of whatever type. Translators beware! Note that in this tradition the external thing is regarded both as efficient and as formal cause of knowledge and such a synthesis of efficient and formal causality constitutes what Leibniz had called the principle of sufficient reason.

To summarize so far, it is suggested that from Descartes onward philosophical theories considered ideas as objects of knowledge. Ideas as distinct from percepts were called representations in the sense of referring to sensorially not present reality states. The French-German idealistic tradition continued to use the term "representational thinking" in a wide sense that did not by itself involve a sensory representation. Since it did not concede that non-perceptual knowledge had its sufficient determinant in externally caused information, it had recourse to a sphere of an "idealistic" reality of categories and essences. In this respect it is not amenable to empirical observation and retains in all its forms, past or present, a flavor of pre-formation, of *a priori* and of "supra"-scientific.

The English empiricist tradition, however, came to use the term "representation" in the narrow configurative sense with the implication that ideas or concepts were nothing but imaginal representations. In this view knowledge is directly caused by external events to which the organism responds and no other "formal" explanation is required.

Psychology as an empirical science developed within the causal-mechanistic framework of English empiricism. When psychologists did not relegate the processes of intelligence to a *Geisteswissenschaft*, they almost invariably employed a representational theory of knowledge that assigned a crucial role to the mediating representation, taken in the passive sense of the term. The internal sign, shown in Fig. 2, as that which represents reality, takes the place of things that are outside. Knowledge is likened to a perception of and reaction to interior signs or perhaps to a manipulation of signs that mirror reality. Only clear causal relations are at work: the thing or the exterior sign causes the interior sign by internalization. The person perceives the sign which in this manner becomes the functional object of knowledge. The sign's power to have the person react to it as to the real thing is the peculiar characteristic of representation which, according to a mediating representation theory, explains knowledge.

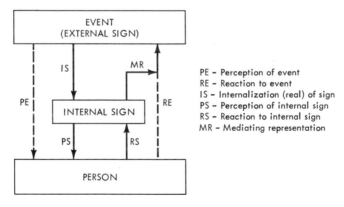

FIGURE 2. Diagram of mediating–representational knowing.

Consistent with the mechanistic-causal model, most of those who reason this way will reject a signal-symbol distinction or at best call a symbol the signal of a signal. In any case, the functioning of a signal, e.g., a learned association, is conceived in terms that are quite similar to the functioning of the interior mediating sign in knowledge. Consequently the representation theory of knowledge is confined to a signal knowledge regardless of whether it labels the mediators images, words, or fractional stimuli. Characteristically it looks for external causes that connect the internal signals with the real things. The combination of an external connection between signs and things, and of internalization, which makes an overt sign covert, provides a sufficient explanation of knowledge. The covert sign, as an internal representation, is the key to knowledge and internalization can now be seen as an important explanatory notion for knowledge, second only to representation.

Internalization in this connection means that something that has been external and observable is gradually withdrawn and takes place in a covert manner. What has been internalized can perhaps be introspectively experienced or registered by special instruments. Essentially internalization as such does not change the nature of the external act, except perhaps by speeding it up or by enlarging its spatial extension. An internally recalled sequence of events can proceed at a rate that far exceeds normal limits, e.g., the imagined mountain trip can encompass in one sweep much more than is accessible to an observer standing in one spot.

Two points can be made concerning the representation-internalization model of knowledge as sketched above. First, this way of thinking strikes the ordinary person in our society as entirely reasonable. It has behind it a history of thinking that goes back for centuries, and it seems as much a part of our cultural heritage as other customs deeply ingrained in our society. As a model it does not seem to call forth serious questions. Open questions relate only to the nature of the internal signs, whether they be images, words, or just neural connections, and to the nature of motivating factors that connect a sign with the corresponding reality. The second point is simply that the explicit or implicit acceptance of such a model makes a more complex model, such as the operative model of Piaget, unnecessary if not incomprehensible.

It remains to relate the foregoing model to some current types of psychological theorizing before contrasting it with Piaget's theory. For this purpose we shall in turn consider the theory of Gestalt as well as later forms of structural theories of knowledge. Subsequently attention will be given to recent neo-behavioristic trends which are particularly concerned with the motoric source of complex thinking processes. Finally special mention will be made of recent theories that rely heavily on verbal mediating support in explaining thinking processes.

The Gestalt tradition was founded on the notion of cognitive structure. The gestalt is a totality inherent in the perceptually given data to which the organism responds. These perceptual gestalten were not considered to be learned in the strict sense but rather to be pre-formed in such a manner that there was a biologically determined isomorphism between external reality, neurological structure, and perceptual response. When the notion of structure was transferred to the field of learning, the pre-formation perspective was dropped and the acquisition and internalization of cognitive structures through reinforcing conditions were emphasized. The internal sign of Fig. 2 would aptly illustrate the mediating function of Tolman's "cognitive map" insofar as it controls outward motoric behavior.

Numerous theorists of the so-called cognitive school of psychology have amplified the notion of internal structure in many important respects. For example Miller, Galanter, and Pribram (1960) introduced a more tightly reasoned connection between the internal image and outward behavior with their hypothesis of a Test-Operate Test-Exit plan. Bruner (1966) related cognitive growth to the development of various techniques by which humans internally represent their experience of the world and organize these representations for future use. For the present discussion it is important to realize that in all these theories, including also the recent cybernetic and computer-based models of intelligence, the internal representation of outside reality is not only crucial but constitutes the chief explanatory factor for intelligent behavior. The internalized sign becomes here a kind of representational sediment which is available for the control of complex behavior. Knowledge is conceived as coextensive with the internalized representations. It does not seem farfetched to relate the ideas and images of the empiricist philosophical tradition— the ideas being derived from experience and constituting the objects of knowledge—with the internal mediators of the representational theories of knowledge as outlined in Fig. 2.

Another tradition that has strong contemporary support derives from the strict stimulus-response theory. Enlarging on the theoretical variables of covert and cue-producing stimuli and responses, psychologists like Osgood and Berlyne emphasize the symbolic character of cognitive behavior. Osgood (1952) postulates the presence of fractional anticipatory goal responses, Berlyne (1965) suggests chains of symbolic covert responses made up of situational and transformational representations. The internal stimulus-response processes are conceived as determinants of outward behavior or as variables that intervene in a complex network of input and output relations. These theorists would hold that the covert connections which determine thinking behavior are basically not different from the overt connections of outward behavior that can be observed and experimentally controlled. Consequently they would be less inclined to speak of an internalized structure or rather they would analyze the internal sign of Fig. 2 as an intricate sequence of covert stimulus and response connections.

Together with the cognitive and neo-behavioristic traditions emerged a third position which considered verbal language as the decisive factor in human intelligent behavior. This trend can be seen as an outgrowth of logical positivism, a philosophical view which holds that the truth of logic and science is essentially a matter of correct use of language. This theory is presented in different forms, such as verbal learning or as second signal system. The decisive point for a general psychological theory of knowledge seems to be its insistence that internalized language is at the base of intelligent behavior. The internal sign of Fig. 2 would then primarily consist of linguistic elements which mediate and determine outward behavior.

Piaget's theory of operative knowledge is unique in dispensing with a mediational representation as far as the essential aspect of critical, objective knowing is concerned. He can describe the structures of his three developmental stages without mentioning the word representation or internalization.

Consider Piaget's diagram of knowing as sketched in Fig. 3. The essential point in the "knowing circle" is the internal structure. The circle assimilates or incorporates the real event into the structure and at the same time accommodates the structure to the particular features of the real event. Only through the closing of the circle is the real event turned into an object of knowing, i.e., an event that is known, and the structure into an active knowing structure. Moreover, the growth and development of the internal structure is primarily due to the coordinating abstraction which feeds back from the knowing activity itself to the enrichment of the structure. Note also that the internal structure is not something that

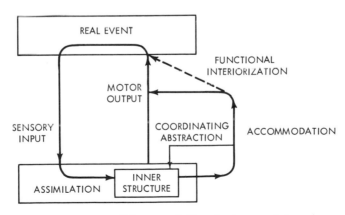

FIGURE 3. Diagram of Piaget's theory of knowing.

at any time was external and gradually became internalized, rather it is developmentally and phylogenetically related to the living organization itself which at no level can be considered as being outside the living organism.

The solid broad lines of the diagram schematize sensory-motor knowing. At that stage the knowing circle is only closed when it is part of an external motor reaction; in other words, knowing is on a practical level only. In fact, sensory-motor knowing is coextensive with the available coordinations that become manifest in adapted exterior action.

However, beginning with the transition to the operational period, one can observe the first knowing activities that are no longer inherently tied to the child's own external actions. The most basic of these activities is the formation of the object-as-such or what Piaget also calls the scheme of the permanent object. It is the beginning of objectivation, the beginning of a different kind of knowledge in comparison with sensory-motor, practical knowledge. This "objective" knowledge will lead according to Piaget to the concrete-operational and finally the formal operational stage.

This new mode of knowing, indicated by the broken line of Fig. 3, is characterized by a growing dissociation between the knowing act and its particular external manifestation. By means of the broken line the knowing circle can be closed without an external action. What I like to call *functional interiorization* is thus the specific condition of a knowing in which the external motor reaction is no longer an essential prerequisite, although it may well remain an accompanying phenomenon. It is this condition which Piaget has in mind when he speaks of interiorization in connection with an operational act. As compared to a sensory-motor act, what is interiorized is not the structure that always was internal but the result of the active inner structure. In the case of a sensory-motor scheme there issues an external act, in the case of an operational scheme, an internal knowing. Piaget refers to the internal knowing by different terms: *operations* when he emphasizes their being part of a reversible structure; *judgment* when he considers the assimilatory activity that assigns an event as belonging to a structure; *concept* when he focuses on the operational scheme as the common source of assimilations. Psychologically all these terms partake of an identical reality status. An active structure, an operation, a concept of judgment are for Piaget one and the same reality and not different reified entities. Moreover, these notions enjoy no reality status of their own, they are merely ways of expressing the only real event which exists, namely the fact that "a person knows something." They have, if you like, a "knowing" existence, as long as it is understood that this knowing is one of the modes of existence belonging to the living organism as a whole.

Is there no room for representation in Piaget's model? Certainly, by means of the representational function the person can make present to himself events that are not present to the senses. Piaget employs representation in the active sense and relates it to the symbolic or semiotic function of intelligence. It is a specialized capacity that lies midway between operational activities and motoric output. Piaget refers to the product of this activity as a symbol (or a linguistic sign). While Piaget distinguishes an imaginal symbol from a linguistic sign, it must not be forgotten that for him both are representational in the sense of being differentiated signs and, therefore, they are not essential elements of operative knowing. As will be pointed out later on, knowing in Piaget's theory is never a mere matter of representation. For a fuller elucidation of Piaget's view on the nature of symbols and on the distinction between the plane of operativity and the plane of representation inherent in the figurative aspect of a symbol, see Reading 4 [Furth (1967)].

Every symbol has two differentiated aspects, a figurative aspect which refers to some sensory or motoric event in itself and an operative aspect which refers to meaning, i.e., to its significate. In its figurative aspect a symbol has a different reality status than the operative knowing. A symbol is, or is experienced as, some thing and Piaget suggests that it derives developmentally by internalization from external motoric imitation. In its operative or meaning aspect it joins the operational circle of knowing. Thus for Piaget the direct significate of a symbol is a knowing or a concept and it is only through this concept that it can be said to represent an external thing.

If these fundamental notions of Piaget's theory are grasped, one can proceed to specify the nature of the various relations: (1) knower to concept and (2) to symbol; (3) symbol to concept; and finally the relations of (4) the real event to concept and (5) to symbol. The word "concept" is here used for the active knowing operation as mentioned above, and the real event is taken to include both physical and symbolic external events as well as internal events; in short, anything that can become an object of knowledge.

(1) The relation of the knower to concept does not imply two factually different entities. To understand this statement better, the reader is referred to the above-mentioned elaboration on *operations, judgments* and *concepts*. The concept has as much reality as the person who is conceiving it and the concept stays fully within the plane of operative knowing. (2) The relation of knower to an active symbol is partially different insofar as the symbol in its figurative aspect is on a different plane of reality which we can call the plane of representation proper. The genetic derivation of the figurative aspect from motoric imitation was already

mentioned. Here we can add that in symbol formation the knower "makes a known thing present" by means of a figurative thing which thereby becomes a representational symbol. From this it follows that (3) the relation symbol-concept is the essential meaning relation which expresses the dependence of a symbol on operativity.

Leaving the most difficult to the last, (5) the relation symbol-real event can be called a relation of representation as long as it is understood that representation is not passively inherent in the symbol but only functions via the operation which has produced or comprehended the figurative thing as a symbol in the first place. Consider now the relation (4) concept-real event. This is not a relation of representation except when the word "representation" is taken in the widest and most general sense of signification. But actually this use of the term is here doubly inappropriate, since according to Piaget we would have to call concept an undifferentiated signal. It is undifferentiated because it is not first known in itself and subsequently leads to the knowledge of the event. Secondly, while all significates are in the last analysis concepts, in this case one would have to call a concept a signal or symbol and the real event the significate. For these reasons one should not describe the relation concept-event as a relation of representation. I submit that this is a relation of a special kind, different from causal and representational relations. Indeed, this is the essential knowing relation which Aristotelian philosophers referred to by the term intentionality. Since this is just another word for this relation of knowing, there is no particular advantage in substituting an unfamiliar and possibly misleading term instead of calling it what it is, a relation of knowing.

It would seem that this short summary would suffice to highlight the difference between Piaget's theory and the current representation theory of knowledge. Unfortunately Piaget's writings are at times not as lucid as one could wish and his choice of terms frequently leads to misunderstandings.

Concerning interiorization there is no doubt that for Piaget the *real* internalization of an imitative movement is something different from the *functional* interiorization of a sensory-motor act. Yet he keeps using the same French word *intérioriser* and does not warn the reader to interpret it differently. In English we do have two words that could be employed for the two different meanings, at least in connection with Piaget's theory. We could use "interiorize" for the functional dissociation between general schemes of knowing and external content and the word "internalize" for the real literal diminutions of imitative movements that according to Piaget lead to internal images or internal language.

With regard to the word "representation" Piaget has only once made an explicit statement distinguishing representation in the wide and in the narrow sense:

> In fact, the word 'representation' is used in two different senses. In the wide sense, representation is identical with thought, that is, with all intelligence which is not simply based on perceptions or movements (sensory-motor intelligence), but on a system of concepts or mental schemes. In the narrow sense, representation can be limited to the mental image or to the memory-image, that is, to the symbolic evocation of absent realities. Moreover, it is clear that these two kinds of representation, wide and narrow, are related to each other insofar as the concept is an abstract scheme and the image a concrete symbol; even though one no longer reduces thought to a system of images, it is conceivable that all thought is accompanied by images. For if thinking consists in relating significations, the image would be a 'signifier' and the concept a 'significate.' (Piaget, 1946, p. 68).

This distinction between representation in the wide and narrow sense conforms to the earlier mentioned double sense of the word representation, that is common to the French but unfamiliar to the Anglo-Saxon philosophical tradition. In the narrow sense there is for Piaget a sensorial, that is, an imaginal representation; in the wide sense representation stands for any kind of thinking that is not entirely based on perceptual or motoric involvement. Thus representational thinking in the wide sense means simply operative thinking above the sensory-motor stage with no intrinsic connection with representational thinking in the narrow sense. Unfortunately neither here nor in subsequent works does Piaget consistently keep the two meanings separate and his failure to mention explicitly the place of arbitrary linguistic signs can easily lead to misinterpretations. It could be thought that representation in the wide sense means just such conventional signs. This is, however, not the case: Piaget's distinction between representation in the wide and narrow sense has nothing to do with the distinction between what Piaget calls an imaginal symbol and an arbitrary linguistic sign.

In fact, I would not hesitate to call Piaget's distinction between the two meanings of "representation" ontological, implying different levels of reality. Representation in the wide sense has to do with the plane of operative knowing, representation in the narrow sense with the plane of representation proper. It is instructive to note that Piaget holds to this distinction and gives it scientific underpinning; a distinction that the philosophical tradition has blurred since Descartes first introduced "l'idée représentative" as the object of knowledge. While in the idealistic tradition the notions of the idea and representation were—uneasily and not unambiguously—differentiated, the empiricist tradition, on the other hand, rejected completely a difference in status between knowing and imaginal representation and considered knowledge as being essentially representational and as entirely determined by mechanistically conceived causal factors.

Piaget, however, has never lost sight of the basic distinction between the relation of knowing which is on the level of action and constructs the objectivity of a reality state, and the relation of representation which focuses on the reality state as such. At the same time he likes to emphasize the relation between knowing on the one hand and representation in the narrow sense on the other hand. While the *fact* of this relation is obvious, the *how* is the crucial question on which he differs from others. In the passage quoted, Piaget somewhat beclouds the issue by adding that conceivably all thought is accompanied by images and calling images symbolic signifiers and thought or concepts significates. Taken literally, such a sentence would place Piaget on the Wundt-Titchener side of the imageless-thought controversy. On the contrary, Piaget stresses in this passage that the meaning of a symbol is to be found in the operative scheme. His additional remark about the presence of images, here and in other places, seems to refer to the everyday, global situation of thinking behavior in which some representational and imaginal elements in the narrow sense are present as ordinary auxiliary concomitants, as indispensable means of communication or of interior attention, but not as constitutive elements of thinking proper.

The plausibility of such an interpretation can be illustrated by numerous texts of which the following two are recent examples. In their book on the mental image, Piaget and Inhelder (1966b, p. 446) conclude, "the image is not an element of thought, but functionally similar to language . . . it can be in spatial domains a better symbolic instrument to signify the content of operational thinking." The authors continue: "All representational knowledge (this term being taken in the wide sense of thought, as distinct from sensory-motor and perceptual knowledge) supposes the activation of a symbolic or better, semiotic function. . . . Without this semiotic function thought could not be formulated or put into an intelligible form, neither for others nor for the self (inner language, etc.)."

When the authors speak here of representational knowledge they refer to thinking that is put into communicable form. While a symbolic articulation is certainly a true and vital characteristic of all thinking, taken in the totality of the behavioral situation, it is not for their theory a constitutive element of thinking. In a contemporaneous work in which the word "representational" is employed throughout in a sense that is not consistently or easily definable, Piaget and Inhelder (1966a, p. 55) assert after mentioning the "imageless thought" controversy: ". . . one can have an image of an object, but the judgment itself which affirms or denies its existence is not an image. Judgments and operations have no imaginal component but this does not exclude that images can play a role, not as being elements of thinking, but as being supportive symbols that complement the function of language." These quotations illustrate the type of possible misunderstandings due to a somewhat ambiguous use of words.

For the representation theory of knowing, the representational sign is considered as an object of knowing, as that to which the person responds. The sign is said to have become internal by a real process of internalization and it constitutes an internal copy or representation of an object that is originally external to the organism. This is the crux of the empiricist position: knowledge has its adequate source in external reality or external actions and resides in internal re-presentations.

For Piaget's theory at all developmental levels knowledge is basically linked to the biological internal organization. Knowledge does not merely derive from the taking in of external data; the organism in interacting with the environment transforms or constructs external reality into an object of knowledge. It would be helpful if in Piaget's theory the use of the English word "representation" were limited to the narrow sense. Representation would then always refer to the direct product of the symbolic or semiotic function (e.g., image, language) and would be connected in its figurative aspect with the real, literal internalization of external actions. In contrast, the operative aspect of thinking, which for Piaget is the essential aspect of logical or prelogical constructive knowledge, would then be seen as clearly separate from representation without denying that both aspects are parts of the global behavior of intelligent thinking. The increasing developmental dissociation between the generalizable forms of internal schemes and a particular content is the meaning of the functional interiorization that leads from external sensory-motor acts to internal operations. If Piaget uses expressions like "thinking in symbols or in words," this is to be understood in the sense that thinking makes use of representational instruments, not that any representation is either a constitutive element or the object of thinking. For Piaget operations or concepts as such are not reified objects which we know but rather that through which we interact intelligently with the world and society and constitute them as an objective reality vis-à-vis our own person.

Recall the interminable speculations and verbal arguments concerning a theory of knowledge based on philosophical preconceptions. When one compares these abstractions with the fruitful results of scientific thinking that is open to a search for facts and recognizes the legitimacy of many philosophical questions, Piaget's theory can be appreciated as productive of relevant factual data on human knowing and as incorporating trends that have been expressed in philosophical theories throughout the centuries. Only now we are no longer dealing with a philosophy that is primarily subjectively determined but with a scientific theory that is open to critical objective verification.

REFERENCES

Berlyne, D. E., *Structure and Direction in Thinking*. New York: Wiley, 1965.

Bruner, J. S., R. R. Olver, & P. M. Greenfield, *Studies in Cognitive Growth*. New York: Wiley, 1966.

Furth, H. G., "Concerning Piaget's View on Thinking and Symbol Formation," *Child Development*, 38 (1967), 819-826. (Reading 4)

Miller, G. A., E. Galanter, & K. H. Pribram, *Plans and the Structure of Behavior*. New York: Holt, Rinehart & Winston, 1960.

Osgood, C. E., *Method and Theory in Experimental Psychology*. New York: Oxford University Press, 1953.

Piaget, J. *La formation du symbole chez l'enfant*. Neuchâtel: Delachaux et Niestlé, 1946 (*Play, Dreams and Imitation in Childhood*. New York: Norton, 1951).

Piaget, J. & B. Inhelder, *La psychologie de l'enfant*. Collection "Que sais-je" No. 369. Paris: Presses Universitaires de France, 1966 (a).

———, *L'image mental chez l'enfant*. Paris: Presses Universitaires de France, 1966 (b).

# III

## Symbolic Knowing

# 5
## *symbolic behavior*

The preoperational period of intellectual development could well be called the symbolic period. The child's nascent operational thinking is largely dominated by symbolic behavior that partly manifests and partly distorts adapted thinking. It is one of the ingenious insights of Piaget to have discovered the unifying symbolic character of such different activities as images, play, imitation, and language and to have related these to the development of operative intelligence.

For Piaget, the essential aspect of intelligence is found in operativity that transforms a given reality state and leads to such constructs as classes, numbers, and other logical notions as were described in the previous chapter. Operative intelligence as it occurs is always accompanied by another aspect of knowing which relates to the particular event. Piaget uses the term "assimilation" to imply a kind of signification or comprehension which is more directly related to the transforming, structuring aspect of knowing. He uses the term "accommodation" to refer to the outgoing direction of knowing, the application of an active scheme to a given event. When this event has a sensorial content, Piaget calls knowledge bearing on the configuration of a sensory event *figurative*. It is distinguished from the *operative* aspect of knowledge which has just been referred to as transforming, structuring, or for short, action knowledge. Note that the term "operative" includes the whole range of action knowledge, from sensory-motor through formal operational intelligence.

The figurative aspect is most conspicuous in perceptual behavior, so much so that one is tempted to neglect the operative aspect altogether. When a three-year-old child perceives a certain toy he obviously pays more than passing attention to its figural aspect. This much is admitted by everyone, but where is the operative aspect of intelligence in such behavior? It is found in that basic structure of coordinating intelligence that provides the object as known. Because the operative intelligence of this three-year-old can structure the seen event into an object that he knows to exist—apart from more differentiated assimilations that confer on it the meaning of being a toy, etc. —one can speak of an object of perception. Only within an operative framework is the figurative aspect even of perceptual objective knowledge conceivable. Figurative aspects of knowing are not limited to perception of things present to the senses. The newly acquired ability to know things that are present is soon followed in the two-year-old child by the ability to represent that which is known. It is this activity which Piaget calls *symbolic function*, a term which for lexical and also theoretical reasons we shall retain, even though Piaget has in recent years labeled it *semiotic function*.

Some deviations from Piaget's terminology in conformity with semiotics, the science of signs, will also be noticed in what follows; Piaget's terms appear in parenthesis. A quite general notion is that of a sign (signifier). It can be described as any thing or event within a behavioral situation that provides some knowledge to an organism about another thing or event; on the basis of this knowledge the organism behaves adaptively towards that other event. In this sense a sign is an event that points to something beyond itself. The event about which it provides information is called a significate (signified). The relation between a sign and a significate is its signification so that one can summarize thus far by saying that every sign signifies a significate.

Piaget, in line with other scholars, recognizes two great subdivisions of signs: signals and symbols. Signals, also called indices, are signs that are not produced by the organism; the organism behaves towards signals by more or less automatic external movements. Symbols, however, are signs that are produced or reproduced by the organism and directly follow from or lead to an internal action of knowing. Within the wider symbol category, for which Piaget has no specific word, he further distinguishes signs from symbols in a narrower sense. Arbitrary, conventional symbols such as language are termed "signs" while what he calls symbols in the narrow sense are motivated and self-related signifiers. I shall play down this last distinction for reasons which will become clearer in the next chapter. The immediate advantage of so doing permits us to use the word "symbol" in the wide sense in which it is actually used in most scholarly writing.

We can schematize the two great subdivisions of signs according to the following diagram in which the essential sign functioning is indicated.

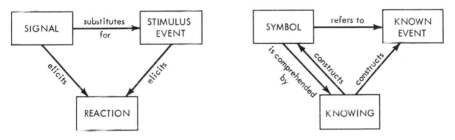

FIGURE 4. Sign relations: The difference between signals and symbols.

A signal is seen to function as a stimulus substitute that elicits a behavioral reaction similar to the original stimulus. As far as the subject is concerned the signal-stimulus relation is undifferentiated: the sound of a bell to which a hungry dog is conditioned works with a total disregard of whether or not the specific occasion brings the food to which salivation is adapted. In like manner, the smell of fire that informs an animal of a fire not yet seen is also a signal insofar as it forms part of the total fire-situation. With the symbol, the relation to the real event is differentiated in two respects. First, it is indirect and mediated by knowing and, second, there are involved two reciprocal relations of active constructions: just as intelligence constructs and transforms a sensory event into a known object, so a symbol refers directly to the knowing of an event, precisely because it is constructed or comprehended as a representation by means of the same scheme of knowing that was operative in constructing the known event in the first place.

When you hear the word "fire" you will respond to it in a more or less knowing fashion according to circumstances which may or may not entail any external action at all, in a manner analogous to a seen fire to which your response will also vary according to your intelligent grasp of the perceived situation. There is thus no fixed, rigid relation between the symbol and any particular event, even when the symbol is highly specific. Signals at the level of practical intelligence, however, have a more or less immediate and specific connection to certain reactions. Thus animals cannot perceive the species-specific fleeing signal without themselves participating in flight. Compare this with your reaction, or rather lack of reaction, to the following very specific message: "The ceiling of the room in which you now sit is going to fall on you this very moment." It is unlikely that you stir at all or even glance upwards.

The reader will have noticed that the signal-symbol division of signs exactly parallels the difference between intelligence on the sensory-motor and on the operational plane. In general, we can state that a sign is as good and as functional as the intelligence which it serves. If intelligence is limited to practical, external activity, sign behavior will also be geared towards external reaction. When intelligence begins to transform things into objects of knowledge, sign behavior will likewise take place on the level of knowing. For short, signals stand for external events, symbols for known events; signals substitute for things, symbols for "objects."

In our discussion so far as we have taken two extreme cases on the signal-symbol continuum in order to emphasize their functional difference. However, in real life the emergence of operational thinking is not a sudden transfiguration of a child's thinking but rather a slow imperceptible transition from less to more developed structures, with later structures building on and incorporating earlier ones. We can clearly see the direction of this growth and speak of qualitative differences between main stages of development without being able to point to two proximate pieces of behavior during a transitional period and call the first clearly sensory-motor and the second clearly preoperational. Such measurable discontinuities do not occur in living organized phenomena.

We can therefore expect that sign behavior of later stages, just like any other behavior, has its roots at the sensory-motor level and that in development sensory-motor reactions are not simply discarded as operational activities take their place. Piaget demonstrates, by the symbolic behavior of the preoperational period, the difficulties which operativity experiences in transforming signals into symbols. Just as the formation of the permanent, independent object is only the bare beginning of operational thinking which will not reach a strict operational level until about five years later, so also the first manifestations of symbol functioning are still far from mature forms of symbol use as exemplified in rational language, in science, or in art. Yet there is a rather dramatic observable change in sign behavior between the preverbal one-year-old and the verbal child one year later. To attribute this change merely to the acquisition of language is to take a partial result for the main cause. For Piaget, language forms part of a whole series of recently acquired behavioral skills that manifest a new mode of intelligent behavior. He calls it the symbolic function and defines it as the capacity to represent things by means of differentiated signs, i.e., symbols.

Where does Piaget look for the sensory-motor precursor of this function? In those modes of behavior where the child's attention to the figural aspect of an event spills over, as it were, into overt imitation. This behavior was mentioned in Chapter 3 as a special development during the second half of the sensory-motor period, and its close relation to the accommodative pole of adaptation was pointed out. As imitative movements become separated from the context of the perceived original, Piaget considers such deferred imitation to be the first manifestation of symbols. The child who reenacts a scene from yesterday *represents* through *symbol* formation the event which was yesterday *present* to him through *object* formation.

The ability to represent widens the knowing life of the child to an unprecedented degree. It provides him with the accommodative-figurative dimension to which his newly acquired power of object formation can be applied. It gives food to his growing operative thinking which otherwise would be limited to perceptual events of here and now. In a relatively short while the child's mind is literally filled with images of those things and events that he encounters in his progress of knowing. From now on the internal symbolic environment is built up in each person for better or worse, an environment with which he must reckon and learn to live the rest of his life.

Piaget's and our concern is with the main direction of growing intelligence and thus we do not study symbolic behavior in its own right, but mainly as a manifestation of intelligence. Images, according to Piaget, are internalized forms of imitation. Piaget uses the word "image" to include those of any sensory modality, including particularly the most fundamental, the kinesthetic image. The internalization of which we speak here is to be understood in a literal, physiological manner in contrast to the functional interiorization that characterizes the progress of operativity. The external movements of the hand muscles that overtly imitate the shape of a ball are similar in nature to the covert muscle movements that we may experience invoking the image of a ball. In a similar manner, the overt movements of the eye that can be observed by appropriate instruments become less large, less detailed during evocation of a visual image but are still directly related to the more easily observable movements during perceptual looking. In short, deferred imitation that is internalized and reduced in its overt activity is for Piaget what we commonly experience as images. These images are one basic form of symbols, functionally certainly the most important ones, without which a normal development of intelligence would be unthinkable.

A second basic form of symbolic behavior is observed in children's play, easily the most typical activity of children during the period of two to seven years. Play uses external things and imitative gestures as symbolic representations in the service of that which the play signifies.

Language is the third basic form of symbol behavior, the discussion of which is reserved to a separate chapter. It differs from the other two kinds of symbols in that its specific form is not indigenous to the child but is presented from without by society. Moreover, it constitutes a relatively autonomous system of symbols which the child has to learn—at least so it seems to an outside observer—in a radically different way from the spontaneous manner in which other intellectual achievements are acquired. Language, however, is not the only symbol system that society presents. Our entire social life is shot through with symbolic events, the manner we greet a person, the way we dress, behavior at meal time, expressive gestures, moral customs, personal idiosyncrasies, not to mention art, ceremonies, rituals. These things, too, the child acquires as part of his symbolic environment.

In fact, symbols and symbolic behavior are as broad and as wide as operational intelligence. Operational knowledge is taken here to include not only reflective or verbal knowledge, but also the grasping and exploring knowledge of a three-year-old. All this can be represented by the symbol-forming intelligence. For it is characteristic of a symbol that the knowing organism can construct it in the service of representation.

Such a broad definition of symbol is not explicitly taught by Piaget, but it is here suggested as an all-encompassing term for designating one of the two kinds of events with which intelligence deals. By this I do not mean to set up a clear dichotomy but merely to indicate that Piaget's theory of symbol behavior can be adapted to wider areas than the symbolic representation of logical or prelogical thinking. When knowing behavior adapts to events according to their functional nature we have a type of knowing which can be called thing-oriented. Thus would be a person's perceiving a tree as a tree, or a person's use of a plank to cross a stream, or the correct inference that John draws concerning his chances to beat Tom when he watches Tom beating Jim and knows Jim is stronger than himself. In these cases things and events are treated for what they are. But when a person sees a century-old oak as a sign of majestic strength, or when he uses the map of the stream to plan the location of the plank, or when the manner of setting the table for dinner indicates the arrival of an important visitor, and of course whenever any conventional language or symbolic construct is used, things are responded to as symbols. Note that for the existence of a symbol it is not necessary that the person who behaves symbolically does so consciously. Neurotic symptoms which the person denies are, for the specialist, communicating symbols nonetheless that may refer to a past knowledge of events as clearly as if it were recorded in conventional language.

According to this view there are some things that are expressly constructed for symbolic use, e.g., language or pictures, and their function is to represent. There are other things to which a thing-oriented response is indicated, a reaction to things for what they are in themselves. But all these real things can be turned into symbols when a person responds to them not for what they are but for what they represent to him. Moreover, while there is usually only one or a limited number of reality-oriented reactions, the levels and varieties of symbolic reactions are truly infinite, and a simultaneous functional and symbolic reaction is in real life the rule rather than the exception.

In spite of this immense variety of symbols, they all seem to fit into the model of symbolic relation that was illustrated earlier in the chapter. All symbols refer directly to some object of knowing and only via the knowing to the external event. We have asked before what is the product of knowing and the answer was the known event, the event as transformed by and assimilated to the knowing scheme. If we ask now what is the functional product of a symbol we can say it is this same knowing scheme which has turned the event into an object of knowing. Thus far the language is clear. Symbols signify or refer to the knowing of an event and nothing appears to be wrong in saying that symbols represent the known event.

A simple and uncritical acceptance of the foregoing analysis can easily lead one to conclude that the entire theory of operational intelligence is an elaborate explanation of developments that could be more parsimoniously dealt with by the traditional assumption that language acquisition results in symbolic representation, which in turn explains all the facts subsumed under the concept of operational intelligence. That Piaget's notion of operations is not a dispensable artifact can only be appreciated by consideration of the causal-temporal relation between constructive, operative knowing and symbol formation.

The problem lies with the word "to represent." Has the reader noticed that in the last sentence of the previous paragraph the symbol is said to represent, while originally it was always the person who represented something by means of symbols? We need only go one little step further and leave out the word "known" and put in its place, at least implicitly, the word "external" and we have left Piaget far behind. One more substitution in the sentence "The external world is represented by symbols" and we end up at the opposite pole of Piaget's position with the following statement: "The external world is known through symbols." With this last change we would have effectively demolished the basic structure of Piaget's operative theory as outlined before.

As was said in Chapter 4 and Reading 3, the unique knowing relation of knower to known is a subtle one and escapes direct introspective evidence. The tendency to give the known object a real, separate existence, external to the act of knowing, is constantly present to our way of thinking. Once symbols are endowed with the power to represent so as to take the place of things outside, the temptation to treat them as functional objects of knowing is almost irresistible. Knowledge becomes then, if not a mere looking on, at best a manipulation of symbols that mirror reality. With this the ultimate explanation of knowledge is taken away from the constructive and representing activity of the intelligent knower and delegated to these symbols as so-called mediators or objects of knowledge.

Notice how Piaget's theory is turned into a travesty if symbols can do so readily what operative constructs accomplish only by devious ways. With knowledge explained in terms of representation, why call in operations and operational constructs to represent reality if symbols in themselves are equipped to do so? Of those who reason this way, most will frankly admit that the symbol-signal distinction is of no relevance and in this statement they appear quite consistent. For only signals work by themselves; they are undifferentiated aspects of a global stimulus situation that elicit an external reaction. A symbol as representation needs a living person who constructs the representation, or in comprehending reconstructs it. As was pointed out in Reading 3, a representation theory reduces knowledge to a signal reaction even when it calls its mediators images, words, or symbols, and it leaves unexplained the active relation of the knowing person to the representation which would be inherent in any true symbol behavior.

The relation of knower to known as being different from the relation of knower to representation as well as from the more familiar relation of material cause and effect lies at the heart of Piaget's entire work. For this reason the reader will bear with me if I attempt by yet another diagram to clarify his theoretical approach towards these relations. I do this with a certain amount of hesitation, knowing full well that operative intelligence almost by definition cannot be adequately represented in a figural manner. (Figure 5, p. 94)

In the field of reality we have the external thing and the living person. The active person constructs the phenomena of the other fields and confers on them whatever reality status they can be said to possess. The three steps in the field of operative knowing are three aspects of the same phenomenon and not really distinct. Schemes or operations form the internal knowing structures, an internal act of knowing can be said to derive from the active structures, and the concept or known thing is shown as a final result in the field of knowing

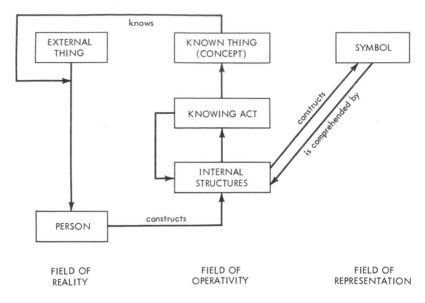

FIGURE 5. Three different fields of reality status in Piaget's operative theory of knowledge.

proper. More importantly the known thing, the final construct of operativity, is related to the external thing not as a symbol that signifies, but as that through which the external thing is known. This fundamental knowing relation is indicated in the diagram by the arrow that feeds from the operativity field back to the thing-person input. The formal abstraction that leads to the building up of knowing structures as discussed in the previous chapter is here shown as a feedback from the operative act to the knowing structures.

In distinction from the construction of the known thing, which stays internal to the knowing activity, the symbol is constructed by means of the scheme of knowing in order to make present, to represent the known thing in a field that is different, not only from the original thing but also different from the field of operativity. Thus while the object of knowing is internal to the operative field, the symbol in its totality is external to operativity. It can have an independent status of external reality as in symbolic play or gesture, a written word, an external ceremony, or it can remain within the person as an internal image. Only by having an aspect external to operativity can the symbol fulfill its function of representation, of making something else present in a new medium. Only by being tied to the operative structure is the active relation of knower and representation assured.

Reading 4, after this chapter, illustrates some common misunderstandings of Piaget's theory due to a failure to distinguish the operative scheme from a representational symbol. It also explains why the present author has discontinued the practice of translating Piaget's *schème* by the English word "schema" and uses instead the word "scheme." A different and superficially much simpler notion of representation underlies the representation theory of knowledge as outlined in the preceding Reading 3. There everything takes place in the field of outside reality where knowledge is supposedly read off with the internalized sign playing the key role. Instead of Piaget's constructive relation of knower-symbol, we have a causal-associative relation of thing to sign and vice versa.

It remains to illustrate how according to Piaget the child employs his symbolic function and in what manner this function interacts with the main progress in operational intelligence. Consider within the most typical activity of the preoperational child one that is surely among the most common: playing with dolls. That the activities represented during doll play hold a special personal interest for the child goes without saying and so does the fact that the child often employs play in the service of his emotional life. In fact, play in children is functionally analogous to dreams and reveries in adults, according to Freudian psychoanalysis. But what has doll play to do with growing intelligence?

A common misconception which has been only partially overcome by recent developments holds that intelligence by itself lacks motive force which therefore must be supplied by outside rewards, such as parental approval or some practical goal. While not discounting outside motivational influences, Piaget insists on the intrinsic biological need for acting and knowing. He compares a sensory-motor or an operational structure to a hungry animal that seeks suitable food. For Piaget one of the specific adaptive functions of symbolic play is the use of external things or actions in the service of the child's structures of knowing. This the child accomplishes by means of symbol-oriented reactions towards things with a functional disregard for an adaptive thing-oriented reaction. Thus, in play a box is not treated as a container but, depending on the situation, it is reacted to as a bed, a table, a chair, a carriage. The child makes present or represents something else by means of a medium that has some figural correspondence to the original. In our case the rectangular shape of the box shows sufficient material correspondence to be employed as a symbol for any of the things mentioned.

Since the child's purpose in symbolic play is to assimilate things to his own schemes without accommodating to their "real" character but rather treating them as symbols, Piaget sees in play a preponderance of assimilative activity over accommodation; as such it serves primarily the need to exercise the growing schemes of knowing and is functionally analogous to the reproductive assimilation of the sensory-motor period. Yet this assimilation to the self is not blind after the manner of a baby who puts everything and anything into his mouth. When a baby assimilates a box to an oral scheme this is due to immaturity, but such is not the case with the doll-playing child who takes the box for a bed. On the contrary, he knows what a bed is and what a box is; precisely because of this double knowledge he can use one as a symbol for the other.

Every functional use of symbols reveals a variety of assimilative and accommodative relations. A box as symbol signifies a bed insofar as it is assimilated to the operative scheme of bed, the identical scheme by which the child knows a bed. But at the same time there is a figural or material correspondence between the symbol and the referent; in distinction from a signal, not just anything can become the symbol of anything. The similarity in the child's accommodations to the figural aspect of the bed and the box is a decisive factor in symbol formation. This explains why a box, but not a ball, is used symbolically as a bed. In a sense, as far as the symbol itself is concerned, the accommodative activity appears preponderant over assimilation. This has to do with the fact that the symbol as some thing or some event, has a static, figural aspect. This aspect is likewise implied in the representational function of a symbol. Just as a perceptual presence, so a symbol insofar as it implies a representational presence, always has a figural aspect.

At the beginning of the preoperational period, the child's operativity has only just begun to manifest itself in object formation, which is the first stable bit of knowledge resulting from the coordinating of a multiplicity of object-centered external actions. Growth of intelligence continues now by a gradual transformation of practical schemes into operational schemes. The one-year-old who can handle a spoon and wants to manifest this practical knowledge by using the spoon himself will be much more insistent when two years old because now he begins to *know* that he can use the spoon. The sensory-motor scheme of using a spoon is here illustrated in the process of being interiorized, in the sense of becoming an object of knowledge. This knowing to use a spoon is not a self-reflective knowledge but is an extension or application of the fundamental knowing of a general object to one particular object.

As the first preoperational schemes multiply, they in turn are co-ordinated among themselves into higher structures that reveal more general aspects of coordinating actions. As on the sensory-motor plane the practical recognition of end-means relation marked a high point of achievement, so at the preoperational level Piaget has recently dis-covered a form of prelogic which he calls a *logic of functions*.[1] This refers to the child's ability to understand not merely simple cause-effect relations such as fire-heat, cooking-dinner, but functional corre-lations of dependency. A four-year-old child will know that the relative size of different containers determines the quantity of fluid he can pour into them or that the force of a push required to displace an object is proportional to its weight. In these law-like generaliza-tions there is a clear affinity to more mature logical and causal con-cepts and a stopping short of the mature operational level. Since this preoperational logic, like all natural logic, derives from actions, and since external actions are sequentially ordered in one direction, pre-operational functions lack reversibility by being limited to a specific direction. The reason for this is that preoperational knowledge in general is still tied to external action, not exclusively in a sensory-motor sense, but mainly through too great a dependence on symbolic representation.

Here we realize the essential function of symbols both for what they contribute, and in which respect they must be brought under operative control. Preoperational knowledge in its totality is still de-pendent on some external aspect of action, even though it is no longer mere knowledge in action. As was said before, in the absence of real objects, it is symbols that serve as representative objects on which operativity acts. Yet the symbols derive most closely from personal,

---

[1] Logic of functions is briefly described in Vol. 20 of the *Études d'épistémologie génétique* and an entire issue on this topic is in preparation.

individual actions that emphasize the particular here-and-now aspect of an event. They are internalized individual imitations and retain the personal flavor of the particular accommodations. The more knowledge is dependent on such symbols, the more it is ego-centered, that is, centered on the child's viewpoint.

Piaget suggests that the peculiar difficulties of the developing intelligence during the preoperational period are in large part due to the multiplicity of relations between reality-oriented and symbol-oriented schemes. One could expand this notion by naming three related factors that contribute to the slow progress of symbolic decentration. First, the experience of symbols, insofar as they are objects of knowing, is something new and fascinating to the child. Being actively produced by the child, symbols thus enjoy a preferred existence to schemes of knowing that are primarily reality-oriented. Secondly, symbolic behavior becomes quickly the favorite sphere of affectivity and emotions. Schemes that serve affective needs are frequently in opposition to schemes that are thing-oriented. Thirdly, even where no affectional distortions prevail, ego-centered schemes are constantly nourished and maintained by the assimilation-dominated use of symbols, such as in play or in early verbal behavior, without being thereby intellectually improved.

It is only around age six that the first true operational structures appear. As a consequence the child now develops reversible operations, e.g., a classificatory system which is not distorted by personal symbols though it may well be accompanied by it. Thus the progress of operative intelligence is always a decreased dependence on one's own actions and a greater freedom from and control of symbolic signifiers.

# Reading 4

## Concerning Piaget's View on Thinking and Symbol Formation[1]

### HANS G. FURTH

Piaget's symbolic function is examined in the light of some American interpretations and of recent theoretical developments. Piaget differentiates within cognition two aspects: operative, acting on and transforming a reality state, the basis of intelligent understanding; figurative, referring to the static configuration. Symbolic functioning includes both aspects: a symbol as signifier with a figurative content different from and assimilated to operative intelligence which is the symbol's source and referent. While symbolic functioning is indissociable from human cognition, a particular symbolic product (e.g., image, language) can be considered a supportive but not a constitutive element of operativity.

Growing interest in Piaget's developmental psychology is evidenced by three recent articles (Ausubel, 1965; Inhelder, Bovet, Sinclair, and Smock, 1966; Sutton-Smith, 1966) that ask for or offer explanations on specific aspects of his theory. While this note is partly addressed to Ausubel's paper, it deals primarily with some critical points of Piaget's position on logical thinking in relation to symbolic functioning. For this purpose use will be made of some recent books not yet available in English translation and of Piaget's (1966) own reply to Sutton-Smith which is precise but perhaps too concise and bears enlargement.

Ausubel contends that the symbolic function, according to Piaget, uses internalized actions as signifiers and in early development is dependent on these actions; however, "once verbal symbolization becomes consolidated,

[1] Reprinted from *Child Development*, 38 (1967), 819-826 with permission of the publishers. This essay was written during the author's sabbatical at the International Center of Genetic Epistemology at Geneva, Switzerland. Thanks are expressed to the collaborators at the Center, particularly to B. Inhelder for critical discussion and reading of the manuscript.

such actions no longer serve a signifying function." Consequently, for symbolic behavior there is apparently a discontinuity between early action-dependent and later verbal-dependent functioning. Concerning the development of thinking, however, Piaget is said to postulate a qualitative continuity between the action- or motor-basis of early and late manifestation of thought. Ausubel makes the plea that a contemporaneous dependence of mature thought on symbols in the form of internalized action seems incongruous to Piaget's view on symbolic development and his general system. Ausubel considers Piaget's position on the continuity of thought development and the discontinuity of symbol development a currently unresolved contradiction.

According to Piaget the primary purpose of the symbolic function is one of differentiation between a signifier and that which the signifier represents. A symbol, as something that represents and signifies, must be some thing or event that has a descriptive or figural component, for example, the observable movements of playing, the reportable visual image, the audible and motoric conventional linguistic utterance. As these examples show, symbols may be either overt, accessible to public observation, or merely covert, reportable as private experiences. Piaget speaks of symbolic instruments and classifies them as derived from accommodative imitations of two sources: (a) gestural or imaginal, (b) linguistic.

The operative as distinct from the figurative aspect of a symbol is given in two characteristics of a symbol: (a) the basic act of differentiation between the signifier and the signified, and (b) the symbol's assimilation to operative schemes, that is, action schemes in the form of preoperational schemes or logical operations. Thus, the symbolic instrument, that is, the symbol in its figurative aspect, is not to be confused with symbolic thought, a term that refers to symbolic behavior in its actual totality, including the figurative and the operative component.

In distinction from symbols, thinking for Piaget is not a descriptive event, not a representation, not some event that can be observed. Thinking is a process or an action, specifically an action that transforms overtly or covertly one reality state into another and in so doing leads to implicit or explicit knowledge of the state. "In fact, to understand a state one must understand the transformations from which the state results . . ." (Piaget, 1966). This active, transformational aspect of thinking within the context of a structure, increasing in scope and internal complexity, is the unifying link between the earliest manifestation of intelligent thinking (preoperational action-schemes) and mature logical thinking (formal operations).

Piaget (1951, p. 67) warns us not to confuse the figurative representation which belongs to a symbol with the transformational component present in all thinking. "We use the word 'representation' in two different senses. In its broad sense, representation is identical with thought, i.e., with all intelligence which is based on a system of concepts or mental schemes ... In its narrow sense, representation is restricted to the mental or memory image, i.e., the symbolic evocation of absent realities." In the next paragraph this distinction is employed to contrast the emergence of conceptual representation (in the broad sense) from sensory-motor schemes and the emergence of symbolic representation from imitation.

Piaget expresses the transformational action-character of intelligent thinking by the term "operative intelligence." Knowledge of an event at all levels of development consists in the assimilation of the event to an operative scheme and in the accommodation of the scheme to the event. Schemes in this sentence are interiorized coordinating or transformational actions, that is, not just any external actions as such, but the generalizable functional coordination of these external actions. Only by misunderstanding that particular coordinating aspect of external action which is interiorized in schemes and expressed in subsequent imitation can Sutton-Smith (1966) attribute a "copy" theory to Piaget. Actually it is incorrect to assert that early motoric coordination is *merely* external in contrast to later interiorized thinking. Strictly speaking, even the most primitive coordination of action is not just "out there" and given; rather it is already constructed from the subject's viewpoint and inferred by the observer.

Consequently, when Ausubel asserts that the mature thought processes of operations should not remain contemporaneously dependent on internalized actions, it seems that he has not fully understood Piaget's straightforward statement, quoted by Ausubel himself, that "operations are nothing but interiorized actions." When operations are said to be actions, there is no room for further asking whether they depend on these actions. The full impact of Piaget's statement escapes all too readily those scientists who wish to avoid a "mentalistic" concept of thinking by means of observable (i.e., figurative) mediating variables. There is empirical and philosophical soundness in Piaget's view which at no level of the biological development of intelligence admits the artificial dichotomy of mental and physical.

Ausubel's summary of Piaget refers indiscriminately to internalized actions as the source of thought as well as of symbol. Consequently one may well wonder what the difference between the symbolic and the thinking function is if both derive from an identical source. Hence, also, Ausubel's surprise that two such similar functions should receive dissimilar treatment from Piaget. It is, however, not exact to state that symbols derive from action. Rather Piaget would say that symbolic signifiers derive from the accommodating aspect of imitation, that is, from the accommodation of a preoperational scheme to the figural-descriptive aspect of a state of reality. For instance, the scheme of moving the hand across the face (itself a development of sensory-motor coordination) is applied to the observation of father's shaving, is subsequently performed in the absence of the model and internalized as a kinesthetic-visual image. This image becomes a symbol for the child when he uses it to represent his knowledge of shaving. In other words, the figural movement or image is the signifying symbolic instrument which is assimilated to the operative scheme of shaving. In another instance, the linguistic expression "second helping" can be meaningfully imitated, that is, it becomes or is employed as a symbol, once the child, having mastered certain basic auditory and phonetic schemes related to language acquisition, assimilates the imitative accommodation of the particular sound sequence to the thinking scheme of "wanting more." Note that in every instance the assimilative dependence on the cognitive scheme is such that without it one could not speak of symbol at all.

A symbol is thus an observable state that derives from accommodating imitation and, as a symbol, represents something other than itself. Does a symbol represent directly the objective state which was originally imitated? Such a view would lead to serious epistemological difficulties that need not concern us here. Rather, Piaget (1966) states that the symbolic function represents figurative and cognitive schemes, that is, symbols refer directly to thinking schemes and only indirectly to objective events. Concerning Piaget's use of the apparently overlapping term "figurative scheme," the recent book on the mental image (Piaget & Inhelder, 1966b, p. 431) makes an interesting distinction between a figurative *schema* and an operative *scheme*. A figurative schema is recognized as the symbolic-imaginative support for a knowledge that is directly focused on the figural aspect of an object, for example, in spatial concepts. The spatial image is then a true schema or schematic outline, while the intelligent structure from which this schema derives can be called a figurative scheme.

English versions of Piaget's books do not consistently translate the French *schème*, although most commonly it is translated as *schema*, so that the above distinction could not easily be articulated. Is this use of the word *schema* perhaps another subtle indication of how Piaget's expressions can become assimilated to a different cognitive framework with the result of fundamental misconceptions about Piaget's position?

An illustration of such a misunderstanding is given in the following sentence, taken from a paragraph which purports to summarize Piaget's developmental theory: "These complex sensorimotor schemata and imitations become internalized as images, and these in turn become coordinated as intuitions. These intuitions are gradually 'decentered' and grouped into reversible and associative operations with concrete objects and materials" (Hunt, 1961, p. 288). In a similar manner, Sutton-Smith (1966) writes: "In due course...these imitations become interiorized as images, and then, later, when these images become attached to, and differentiated from, external symbols [2] during intelligent activity or during play, they are transformed into concepts."

Is it not clear that in these two quotations images are considered to function within a developmental-hierarchical arrangement on a par with sensory-motor schemes, concepts, and operations? This seems a far cry from Piaget, for whom the symbol as such is outside the operative-transformational component of the developing intelligence.

Once symbolic functioning and operative thinking have been clearly delineated, it is proper to ask the question whether there can be operative thinking without any contemporaneous symbolic support. Symbol is here taken in the broader sense of including besides gestures and images also socialized language. This is quite a different question than asking whether thinking can take place without internalized actions. Furthermore, questions about the nature and the relation of this support become meaningful. Piaget in his early writings did not directly concern himself with this problem. Yet it is a fair statement that today a majority of psychologists of different persuasions base the developmental and theoretical explanation of mature logical thinking processes on the presence of symbols, particularly the verbal language of one's society.

In order to clarify his position on this point, Piaget now speaks more clearly of the figurative component of the intelligent grasp of reality as contrasted with the transformational-operative component. Only in two recent books which summarize empirical and theoretical investigations on perception and imagery has Piaget fully elaborated on this distinction. When Piaget (1966) now says that perceptual presentation is figurative but not symbolic, linguistic representation is symbolic but not figurative, while imaginal or gestural representation is both figurative and symbolic, this statement must be understood as to the relation between the represen-

---

[2] It seems astonishing that one can attribute to Piaget the notion that "images become attached to...external symbols" when from cover to cover of his book *Play, Dreams and Imitation in Childhood* Piaget proposes that images *are* symbols. Piaget's original title expresses clearly this concern to search for the common symbolic factor underlying different behavioral manifestations. For some reason this title has been withheld from the English public who knows the book only by a part of its subtitle. Here is the full title in literal translation: *The Formation of the Symbol in Children.* (Subtitle:) *Imitation, Play and Dreams, Image and Representation.*

tation and the object itself. In itself any symbolic event, whether imaginal or linguistic, partakes of a figurative and an operative component. It is the operative component, present in any perceptual or symbolic behavior, which primarily determines the level of understanding reality. Thus neither symbolic nor figurative functioning can explain intelligence since these cognitive aspects are fully tied to and dependent on the level of operative thinking.

To illustrate the role of symbols and the fact that operations are real actions, Piaget (1963, p. 56) considers the addition of two numbers $(2 + 3 = 5)$. When the operation of addition is performed on symbols, the specific symbols 2, 3, 5, +, = constitute the figurative aspect of thinking and are tied to the representation and communication of specific states. The transforming operation of combining as such is, however, as real when it is done on symbols as when it is done preoperationally on two external things to which three are added. The reason for this functional identity ("as real") is the fact that in both situations the combining addition as such is not simply given but is constructed by the thinking subject.

This example illustrates at the same time the manner in which it is legitimate to consider symbolic functioning essential for the manifestation of thinking processes. By what other means than external symbols could a problem of addition be communicated and represented? By what other means could states be evoked that are not actually perceived? However, verbal language as such does not have a privileged place with respect to the development of representational thinking. Piaget puts it like this in the article expressly devoted to the language-thinking relation: "If it is legitimate to consider language as playing a central role in the formation of thought, it is insofar as it constitutes one of the manifestations of the symbolic function while the development of this symbolic function is itself dominated by the intelligence in all its aspects" (Piaget, 1963, p. 57). And in the book in which Piaget discusses the role of the mental image one can cite this summarizing statement: "If the image is not an element of thought, it nevertheless serves on a par with language as a symbolic instrument to signify the content of the cognitive significations; for spatial concepts the effectiveness of the image is particularly evident" (Piaget & Inhelder, 1966b, p. 446).

With statements such as the above, Piaget clearly puts himself in opposition to any view that considers any particular symbolic product, including verbal language, as a central, constitutive component of operative thinking.

This of course in no way implies that general symbolic functioning is of no import in intellectual development. On the contrary, symbolic functioning is characteristic of and indissociable from human thinking from the second year onward. This symbolic function, or as Piaget recently prefers to call it (Piaget & Inhelder, 1966a), the semiotic function, makes possible the evocation and representation of states by means of differentiated signifiers. Consequently, symbols, as signifiers, have a status different from that which they refer to, namely operative schemes. Operative thinking, it will be recalled, does not represent but implicitly transforms a reality state according to its own structure; this internal action constitutes the basic aspect of intelligent understanding.

While there is no good empirical method of controlling the private symbols of images and gestures, one can find and observe children who are normally equipped to develop symbolic behavior but grow up without the benefit of being steeped in the verbal language of society. With such a natural "deprivation" experiment one can readily test whether or not a deficiency specifically focused on language leads to a serious and general deficiency in intellectual development. If Piaget's view on the dependent role of symbolic functioning, including the role of language, is correct, the answer should be "no." It seems that our own investigations with deaf people (Furth, 1966) provide a fair measure of empirical confirmation of Piaget's position on this critical issue.

In summary, according to Piaget the cognitive operative component of intelligence constitutes the basic aspect of intelligent knowing. It dominates and determines increasingly all other aspects. While its development shows structurally the well-known stages which are clearly differentiated, functionally there is continuity derived from the increasing interiorization of coordinated action-schemes.

The figurative and symbolic aspect of intelligence does not exhibit a similarly unified development. Perception is present from the first period regulated on the cognitive side by perceptual activity of the sensory-motor intelligence. The emergence of symbolic activity in the form of signifiers, different from and outside the operative activity, requires the cognitive dependence on at least preoperational schemes. Language is recognized as a special kind of symbol that is not figuratively related to the objective configuration but it too is part of the symbolic function and does not enter directly into the operative component.

There is, of course, constant interaction between these various activities as well as reciprocal influence of operative on figurative-symbolic activity. But these latter activities lack the functional continuous development of the former and cannot be said to derive or develop one from another, much less to be determining stages in the growth of operative intelligence. The particular stage of thinking in its operative aspect is the basic source and explanation for the production and comprehension of any symbolic behavior.

REFERENCES

Ausubel, D. P., "Neobehaviorism and Piaget's Views on Thought and Symbolic Functioning," *Child Development*, 36 (1965), 1029-32.

Furth, H. G., *Thinking Without Language: Psychological Implications of Deafness*. New York: Free Press, 1966.

Hunt, J. McV., *Intelligence and Experience*. New York: Ronald, 1961.

Inhelder, B., M. Bovet, H. Sinclair, and C. Smock. "On Cognitive Development," *American Psychologist*, 21 (1966), 160-64.

Piaget, J., *Play, Dreams and Imitation in Childhood*. New York: Norton, 1951.

———, "Le langage et les opérations intellectuelles," in *Problèmes de psycholinguistique*, Neuchâtel: Symposium de l'association de psychologie scientifique de langue française, 1962. Paris: Presses Universitaires de France, 1963. (Reading 5)

———, "Response to Brian Sutton-Smith," *Psychological Review*, 73 (1966), 111-12.

Piaget, J., and B. Inhelder, *La psychologie de l'enfant*. Collection "Que sais-je," No. 396. Paris: Presses Universitaires de France, 1966 (a).

———, *L'image mental chez l'enfant: Étude sur le développement des représentations imagées*. Paris: Presses Universitaires de France, 1966 (b).

Sutton-Smith, B., "Piaget on Play: A Critique," *Psychological Review*, 73 (1966), 104-110.

# 6
# language
# and verbal
# behavior

Without doubt the biological function of speech is intra-species communication. The vocal chords have evolved for the biological function of vocal expression. As a means of communication speech must be something externally expressed and discriminable that can be given by one and received by another. For many species the speech or song system consists in rigidly built-in signal behavior. As we go up the evolutionary ladder in the direction of less immediacy and less specificity of adaptive actions, we also find a similar progress towards greater freedom from immediate signal behavior and greater finesse in varying the signal in accord with the event to be communicated. If there were measures available, one could certainly observe a general correlation in animals between complexity of practical intelligence and vocal communication, but such a relation would be inconsistent in many particular cases. Thus, the most evolved vocal system among the monkeys is not found in the primates. Similarly, complexity of social life in animals is not a reliable indicator of an evolved vocal communication.

Taken as the totality of speech behavior typical of a society, language in the human species is characterized by a freedom from immediacy that is the mark of a symbol as distinct from a signal. Moreover, it presents itself to an investigator as an incredibly complex system both on the phonological and on the grammatical level. At first thought there seems to be something here for the child to acquire which is totally different from any other thing he has achieved so far. It is different from so-called objective reality and requires a symbol-oriented, not a fact-oriented response. The preceding chapter has shown that in Piaget's system a playing child also makes a symbol-oriented response when he treats a stick as a jet plane. We can understand this play as a self-produced activity that confers a borrowed meaning on the stick and turns it into a symbol. But in language the meaning is conferred from outside. In other types of symbol behavior we speak freely of the production or formation of symbols; with language it appears to be first a problem of comprehension, followed only afterwards by expression or production.

It was pointed out before that Piaget uses a different term for linguistic as compared to other self-produced symbolic behavior. He does so following the tradition of Saussure, an influential linguist who flourished at the time of Piaget's youth in the same institution where Piaget is today, the University of Geneva. Saussure's approach to language was diametrically opposed to Piaget's approach to intelligence. Saussure investigated language as a finished product; studied its organization in a static, classificatory manner apart from the meaning context and was not concerned with developmental considerations. He assumed *a priori* that language is the essential instrument by which thinking is structured into an organized, rational whole. As he endowed language signs with the power to structure thought, he separated them sharply from other symbolic signs. He called them conventional or arbitrary "signs" as distinguished from self-motivated "symbols."

Piaget adopted this nomenclature at an early time of his work when he was also seriously considering the hypothesis that the final stage of logical thinking may be intrinsically dependent on verbalization. Yet having accepted the distinction, he started publishing book after book in which he showed that the language use of the small child is thoroughly permeated by ego-involved, subjectively motivated factors. Later on with a clearer insight into the action-derived structure of operational thinking he found little room for bringing language in as an explanatory principle. Today Piaget finds himself as perhaps the only exponent of logical intelligence who does not see language as an intrinsically necessary element of operational thinking.

Thus I think that Piaget does himself a disservice by adopting the label that has been used in connection with an assumed thought-structuring property of language and then sets out to demonstrate, against the overwhelming majority of other scholars, that neither language nor any other symbolic sign has such a property. From the child's viewpoint—the viewpoint which Piaget has consistently taken in his developmental considerations—it seems irrelevant whether the sound sequence to which he is exposed has an arbitrary conventional meaning, whether it is inherent in a melodic and rhythmical song or whether it has an intrinsic natural connection with its source, as the roar of an airplane that is taking off. Developmentally a sentence does not appear more arbitrary to the two-year-old child than a thousand other facts, such as the fact that he is not allowed to jump on the sofa, that there are three meals at specified times of the day, or that daddy does not work on weekends. Biologically as a general function, and historically as the acquisition of a special language, language has all the characteristics of a living, ongoing process, something that is functionally organized and fitting the nature of man. Finally, modern linguists indicate that human languages have some general structural properties which arbitrary systems need not have, so that the attribute of arbitrariness should not be applied except perhaps to the semantic aspect of language. It is even considered that the main task of linguistics lies in discovering the universals underlying natural languages. Leading scholars in the field look for the roots of the more essential structural aspects of language not in society's convention but in the biological system of man.[1] In what respect are any conceivable deep

[1] The linguist's recent interest in the generative, structuring aspect of linguistic behavior should not obscure the fact that Chomsky's model (as for instance outlined in Lenneberg, E. H. *Biological foundations of language.* New York: Wiley, 1967) follows an analytic and not a genetic approach. Hence we observe Chomsky's apparent insistence that linguistic rules are innate, "...that [a particular linguistic principle] is not learned at all, but rather that it is simply part of the conceptual equipment that the learner brings to the task of language acquisition" (p. 415). The view that language is not learned is compatible with Piaget's distinction between learning in the strict sense and development (see Chapter 13). But the issue must be carried further than innateness as the only alternative to learning. The development of linguistic structures must be related to the overall development of non-linguistic structures and symbols. There is little hope that linguists can do this as long as they are satisfied

structures of language related to a logical or prelogical deep structure of thinking? In what manner do these two structures imply a common biological matrix? These are questions that at the present state of the science can only be asked and left open.

Last but not least the view that language behavior is found within the same context as other forms of symbol behavior is one of the most important new insights of Piaget. Instead of stressing this unity by the one common name of symbolic behavior as is done here, his verbal distinction between signs and symbols seems to relegate symbols to a lower ego-centered phase. As a consequence Piaget's distinction between symbols and signs can at times give the impression that mature symbol behavior is not only disregarded but does not fit into his theory, while language is a determining factor of the rational phase. Though Piaget himself in other places denies this role to language, such wording plays into the hands of those who according to the representation theory of knowledge endow signs with structuring properties as the basis for intellectual growth.

In Piaget's model the symbolic function is an integral part of intelligence in its totality. We recall from previous chapters that the capacity to represent resides in the same knowing structure that constructs the known object. While this object stays within the plane of knowing, the symbol as a product, as a thing, can be clearly distinguished from the symbolic function. By being outside the thinking process, a symbolic instrument can become a means of communication between persons and thus form part of the external symbolic environment to which a person responds. Knowing as a living process cannot be experienced or observed in itself, but only inferred from its manifestations; a symbol, in contrast, has an integral part that is external to thinking. This external part can be observed by another person, as in a spoken word, a visual gesture, or a picture. Even if the symbol remains interior to the person as in a mental image or an inaudible word, it can be introspectively experienced as something which one sees or which one senses. But, as Piaget points out, introspection is deceiving when it reports that intelligence is nothing but these external parts of covert symbols. For just as introspection does

---

with rejecting a mechanistic-association model of *language* acquisition and at the same time implicitly accept such a theory for *knowledge*. The description in this chapter of linguistic acquisition within the totality of Piaget's developmental theory is an attempt to suggest areas of contact that could be elaborated in greater detail.

not experience the knowing transformation which results in the known thing, neither can it experience the transformation by which the external event of a sound sequence or a visual form is turned into a meaningful symbol. The act of comprehending a symbol is similar to the operative process by which we know the referent. This is the deep reason for the previous statement that a sign is only as good as the knowing structure which uses it.

Piaget, as is well known, first studied the thinking of the young child mainly by means of verbal questions and answers. In these procedures he took the adequacy of children's linguistic knowledge for granted. In fact in the few examples that follow here, one will not find any *linguistic* difference between logically correct or less correct answers. When children reply that the sun is named sun "because it is yellow," or "because the sun gives more light than the moon and people thought it was the best name," or "for no reason, it's just a name," these statements are equally well-formed English sentences. Piaget's purpose in studying the verbal behavior of the children has therefore no bearing on language as such, except to indicate in a rather decisive manner that progress in logical thinking is in no *obvious* way linked with progress in linguistic ability.

The above examples express replies of children with increasing age to the question: Why is the sun called "sun"? Note the early belief of children that names are part of the essential nature of objects and adhere to the objects as an invisible quality. Piaget calls this *nominal realism*. While children at the age of nine or ten were observed to recognize finally that names had a subjective reality as distinct from the objective reality of the referent, it was only when two years older that the intrinsically arbitrary nature of names was generally admitted.

In these and other investigations Piaget not only presupposes adequate linguistic competence but, more crucially, he believes that children adequately express what they think. One frequently hears the argument that the answers of the children may be due merely to a semantic confusion and not to a lack of logical comprehension. A detailed study of children's verbal behavior will indicate, however, that this argument is not well founded, certainly not in the vast majority of cases. Take the case of four-year-old Jim who is cooperative and replies negatively to the question whether or not he could be named Bruce rather than Jim. At the same time he replies affirmatively to the question whether or not he could live in a house different from

his own. The two different responses on the part of the child permit
one to infer that semantically he understands the questions quite correctly and replies according to his knowledge about the function of
names.

As a further illustration of verbal thinking in children, consider the
simple "test" of vocabulary, since Binet's time still the one single best
indicator of IQ. First, children will not speak at all but simply point
or make a gesture. At a second stage they will respond with a phrase
indicating a function, e.g., a car is to go for a ride, mummy is to cook
dinner, etc. This is an example of the ego-centered stage of thinking
at which the child cannot free himself from his own viewpoint. Of
course, Piaget's ego-centrism has nothing to do with selfishness or an
overly keen regard of self or with a frequent verbal use of "I" and
"me." At this stage one can hardly speak of knowledge of self as an
independent social person. Since his knowledge of things derives from
his own actions, it is not surprising that the child begins by thinking
of things in terms of his own subjective activity. Thus, as Piaget likes
to put it, seeing himself in all things, he is least able to know his self.

There follows a third stage in vocabulary when the child gives a
logical answer but in a global fashion where the decisive logical difference is left out: mummy is a lady, a brother is a boy. Interestingly at
the same age children will mistakenly give differences even when
asked for similarities, that is, for the general superordinate class: In
which way are an apple and a pear alike? Reply: "An apple is round,
a pear is oval." In which way are a lion and a squirrel alike? Reply:
"One is strong, the other is weak." Such illustrations show that the
reason why a five-year-old fails in giving a logically adequate verbal
definition is not lack of linguistic but of operative knowledge. He has
not yet adequately constructed the general logical framework of
classification, a first structure of true operations, within which he can
freely move from superordinate class to subordinate class and vice
versa. It is only when and because the child's intelligence has reached
this stage of operations that adequate logical definitions are forthcoming.

It seems hardly necessary to give more examples that show how
children's verbal concepts do not conform to adult usage. The child
who is beginning to speak may call all ladies mummy or every kind
of meat chicken and may widen or narrow the meaning of words in
a fluid, unstable manner. Even two or three years later when he seems

to use language in an adequate fashion, one encounters frequent mis-understandings. Piaget reports how children when faced with a collection of some circles all of which are blue, and a number of squares some of which are blue, others red, will consider the statement: "All circles are blue" as false. Because of his incapacity to differentiate clearly between comprehension and extension, the young child apparently takes the word "all" as pertaining to the predicate and mis-understands the sentence as meaning: "The circles are all the blue things."

An associate of Piaget has recently discovered some interesting structural correlations between language and operative thinking which open up a new and fruitful perspective in viewing the language-thinking relation. H. Sinclair (1967) found that linguistically higher-order structural devices were used by children who had reached a higher operative stage of thinking. Children were asked to describe the difference between two pencils, one short and thick, the other long and thin. Some children who had not reached the stage of ele-mentary concrete operations showed an inadequate use of lexical items by describing the difference in terms like "one is big, the other is a bit small." Other children, still in the preoperational stage, already used the two terms of opposites, long-short and thin-thick. However, their description was linguistically relatively unstructured. They singled out one difference in two positive, complete sentences, "this pencil is long, this one is short" and then remarked on the other differ-ence "this pencil is thin, this one is thick." By contrast, children who had operationally mastered conservation of quantity expressed the double difference in one all-embracing statement. Thus from a lin-guistic viewpoint their utterance used structurally more complex de-vices of comparative markers and of a coordinated structure: "This one is longer and thinner than the other one."

Similarly, Sinclair observed that concrete-operational children used operator-like words such as "more" or "less" to describe a difference between two continuous quantities whereas preoperational children preferred the use of positives like "a lot" and "a little." In these simple situations no judgment of conservation was needed to notice the dif-ference in question; moreover, the preoperational patterns of verbal descriptions were not due to any linguistic ignorance, since all chil-dren not only comprehended comparatives but spontaneously used them in situations which they could master intellectually, such as adding something to a given quantity. Some children used comparatives ("more," "less") even in conservation problems as long as discrete elements were employed but switched to positives ("much," "little") when conservation of continuous quantity was tested. An explicit drill in the comparative and coordinate use of language was found to have very little effect on the conservation performance—a rather clear indication that the linguistic factor was not decisive in the emergence of operational behavior.

In view of the immature use of language it is a rather astonishing fact that the basic knowledge of language, i.e., linguistic competence, is present in any typical four-year-old. However, linguistic competence refers to a person's ability to comprehend the basic phonological and grammatical structure of a language, it does not refer to its adequate use. Grammatical structure is understood as the sequencing of words, phrases, the use of nouns, verbs, gender—in short, all the principles by which a native speaker recognizes a sentence as grammatically correct or incorrect. These principles which are acquired by all of us at an early age are still far from being known by scientists in an explicit, formal manner: an apt illustration that the successful acquisition of linguistic structures is not tied to explicit verbal statements of the rules. On the phonological level, audiologists study the complex nature of the discrimination of the sound elements of speech, of the sequencing of these elements and their vocal reproduction, all of which reveal the great complexity of analysis and synthesis that is characteristic of speech behavior. However, there is no reason to believe that other knowing and symbolic behavior that the child acquires as early as language does not require equally complex activities on the part of the child.

Piaget has not directly concerned himself with the problems of language as such, and even his most explicit treatment in the essay translated as Reading 5 is limited to the general relation of language and operations. What follows should be clearly understood as an attempt on my part to employ the constructs of Piaget's theory in a more detailed analysis of a linguistic situation. In whatever way the acquisition of language is explained, Piaget's theory reminds us that any specific symbolic behavior is inherently dependent on knowing activity and on the symbolic function in general. In this perspective language acquisition is not unlike image formation. The main difference between these two processes is that language imitates a "symbolic" event, image a "real" event. But let us assume that an operative, assimilative contribution is needed in both cases and that this assimilation can be at a very imperfect level, i.e., the child can imitate something of which he has only a very imperfect understanding. Under these conditions the difference is not as big as we adults imagine it to be. Adults are overly impressed by the difference between the invisible image and the physical stimulation of audible sounds. Children do not learn language in the way in which a high school student learns to memorize a list of Latin words. They learn language in the same way in which they adapt to customs and regulations within the family or society, such as the daily routine, the differences between what the child himself, his siblings, friends and adults can do, rules for walking across the street, rules of games, particularly also responsiveness to signs of interpersonal communications other than speech, including of course expressions of feelings and emotions. In brief, once the child has reached a stage where he can make a symbol-oriented response, he is ready to respond meaningfully to the total situation of which spoken language is a part and as a by-product he learns language.

Early schemes of hearing, voicing, of reciprocal eye, ear, voice and movement coordinations have prepared the child for some of the phonetic phases of the language situation. Another prerequisite for language acquisition is undoubtedly the grasp of time sequences within practical actions. Sequencing is inherent in his own or other people's motor acts or events, e.g., the child's familiarity with the expected sequence of the washing, preparing, filling, and closing of the bottle. Sequential ordering is of paramount importance for hearing the difference between TOP and POT or for paying attention to sequential rules of grammar. Most importantly, the basic mechanism of symbol acquisition, which derives from accommodative imitation, is equally at work in the linguistic as in other symbol-forming situations.

Accommodation to the global situation in which a little girl just broke a cup and spilled milk on the floor consists in paying attention to the particular visual and auditory events, part of which is hearing a sentence like "How terrible, you broke a cup and spilled all the milk on the floor." The auditory mechanism accommodates to the sound sequence and the voice organs begin to shape themselves in covert imitation of the heard speech with reciprocal influence of these two processes. Then there is also visual and kinesthetic accommodation to the seen movements of the other members of the family, probably also to the shape of the puddle of milk on the floor that strikes the child's eye as an unusual and interesting sight. At the same time the child responds to the social and emotional situation by interior reactions that correspond to the autonomic reactions of the bystanders. These are a few of the outward-directed activities of accommodation on the part of the child within the given situation.

There is a corresponding assimilative activity which confers meaning on the total situation by transforming the sensory input into things and events that are known according to the structures available to the child. It is impossible to enumerate exhaustively the varieties of active schemes at this moment. Schemes corresponding to the table, the cup, the milk, the family, the room, the social events of eating, of scolding, of hearing the speaking of others—these and many other structures interrelate in a tight network of the child's particular organization of knowing. Perhaps the child has only recently begun to show some specific vocal reactions to language. When the child now suddenly responds to the situation by emitting the sound sequence "Cup broke" in a clear, phonetically correct voice, words which she had never spoken before, can one infer that she has "learned" these two words at this moment?

A number of pertinent questions arise. Why did she put the words in this particular order, since she heard them a few seconds ago in the reverse order? Can one confidently assert that the girl associates the word "broke" with just the event of breaking or does it encompass a whole sequence of events from the taking, drinking, dropping, breaking, spilling to the global situation of there being a cup that arouses a peculiar social reaction? Is the word linked to an undifferentiated situation of something bad or something interesting? Why did she repeat just the two words and not others that were more conspicuously stressed, for instance, the first and the last words "How, floor," or just any two words—"on, broke"? All these considerations seem to indicate that the child approached the particular linguistic situation with a variety of knowing structures without which the particular sentence "Cup broke" would be a highly unlikely utterance. It is apparent that the imitative accommodation was far from being a passive copy of an external event. Accommodation corresponds to assimilation. The particular external accommodations of the hearing and speech organs were already prepared, as the child had previously acquired structures of comprehending sound sequences and grammatical rules of her mother tongue. The child's saying "Cup broke" is but a first external manifestation of a process of comprehension that has been at work for a long time, both in the sense of the growth of intelligence in general, and in the quite specific sense of acquiring specific linguistic knowledge.

This analysis of a single speech situation stresses first the active structure of knowing schemes to which the child assimilates the event, at the same time as she accommodates sensory and motor parts of the organism to the event. The structure includes previously acquired schemes of hearing, voicing, and sequencing, corresponding to the phonological, grammatical, and other levels of a specific language. The child expresses these knowing structures by a sound sequence just as she might with an outward gesture. As far as symbol formation is concerned, the two actions are functionally equivalent. Both can become internalized and serve as differentiated signs, i.e., as symbols, to refer to the event as known by the child.

While emphasizing this essential communality as far as the knowing or acquisition process is concerned, the specific properties of linguistic behavior can be better appreciated. There is above all the linguistic system, the grammatical structure, with its obvious relation to general properties of structuring, characteristic of all operative schemes. The specific relations of operational and linguistic structures are, however, quite obscure. On the other hand it is clear that in distinction from other symbols which serve primarily the knowing function, speech is biologically oriented not to knowing but to communication. Its whole system is geared towards social exchange. It is a misunderstanding of its basic nature to look for a completely consistent reflection of logical thinking in the linguistic organization. Piaget frequently attributes a decisive role in breaking the child's egocentric opinions to social communication as carried on through language. However, he knew better than to build the structure of logical thinking on a system of communication that in its redundancy, its vagueness of meaning, and many other respects is admirably suited for its adaptive purpose but constitutes a veritable trap for critical thinking, as logicians long ago realized.

It has been remarked by Piaget and others that the young child uses language audibly to speak to himself as well as to communicate with others. Some scholars, like Vygotsky, hypothesize that the early speech for self is gradually internalized and synthesized with thinking. In this connection the term "inner speech" is employed in a sufficiently vague meaning to cover a multitude of possible phenomena. On this point I would like to make the following personal observations. While many children, not all by any means, habitually speak to themselves during play or in other non-communicative situations, no normal child at any period of development uses language primarily for purposes of self-communication. On the contrary, the social use of language is always foremost, and the greatest influence of language is undoubtedly in the social sphere. Second, the fact that the child uses language as a symbolic instrument for representing to himself things which he knows is as natural as that he internalizes the accommodation of his eye muscles as mental images. This internalization does not suppress the primary function of the eye, which remains seeing, not forming symbols.

Finally, the mention of inner language [2] and the synthesis of internal speech and thinking can be but a more subtle version of explaining intelligence in terms of the linguistic contribution. If inner language is merely a derivation from external language, if it entails an inaudible talking to oneself in incomplete and fragmentary sentences, then the term is clear and acceptable. But more frequently inner language seems to be understood as a general capacity of internal representation, perhaps identical with what Piaget calls the symbolic function in general. Or is inner language linguistic competence, the acquisition of the rules by which the infinite numbers of possible sentences pertaining to a particular language can be generated? Or is it the knowledge of articulated words, of the names of things and of classes? If it is any of these things, does it include the operative aspect of thinking? In that case, what is the meaning of a synthesis of thinking and inner language when the second term by definition includes thinking and perhaps is nothing but thinking? If it is not included, the crucial question about the relation of intelligence to symbol behavior in general and to linguistic competence in particular remains unsolved. It does not suffice to say that intelligence and symbol formation are related or united. In which way? Which part contributes what?

Let us take an example in the area of verbal thinking and ask a

---

2 "Inner speech" is a favorite term with various scholars in the language area. Its ambiguous and unanalysed use has contributed considerably to the neglect of isolating the relevant variables in the language-thinking domain. See also Furth (1966), pp. 60-64.

five-year-old boy from New York: "Are there more New Yorkers or more Americans?" His answer, more likely than not, will be "More New Yorkers." Just two years later he may give the right answer as a matter of course. In connection with this Piaget-type problem of class inclusion we may ask what language contributes as an integral part of the problem situation. Since the question was framed in linguistic symbols, linguistic competence is of course a prerequisite in this situation. Moreover, the child's general knowledge or lack of knowledge of embedded class systems is expressed by the verbal reply. But is the verbal reply or any linguistic skill in general an intrinsic part of this knowledge of classes? To this question Piaget replies with an unequivocal no. He finds no theoretical reason for bringing in language nor is he able to interpret any known evidence to the effect that language in itself is a decisive contributory factor in developing the first operations.

Some years ago I began to investigate the hypothesis of a decisive influence of language on the development of logical thinking by means of what K. Lorenz terms a "deprivation experiment." Children who are born deaf are not exposed to the linguistic environment as all hearing children are. As a consequence, for about 90 per cent of them the knowledge of their society's language compared to hearing children's linguistic competence is like night to day. If language plays an important role, I expected to uncover marked deficiencies in logical thinking directly related to the linguistic deficiency of deaf individuals. Largely by means of verbal methods, investigators before me had already indicated serious conceptual shortcomings.

When my colleagues and I devised thinking tasks that were not couched in verbal terms, we found to our increasing surprise that the basic manifestations of logical thinking in linguistically deprived deaf children were present without any important structural deficiencies. In a deprivation experiment, even one bona fide example of non-impairment can be as valuable to science as many examples of the expected impairment, since indirect or extraneous factors may produce the impairment. Thus, while we did not find the deaf uniformly equal to the hearing, the number of tasks which showed no difference was impressive, and those tasks on which the deaf failed were not consistently related to specific logical operations. Failure seemed to be due to such types of behavior as intellectual initiative, grasping of instructions, or familiarity with similar problems. We hypothesized that these factors may be a more direct result of inadequate social experience rather than language deprivation. In fact, it is easy to observe that deaf children, with rare exceptions, grow up in an environment that neither readily accepts their handicap nor challenges their intellectual capacity. To test this experiential deficiency hypothesis, we replicated a number of tasks on culturally deprived children and adolescents and observed that they, too, in spite of their linguistic competence, showed a similar pattern of failure and success.[3]

Thus, having set out to explore the nature of the linguistic contribution to the development of thinking, we found ourselves in the awkward position of having to explain the development of thinking without language. We had to look for a theory that made sense of the fact that linguistically deprived deaf persons develop the structures of logical thinking. There are many deaf youngsters and adults who grow up without the benefit of a linguistic environment during their early childhood, who learn language in an artificial manner without much success, and who eventually pick up a kind of gestural language within the deaf society. Perhaps Piaget may not think so, but I am persuaded that the existence of those deaf persons who have developed into mature, intelligent humans without an early linguistic environment and without an orally articulated symbol system, is one of the best pieces of evidence for the soundness of his operative theory of thinking.

[3] The literature on the cognitive development of deaf individuals has been summarized in Furth, H. G. "Research with the deaf: Implications for language and cognition." *Psychological Bulletin*, 62 (1964), 145-164 and more recently in Furth, H. G. "A review and perspective on the thinking of deaf people." *Cognitive Studies, Volume I*, New York: Brunner/Mazel, 1969. This cites more than 100 references.

# Language and
# Intellectual Operations[1]

This article is a translation of a paper which Piaget prepared for a symposium held in 1962 under the auspices of the *Association de psychologie scientifique de langue française* on problems of psycholinguistics. After some general remarks addressed particularly to the position taken by logical positivism, Piaget analyses in section I the proposition that language is a *sufficient* condition in the formation of intellectual operations. After rejecting this hypothesis on the basis of developmental observations, Piaget, in section II, systematically discusses the manner in which language can be said to be *necessary* for intellectual operations. In conclusion he rejects the view that language provides thinking with ready-made structures and emphasizes the collective educative impact of language as a process of social equilibration.

I thank the committee for having asked me to participate in this conference. At first I accepted this invitation with pleasure, but during the preparation of this paper I felt a certain uneasiness. In fact I will not treat language in itself and moreover I have often developed the ideas which I am going to present concerning the relations of language and operations. You should have asked me for this paper some forty years ago at the time of my first works when I believed in close relations between language and thinking and when I studied almost nothing but verbal thought. Since that time I observed the nature of sensory-motor intelligence before the acquisition of language, as well as the results obtained by A. Rey in his

[1] Jean Piaget, "Le langage et les opérations intellectuelles," in *Problèmes de psycholinguistique: Symposium de l'association de psychologie scientifique de langue française* (Paris: Presses Universitaires de France, 1963), pp. 51-61. Translated by Hans G. Furth, by permission of the publishers.

analysis of *The Practical Intelligence in the Child;* subsequently I discovered the inventory of "concrete operations" of classes, relations, and numbers together with their parallel infra-logical structures in the area of spatial relations and measure, all of which develop between seven and twelve years; this takes place well before the stage of propositional operations which alone are capable of bearing upon merely verbal statements. All these facts have taught me that there exists a logic of coordination of actions. This logic is more profound than the logic attached to language and appears well before the logic of propositions in the strict sense.

It is quite possible that language is a necessary condition for the achievement of logical structures, in any case at the level of propositional structures. But this does not by itself make it a sufficient condition of logical formation, even less as far as the more elementary logico-mathematical structures are concerned. If I shall insist primarily on the insufficiencies of language, it is because everybody is aware of its positive contribution. I trust that I recognize sufficiently the importance of this contribution. On the other hand one forgets too often the role of actions and operational intelligence.

It is true that the principal operational structures are inscribed in the natural language in a syntactic form or are inherent in the semantic meaning. First of all, as far as concrete operations that bear directly upon objects (classes, relations, and numbers) are concerned, the linguistic distinction of substantives and adjectives corresponds in a general way to the logical distinction of classes and predicates. As a function of the meaning attributed to different substantives, every language involves relatively elaborate classifications. Simply by keeping to the ordinary sense of the words "sparrow," "bird," "animal," and "living being," the speaking subject can conclude that all sparrows are birds, that all birds are animals, and that all animals are living beings without the reciprocals being true. This in itself constitutes a hierarchical ordering of classes, that is to say, a classification. To affirm on the other hand that whales are "at the same time" mammals and aquatic animals expresses an intersection or multiplication of classes, the principle of multiplicative and not merely additive classifications. Words such as grandfather, father, son, brother, uncle, nephew, etc. suffice to determine the structure of a genealogical tree or co-univocal multiplications of classes or relations. Comparatives such as "bigger than" lead to seriations and the sequence of whole numbers is part of the common vocabulary.

As far as propositional or formal operations are concerned, one can find their principal forms in language: implication ("if ... then"), exclusive or non-exclusive disjunction ("either ... or"). The possibility of reasoning on simple hypotheses is a characteristic of these hypothetico-deductive operations and is produced by a correct handling of the above terms. Syllogistic reasoning can be translated directly into adequate verbal forms so that Aristotle's logic has been criticized for being somewhat dominated by grammar. With regard to structures that are too differentiated and complex to be expressed by current language, mathematicians and logicians have created artificial or technical languages for their use. Psychologically they can still be considered languages.

Consequently it is not surprising that theories have been developed among psychologists as well as epistemologists which seek to reduce to language alone the entire range of intellectual operations, not to say all of thinking, with the sole exception of kinesthetic or visual images. These theories simultaneously include a genetic and a causal viewpoint. It is unnecessary in a meeting of psychologists to recall in this connection the works and tendencies of current behaviorism deriving from Watson. But it may perhaps be of interest to note the complete convergence of its positions with those of the "Vienna Circle," an epistemologic school which originally worked independently of it. After the Viennese immigrated to the U.S.A., this school entered into close relation with behaviorism. R. Carnap, one of the founders of that "logical empiricism or positivism" was the first to propose that the entirety of logic was merely a general syntax in the linguistic sense of the term. Following the example of Tarski, Carnap was led to add to the syntax a general "semantics"; but this fact also does not take us beyond the frontiers of language. Finally Morris has shown the necessity (not recognized by the entire school) to take account of the operative character of logic, and to complete the logical syntax and semantics by a "pragmatics." But here too one is still dealing with rules of utilizing a language and not a logic of action.

If one goes through the *Encyclopedia for Unified Sciences*, the bible of logical positivism, one can only be astonished at the insistence with which logicians, linguists, and psychologists of the school outdo themselves repeating that "mentalistic" concepts such as thought, etc., correspond to nothing, that everything is language, and that the access to logical truth is assured without much ado by a correct use of language. It is worth noting how E. Brunswick expresses himself in a more subtle manner than his non-experimental colleagues.

In general these are psychological questions that can be answered only by experimentation. In this regard, the following two problems can be distinguished.

1. Language can be a necessary condition for the achievement of logico-mathematical operations without being *ipso facto* a sufficient condition of their formation. On this point genetic data are decisive in providing an answer to three questions: a) Are the roots of these operations anterior to language or are they to be looked for in verbal behavior? b) Is the formation of thinking tied to the acquisition of language as such

or to symbolic functioning in general? c) Is verbal transmission sufficient to establish operational structures in the child's mind or is that transmission effective only if it is assimilated thanks to structures of a more profound nature (coordinations of actions), not transmitted by language?

2. If one considers language as a necessary but not sufficient condition for the formation of operations, the following three questions can be asked: a) Do operations function only in a linguistic form or do they have to do with "group structures" or dynamic systems, which as systems are not formulated in the current language (as distinguished from technical languages)? b) In any case is the role of language in the eventual achievement of these operative structures necessary as a constitutive part or merely as an instrument of formulation or "reflection"? c) If it plays a constitutive role, does this mean that language as a system of communication involves checking rules and precorrections of errors or that logical structures are preestablished in ready-made language?

I. Concerning the first problem, one can already note the following facts while recalling that some questions are not solved and experiments remain to be done. We shall mention some of these at the end of this paper.

a) At sensory-motor levels preceding language one already notices an elaboration of a whole system of schemes that prefigure certain aspects of the structure of classes and relations. A scheme is, in fact, that which is generalizable in a given action; for example, after having reached a distant object by pulling the blanket on which it is placed, the baby will generalize this discovery by utilizing other supports in order to bring near to him other objects in varied situations. The scheme thus becomes a sort of practical concept, and in the presence of an object that is new to him the baby will seek to assimilate it by applying to it successively all his available schemes, as if it were here a question of "definitions by usage" characterized by the words "it is for . . . , it is to . . . ," the kind of definitions which Binet has pointed out at a much later stage.

By generalization, schemes constitute at first quasi-classifications. For example, one and the same goal can correspond to a number of means capable of reaching the goal and equivalent among themselves from this viewpoint; or again, one and the same means can lead to various goals. The classes involve a "comprehension" from the subjective viewpoint, that is, a group of common qualities upon which the generalization is based; the classes also involve an "extension" (the totality of situations to which they can be applied) but merely from the viewpoint of behavior observed by the experimenter. The subject is not capable of representing to himself this extension which he will be capable of attaining only after reaching the level of symbolic functioning.

Moreover, schemes involve, of course, a great variety of active relations that prefigure the logic of relations which will develop eventually on the plane of representation. These relations can even result in a kind of sensory-motor seriation as in the series of blocks of decreasing size (cf. the baby tests of Ch. Bühler).

The coordination of schemes leads further to practical inferences. When an infant of 16 to 18 months looks for an object under a small towel under which one has previously placed a hat, not seeing the object when he removes the towel, the infant will immediately conclude that the object is under the hat. He infers this from the fact that the object was put under the towel and he does not see it when the towel is removed.

Above all, the sensory-motor schematism results in prefigurations of the later notions of conservation and operational reversibility. Thus, between the middle of the first year and of the second year there develops the elementary form of conservation which is the scheme of the permanent object. This scheme already constitutes a kind of "invariant of a group." In fact the search for the hidden object is a function of its localization, and localizations are only assured by the constitution of a "group" of displacements that coordinate detours and returns (corresponding respectively to associativity and reversibility of the group).

Therefore, before the operations formulated by language, there is a kind of logic of action coordination. This logic is characterized by order relations and by the hierarchical linking of the part to the whole. On the other hand, on the plane of more mature representation and thinking one can distinguish a figurative aspect tied to the representation of states and operations involving actions and their interiorization. A genetic relationship can then be postulated between these operations and the above-mentioned logic of action coordination. For example, the operation of adding two numbers $(2 + 3 = 5)$ derives from the action of uniting objects; if one must call this uniting symbolic, this is insofar as the terms 2, 3, 5, + and = are signs and not things; but the addition that is applied to these signs is as real a uniting in the strict sense as an addition applied to objects.

Furthermore it is germane to the discussion to mention the fact that operations insofar as they result from the interiorization of actions and from their coordinations, remain for a long while relatively independent from language. Thus between seven and twelve years, that is, before the formation of propositional or hypothetico-deductive operations which become closely linked to language, one observes a long period that is characterized by concrete operations (classes, relations, and numbers) tied to the manipulation of objects. These operations are manifest by the formation of more general notions of conservation than the notion of the permanent object: for example, in the conservation test with clay one observes conservation of substance at seven to eight years, conservation of weight at nine to ten years, and conservation of volume at eleven to twelve years. In spite of these chronological disparities the child justifies his successive conservations with exactly the same arguments when translated into a rigorously identical verbal expression: "one has only lengthened it" (the ball transformed into a sausage), "one has not taken anything away nor added anything," "this is longer but it is thinner," etc. Such facts indicate that these notions do not merely depend on language. On the contrary, it is here a question of a progressive structuring of the object according to its different qualities. This structuring as a function of systems of active operations derives from actions directed to the objects and not from verbal formulations.

b) The formation of thinking as conceptual "representation" assuredly goes hand in hand in the child with the acquisition of language; but one should not see in conceptual representation a simple causal result of language, for both processes are linked to a more general process which is the symbolic function. In fact, language appears at the same level of development as symbolic play, deferred imitation, and probably the mental image insofar as it is internalized imitation. The characteristic of the symbolic function in its various aspects is the differentiation of signifiers and significates, and the capacity to evoke, by means of these differentiated signifiers, significates that are not actually perceived. These two characteristics oppose verbal signs and the symbols used in play, gesture, or images to sensory-motor indices, or signals that are not differentiated from their significates and therefore cannot evoke objects or events not actually perceived. The transition between sensory-motor behavior and symbolic or representational behavior is probably tied to the presence of imitation (a thesis which we have in common with Wallon). The deferred extension and internalization of imitation makes the differentiation of signifiers and significates possible. It is noteworthy that language is acquired in a context of imitation and this imitative factor seems to constitute an essential support. If language acquisition were only due to conditioning it should take place at a much earlier age. But if the development of imitation is itself linked to the development of intelligent behavior in its totality, it is apparent that one can legitimately consider language as playing a central role in the formation of thinking only insofar as language is one of the manifestations of the symbolic function. The development of the symbolic function in turn is dominated by intelligence in its total functioning.

c) Once language is acquired it is in no way sufficient to assure the transmission of operational structures ready-made. The child does not receive the structures ready-made from outside through the medium of linguistic constructs. A certain number of facts can be brought to bear on this point 1) In spite of the classifications found in the language, only

* pt. being . if language assures intelligence & logic — why Then does it take till 7 + 8 before the child reaches level of concrete operations. ??

at the level of concrete operations (7-8 years) does a child master the use of inclusive definitions (by genus and specific difference: test of definitions by Binet and Simon) and of classifications in general (3rd stage of Inhelder and Piaget); 2) verbal expressions that refer to inclusion of a subclass within a class, such as "Some of my flowers are yellow," are not mastered until a level when inclusion is established thanks to the interplay of additive and multiplicative operations of classes; 3) the exercise of saying numbers does not suffice to ensure conservation of numerical wholes, nor conservation of equivalences by bi-univocal correspondence, etc.

In short, a verbal transmission that gives adequate information relative to operational structures is only assimilated at levels where these structures have already been elaborated on the plane of actions or of operations as interiorized actions. If language favors this interiorization it certainly does not create nor transmit ready-made these structures in an exclusively linguistic way.

II. The questions relative to the necessary (although not sufficient) role of language in the formation of operational structures can be most clearly investigated at the level of formal or hypothetico-deductive operations. These operations no longer bear upon the objects themselves as do concrete operations, but on propositions, on verbally announced hypotheses, etc. Propositional operations which are elaborated between ages 11-12 and 14-15 are manifestly more closely tied to the exercise of verbal communication. It is hard to conceive how they would develop or, rather, how they would reach an advanced stage of development without the use of language.

a) Note first that, just as operations take root before language in the coordinations of actions, they go beyond language in the sense that the operational propositional structures constitute rather complex systems that are not inscribed as systems in the language even though the elaboration of the structures needs the support of verbal behavior. These systems are, first, a combinatorial system (as opposed to the simple hierarchical ordering of concrete operations), and secondly, the group of four transformations that coordinate inversions and reciprocals, the two forms of reversibility that up to now have been separated in concrete "groupings" (classification, seriation, etc.). These two correlative group structures are manifest in the behavior of the subject by the formation of a series of new operational schemes (double systems of reference, proportions, combinational probabilities, etc.). They provide the functional unity of these manifestations and explain their relatively simultaneous appearance. These superstructures go beyond the language of the subject and cannot even be formulated by means of the current language alone.

b) The elaboration of logical structures raises as yet many problems. It seems best to reserve one's judgment about the truly constitutive or merely indirect and supportive role of language in this elaboration. On this point it is better to wait until the works of the various schools of linguistic structuralism (Hjelmslev, Togeby, Harris, etc.) have reached sufficient points of contact with algebraic and logistic analysis of thinking mechanisms.

c) However it seems already possible, even at the level of formal or propositional operations, to envisage the influence of language as being less the transmission of ready-made structures than a kind of education of thinking and of reasoning due to the conditions of communication and precorrection of errors. "It should be possible," says the linguist Hjelmslev, "to bring together the system of formal logic and of language under a common principle that could be called a sublogical system." L. Apostel has shown that this common system has to do with the theory of coding and assures the precorrection of errors that can come about between encoding and decoding. It is in this direction of a common functioning and of a common probabilistic source that the active influence of language on operations is conceivable. It is to be understood that this influence goes beyond the limits of language and extends the equilibration process which is already active in the domain of coordinations of actions in general, to the area of coordinations of social actions.

> Piaget's final remarks concern three ways of possible research bearing on the thinking-language relation: 1) verbal learning of operations or learning through verbal formulations of operations; 2) study of persons with disturbed development in language or in operative thinking and a comparison of levels attained in either of these two areas, 3) study of intellectual development in deaf persons.

At the end of these few remarks we would like to suggest research that needs to be pursued to solve some of the preceding problems, to confirm proposed solutions or raise new questions.

A fruitful new method in this regard consists in studying the effects of learning verbal formulations on operations that have not been spontaneously acquired by the subject. A first beginning along this line has been made by A. Morf with children at an intermediate level between concrete and formal operations. Morf utilized some reasoning problems with implications, disjunctions, etc. and started by analysing the spontaneous solutions of the subjects. Then he furnished them with a certain amount of verbal information by repeating questions with supplementary details or by providing analogous examples, etc. The result of this additional help has been systematically negative except with subjects who had spontaneously succeeded in solving one or another of the questions by hypothetico-deductive methods. Only these subjects were able to assimilate the meaning of the supplementary information for the successful solution of problems they had initially failed.

Research of a different type has been undertaken by B. Inhelder and J. Bruner in some recent experiments at Harvard. Subjects who had not reached conservation in the case of pouring of liquids were submitted to a verbal learning period focusing on expressions such as "a glass A is at the same time higher and thinner than a glass B" etc.; the aim was to analyse how subjects would learn to comprehend these relations and whether they modified their judgments of conservation (experiments were done apart from the tests of conservation but in the same context). The preliminary results seem to show that: a) difficulties in the progressive comprehension of these verbal expressions are of the same order as the obstacles known in the acquisition of conservation; b) there is little relation between the two domains of verbal comprehension and concrete reasoning, as if at this stage one had to do with two different processes.

A second instructive method is the analysis of relations between the linguistic level and the operational level in connection with deficiencies in the development of one or the other of these two domains. Such an analysis has been made by J. de Ajuriaguerra and B. Inhelder who are presenting a paper on this subject at this meeting. Here I only wish to underline the significance of the paradoxical cases in which a marked linguistic retardation is not accompanied by any trouble in intellectual operations. One sometimes finds the reciprocal: an operational retardation without linguistic troubles.

Finally the method of choice with regard to the problems under discussion is naturally the analysis of the intellectual operations of deaf persons who possess the symbolic function without by themselves attaining articulated language. Some interesting studies by P. Oléron, M. Vincent, and F. Affolter of our laboratory have already demonstrated that the subjects show a varied amount of retardation on several tests when compared to hearing persons. Among other things, the deaf children have less mobility but are nonetheless capable of mastering the essential operations: classifications, seriations, and other operations of order, perspectives (tests of shadow), etc. A new problem has recently been raised by P. Oléron as to a possible considerable retardation of these subjects in the acquisition of the notions of conservation. However the solution of this problem is rendered difficult for methodological reasons. One can ask whether the results of Oléron are not in part due to his technique, especially since the averages indicated for the control subjects do not at all correspond to the norms recently established by various authors in a number of different countries. When F. Affolter replicated this problem with other techniques she seemed to observe an earlier acquisition for the deaf children. This question must therefore remain open as do so many others among those which we have raised.

Piaget could not express himself in more decisive terms against the view that linguistic elements or structures as such contribute substantially to the development of logical thinking. Moreover, since writing these lines, Piaget's associates have done a number of investigations along the line mentioned in the last paragraphs. The results of these studies have confirmed the dependence of correct linguistic behavior on the operational structures and not vice versa. As an example of this ongoing research here is the conclusion of Sinclair's (1967, p. 62) research on verbal learning of a conservation:

"The possession of certain expressions does not structure operations nor does their absence impede their formation; the expressions are acquired and their use becomes functional according to a process similar to the mode of structuring of the operations themselves, namely through an interplay of decentrations and coordinations. The contribution of language must be sought for on another level. Language can direct attention to pertinent factors of a problem, just as it can control perceptual activities, as Luria and his collaborators have shown. In this way, language can prepare an operation but is neither sufficient nor necessary to the formation of concrete operations."

# IV

## Figurative Knowing

# 7

# *perception and image*

If one were to seek areas in which Piaget's thinking goes most clearly against common notions, one would undoubtedly select those that are discussed here under the term of figurative knowing. Having worked through the impalpable zone of operative structures and symbolic significations, the reader may well rejoice to meet at last with the familiar subheadings of perception, memory, images. Piaget likes to stress the difference between his position and those for whom perception and image are the "objectively" given foundations of a theory of knowledge.

The reason for this basic difference in approach has been pointed out before (Ch. 5). Traditionally the external environment and the organism are posited as given, and with such an implicit assumption an analysis is made of how knowledge comes about. Following the empiricist tradition, it is tacitly accepted that our knowledge *within* must have an adequate cause *outside* the organism. By such an initial assumption, we have already preempted the viable alternatives in the essential problem of knowledge and relegated the knower-known relation to a cause-effect situation in which the potential knower is on the receiving end and the efficient cause is the environment. As a consequence, sensations and perceptions both in the developmental sequence and in the analysis of knowing, are seen as coming first, followed by memory to explain learning, and images to explain non-perceptual representation.

Piaget's biological-developmental approach does not start with an empty organism nor with the eventual environment of the mature organism, but with the adaptive action of a living organism in his new environment. Think of the first days of a baby. Who would say that the new-born "perceives" either himself or an object? We outlined in Chapter 3 how Piaget conceives of reflex activity as a coordinated differentiation of global rhythmic activity and how this activity continues to adapt itself by better assimilation and accommodation. In interacting with the environment, the organism builds up within itself coordinated schemes of knowing and gathers correspondingly meaningful knowledge about the outside environment. As these schemes become more tightly organized, more general and less immediately dependent on external actions, so the environment becomes increasingly stable, objective and inter-coordinated.

Such a view does not deny or demonstrate the existence of the real world, but stays consistently on the appropriate level of natural observation. A physical environment to which an organism does not react is simply not an environment from a biological viewpoint. To become a meaningful object, a thing to which one reacts, the organization of the organism must be capable of adapting to it in a twofold direction: by assimilating the thing into its organization and by accommodating the organization to the particular characteristics of the thing. Previous chapters have emphasized the assimilative activity in terms of operative schemes. These schemes assimilate, i.e., confer meaning on environmental events and transform things into objects of action or objects of knowing. In this operative transformation of knowing lies the essential aspect of intelligence. According to Piaget, all other activities of knowing must be viewed in relation to operativity, taken in the wide sense as including operational as well as sensory-motor action schemes. We have seen this already in the previous section where the dependence of symbolic activity on operative structures was emphasized.

Perception has to do with the appearance of the external world in its momentary, yet always changing characteristics. It thus constitutes a particularly clear form of accommodative behavior, accommodation being the outward-directed activity of intelligent adaptation that applies general schemes to the particular here and now situation. Assimilative activity transforms a given input into objects that correspond to the person's structure of knowing. Accommodative activity transforms the organism according to the particular characteristics of the input. When this input, as in the case of perception, consists of sensory data, it is part of the accommodative activity to adjust itself to the particular configuration of these data. Such correspondence to the outside state can be literally observed in the accommodation of sense organs, as for instance in the adjustment of the eye to the various visual characteristics of a seen object, its distance, brightness, shape. It will be recalled that imitation, overt or covert, is a similar phenomenon, a more or less meaningful correspondence of part of the person's motor system to a perceived movement or to his own potential action vis-à-vis a given object.

Whenever in an act of knowing the accommodative activity is oriented towards the organization of sensory data, Piaget refers to that aspect of knowing as "figurative." In distinction, "operative" is the fundamental aspect of knowledge that "operates" on a reality state and transforms it into an object of knowing. Figurative knowledge does not transform a reality state, rather it modifies the organism according to the figural aspect of that state. Consequently one cannot speak of figurative knowledge as such unless this knowledge is embedded in and forms a whole with operative knowledge, which alone confers knowledge in a true sense.

On the other hand not all operative knowledge need be accompanied by figurative knowledge. Where the knowing act does not include sensory data—and this need not necessarily be on any high level of abstraction—there will always be accommodation, it goes without saying, but with no resulting figurative knowledge. For instance, a nine-year-old boy leaves home at three o'clock and walks briskly to his friend's house which is not located in the immediate neighborhood of his home. He arrives there at 3:20. Remembering that he should be back by 6 o'clock he tells his friend: "I have to leave by 5:40." While there are obviously some figurative aspects in the totality of the knowing situations depicted in this story, let us take the boy at the moment when he realizes that it took him 20 minutes

to walk one way. What permitted him to jump to the ultimate conclusion about his departure? The apparently obvious knowledge that,
barring special circumstances, the time taken to walk from A to B is
identical to the time for walking from B to A, an inference which is
based on an even more primitive knowledge that the distance AB
equals the distance BA.

Consider just this one act of knowing on the part of the boy, a
knowing which for the sake of communication and analysis we, but
not the boy, must put into words: the knowing that "time-to-walk
BA equals time-to-walk AB." There is no figurative aspect in this
particular knowledge. Knowing that AB equals BA is not a perceptual
act of seeing or imagining real roads and covertly matching one road
against the other; it is the result of a developing process of transforming the world into a coordinated framework of stable space and
objects. It took most of his nine years to make the boy capable of
such knowledge. This knowing is an operative construction that extended the structures of practical localization achieved at the sensory-
motor period. If spatial notions were just read off from the perceptually given situation, a time span of so many years to make a child
"see what is there" should be a heavy strain on any one's credulity.
Notions of space and time are intimately related. As the preoperational
child lacks stable spatial coordinates, so also is he incapable of comprehending notions of time that go beyond a certain limited duration.
The grasping of the time span of 20 minutes implies a structuring of
time. The active knowledge of the boy in this particular moment is
thus a true operative knowing.

In order to see the assimilative and the accommodative aspect of
this act we analyse it in the following manner. The input is the implicit problem which can be put in words, again only by us, not by
the boy: "How long does it take me to walk BA? I know it took me
20 minutes to walk AB." This problem situation is assimilated to the
child's operational coordinations of space and time. It is thereby transformed so as to become an integral part of a network of reversible
operations. Within these operations the particular operation that leads
to the appropriate solution is found. That particular operation could
be verbalized as "It takes as long to walk a distance AB as the distance
BA." Accommodation consists therefore in the adaptively adequate
selection and application of this operation to the given problem. As
the problem did not in itself include any sensory or perceptual ele-

ment, the resulting accommodation does not lead to any figurative knowledge.

We should now be in a better position to understand why for Piaget the word "perception" has a different connotation than the one to which traditional views have accustomed us. First of all, to consider perception as providing one kind of knowledge and intelligence, another kind is alien to Piaget's way of thinking. He repeats with almost monotonous urgency—whether addressing philosophers or fellow scientists—that there are not different kinds of knowledges, but one continuous evolution that blossoms into mature logical intelligence, and that wherever even the tiniest glimmer of knowing is at work it bears some direct genetic relation to the mature structures of adulthood. To divide knowledge into one category based on perception, another one on intelligence is out of the question.

Since, for Piaget, perception without operative knowledge is inconceivable, it follows that perception is simply one manifestation of intelligence in its total development. It would be radically wrong to think of perception as an autonomous substructure that should be relegated into a primitive period of intellectual development. Piaget only speaks of perception when the figurative aspect forms an integral part of knowing, and when the object of knowledge is immediately present to the senses. Thus, if you look at the open book and perceive the pages of a book, this is certainly a perception. But Piaget considers that, in this situation, your operative knowledge of the properties of a book far outweighs in importance the specific perceptual activity concerned with the figurative accommodation to that particular book.

Consequently, Piaget studies perception in such a fashion that the operative aspect surrounding the figurative knowing is minimized. A knowing act that results in perception in the most narrow sense of the term, as just indicated, is called by Piaget "perceptual activity." Examples of methods by which he investigates perceptual activities would be comparing the lengths of two sticks, adjusting a line so as to appear perpendicular, judging the size of a distant object. It is from developmental data collected on these kinds of tasks that Piaget derives his theoretical notions concerning perceptual activity. Before discussing these in some detail, a word must be said about perception during the sensory-motor period.

There is no doubt that infants of eight months, as well as animals, perceive objects. However, sensory-motor knowledge is practical knowledge, geared toward external, adaptive action. The infant perceives his bottle not as some object he knows to be out there, but solely as an object to which his eyes and other parts of his organism are externally reacting. It is instructive to realize that some perceptual skills are developed long before the formation of the permanent object, that is, before the child can be said to know that objects exist.

In connection with an adequate eye and hand coordination acquired during the sensory-motor stage, there is the peculiar fact that, to the hand, a toy lying on one's lap feels exactly the same as when it is at arm's length. For the eye, however, the difference in apparent size is unmistakable. It easily appears four times smaller when far than when near; yet the size to which the hand adjusts remains the same. Does the coordination have to wait for the development of perceptual size constancy, namely the ability to compensate for changes in apparent size due to distance, or is this a chicken and egg question? No, says Piaget, the practical coordination comes first. He cites experiments as evidence that only after infants develop hand-eye coordination are they capable of choosing the bigger of two objects, even though the apparent size of the bigger object is smaller to the child's eye. Similar considerations can be made about shape constancy as indicated by a child's recognition of an object in different perspectives.

Shape constancy develops after an increased flexibility in practical means-ends relations. On the other hand, shape constancy contributes to the eventual formation of the permanent object at the end of the sensory-motor period. Thus we see how in this period perceptual regulations—for that is what perceptual constancies are—stand in mutual interdependence to schemes of actions. Actually, there is no qualitative difference between schemes of perception or schemes of actions, they are both equally internal structures of coordination and regulation and equally geared towards external action. Piaget is thus justified in speaking of perceptual schemes with reference to those action schemes which are expressly directed to the perceptual configuration of an object.

When Piaget studied perceptual activity at later periods by means of experiments that permitted the perceptual contribution to stand out, he discovered a basic characteristic that did not substantially change with increasing age. He observed that perception by itself was responsible for a slight deformation of objective reality: the best examples of this deformation are the so-called optical illusions. However, many everyday examples are readily at hand. When there are two vertical lines A and B of different lengths in one field of vision some inches apart and we focus our regard on B it will appear bigger than if we had focused on A and estimated the length of B. If one thinks of perception as the primary source of veridical knowledge about the real world, it comes somewhat as a surprise that by itself the exercise of the sense organs misinforms us about objective dimensions. Biologically speaking, the fact that sensorial focusing brings about a relative overstimulation makes sense. Think of the apparent amplitude of a warning signal that must be noticed against background noise. Is this perhaps an indication that our sense organs have not evolved in order to bring us objective knowledge, but in order to provide knowledge which is useful for the adaptive functioning of the organism? The organ for objective truth, for objective knowledge in the strict sense, is the operative intellect, not the senses.

Piaget studied this primary deformation in experiments where due to the short exposure time only a single centration of the eye was possible. He calls the deforming effects that were invariably observed field effects. By this term Piaget indicates that the effects follow from a single centration within one perceptual field and are thus quite basic and present before the eventual contribution of perceptual activities. These activities can be readily comprehended in terms of perceptual strategies. In looking at a picture we focus our eyes successively on different points along the picture and the way in which we organize the successive scanning can of course make a lot of difference in what we see. Perceptual activities compensate in part for the primary deformations of single centrations, and this the more so as the activities come more and more under operative control.

Are these field effects pure figurative knowledge, a kind of basic perceptual datum on which perceptual activities with their implied operative component start to work? If such were the case, we would have a clear split between types of knowledge. Piaget spends the better part of a book from which two sections are translated in Reading 6 to demonstrate that a single field effect is the limiting case of accommodation with but a single sensorial accommodative adjustment. But where there is accommodation, there must be a scheme which is accommodated to the object. And where there is a scheme, there is a previous assimilation that has been generalized and organized into the behavioral structure of that particular scheme. Field effects are distinguished from perceptual activities not by the fact that one is a passive perception and the other an activity. The perception with a single centration is as truly an active perception as the one that includes a whole series of organized centrations. The difference consists in the fact that a single centration limits non-perceptual contributions to a greater degree than other types of perception and is therefore of special interest.

Piaget uses a probabilistic and statistical model to explain perceptual effects. This methodology is contrasted with the apparently more logical model for operative thinking. He bases his perceptual theory on the fact of chance encounters between supposed elements within the sense organs and elements outside in the perceptual field. Characteristically, a regulatory contribution from the active organism is a prerequisite even in these most superficial encounters. That the regulations should be closely related to physiological mechanisms should cause no surprise. For here, as before with regard to reflex activity, we are truly at the border between the psychological and the physiological; both areas are characterized by similar laws of biological organization, laws that dominate the organism-environment interaction. In fact, operational regulations are but a further evolution of the perceptual regulations. Operational regulations involve strict implication and generalizable concepts; perceptual regulations involve the inherent uncertainties of perceptual encounters.

In Chapter 5 we discussed Piaget's theory concerning images, especially their derivation not from perceptual data as such but from accommodative imitation. The close relation between imitation and accommodation was stressed there and was again mentioned above in connection with perception and figurative knowledge. In Chapter 5 we were primarily concerned with the notion that a symbol as far as it is a signifying event, is both different from, yet structurally linked to operative knowing. Assuming this, we shall focus here more on the figurative knowing inherent in a symbol. It is the figurative aspect of an image which makes it representational and assures its privileged status in the spatial area. A mental image of the tree has a figurative resemblance or correspondence to the perceptual configuration of a particular tree. The correspondence comes about via the accommodative imitation during perception; the imitation is internalized and transformed by the symbolic function into a symbolic instrument for the knowing of a tree.

In this connection the following question may be posed: If an image signifies a tree, why not say that perception signifies a tree? A fuller explanation of this would merely repeat the long discussion of Chapter 6 as to why the knowing construct, the known object, should not be said to signify the real object. In an analogous sense, the reader will understand that perception, perceptual activity in its totality, and the perceived thing are one and the same reality. But the mental image is another thing than the perceived thing; because of this differentiation, an image can come to represent the perceived thing. In this way perception, imitation, and image can be called, as Piaget puts it, three instruments of figurative knowledge, or even more precisely, three different instruments of the same figurative knowledge.

Piaget considers that imagery together with linguistic signs are employed in the service of operative knowing not merely during the preoperational period when a figurative support is still required but also later. He suggests that images have a particular affinity to the figural here and now, while linguistic signs are in themselves unrelated to figural aspects and more directly signify general schemes.

However, language obviously has a figurative aspect since it is something that is heard and spoken, even if in and of itself the auditory figural element of the word is unrelated to the visual figural aspect of the object. Moreover, as Piaget and others have shown, language is treated by the growing child as something that is as much part of the total concrete situation as is any other figural component. It gives rise to similar imitative accommodation and is subsequently employed with as much egocentrism and deforming concreteness as any other symbol. For this reason it would seem to me more appropriate to include the language of the growing child in the category of figurative instruments to the same extent as mental images. Moreover, as in all development, the sensory-motor and preoperational characteristics of linguistic symbols do not simply disappear when operations take over. Language, no less than any other symbol, has its deep sensory-motor roots. Linguistic symbols can deform critical knowledge all the more seriously if they are assumed to be free from bias and simply to represent the objective truth. To use language in the service of rational thinking requires no less effort than to dominate imaginal symbols by operational structures.

The theoretical implications of the great variety of Piaget's experimentations on the mental image are our main concern here. They can be summarized under three headings. First, the findings confirm Piaget's theory that images are not just faint copies or traces of things seen, but are partly derived from what the child understands or misunderstands. Children will draw configurations the like of which they have never seen, in fact they will draw according to their level of comprehension even if the model remains in front of them. An ordinary six-year-old child simply does not perceive that the water level in an inclined tube remains horizontal.

Second, for the preoperational child an image is as static as his notion of space. He is preoccupied with the edges or outlines of a figure. He also tends to follow topological rules that pertain to the general "feel" of the shape and frequently predominate over our familiar Euclidian metrics. Outlines and edges play an important role in topological thinking. As an example, the notion of length is primarily determined by the end point, the point of arrival of the child's visual regard. Given two parallel lines which are shown to be of equal length, a child observes how one line is moved slightly to the right. He will now assert that that line has become longer. A similar lack of conservation of quantity is observed in the following image experiment. The child is shown two identical squares one on top of the other, and he is then asked to draw what the squares would look like if the upper square would be pushed slightly to the right. Children of preoperational age will show marked unwillingness to shift the right edge of the top square, even while they correctly move the left edge of the top square to the right. Having seen that the two original squares are identical, the children seem to be concerned with conserving the quantity of the upper square. This preoccupation apparently makes them unwilling to shift the right edge. In general, drawings that copy or anticipate a movement are wrongly executed. At best children show the correct initial and final state but are quite incapable of forming images of the in-between states as, e.g., in drawing the movement of a match stick that is flipped from a table to the floor.

Third, images of spatial relations become adequate precisely at the point at which children acquire the corresponding operational notions. Thus, for instance, only after children, around nine years of age, have mastered the horizontal and vertical system of spatial coordinates do they begin to perceive the horizontal water level of an inclined tube. This spatial comprehension is largely unaffected by their daily experience of pouring milk from a pitcher into cups. Images become flexible and adequately represent or anticipate movement, not because of any intrinsic tendency by which their static figurative aspect becomes more supple, but because of the increasing contribution operative knowledge brings to bear on figurative knowledge. This is but another indication of what was said twice before—that symbols are as adequate as the operative intelligence that uses them.

Finally, it may be opportune to stress, as do Piaget and Inhelder in their introduction to the book on the mental image, that according to Piaget's theory an image cannot be considered in isolation. Because of its symbolic and significative character, an image, like a word or a sentence, is linked to the operative activity of the thinking person. Language has the advantage over the mental image that one can isolate and study its figurative, i.e., phonemic and syntactic aspect, without bringing in semantic, i.e., significative factors. The figurative aspect of an internal image is not easily grasped or defined. Consequently, Piaget's studies of the mental image were directed more towards the "semantic" side of the image, its function within an operative context. As such the peculiar figurative characteristics of the images are of secondary importance. Whether children "really" had a visual or kinesthetic image or whether they simply anticipated and knew a spatial coordination is not a critical point in the general emphasis on the significative, representative aspect of the image.

# Reading 6

## Assimilation and Perception [1]

This is a continuation of the same article from which Reading 2 was taken. In the first section Piaget shows that in the accommodations of a single visual centration the contribution from the interior organization must be considered. Point (1) asserts the continuity between single field effects and more complex perceptual activities. One finds here a characteristic description of accommodative activities as contrasted with the developing schematization. Point (2) explains the processes involved in a single centration. Piaget singles out for special reference the perception of a continuum and of topological relations within a centration. Point (3) distinguishes more clearly effects prior to centration from effects on the same level as centration. The distinction between dynamic and static effects seems analogous to what he will later call operative and figurative knowing. There is also found here a critical reference to interpretations given by the theory of Gestalt.

(*pp. 85-89*) (1) First it is well to be careful with such words as "simple" and "elementary" and to avoid the elementaristic tendencies which can be found even in interpretations that are apparently at the opposite pole (as in the theory of Gestalt). Recall that perceptual activities at a level superior to field effects do not constitute a mosaic or composition of these effects. On the contrary, a centration is but a single momentary episode in the context of the totality of perceptual activities. Since these activities are but a particular instance of sensory-motor activities, "simple" percep-

[1] Jean Piaget, "Assimilation et connaissance," in *Études d'épistémologie génétique*, V (Paris: Presses Universitaires de France, 1958), pp. 85-9, 93-4. Translated by Hans G. Furth, by permission of the publishers.

144

tion can never be considered the source of our knowing. In fact, knowing means the assimilation of an object into sensory-motor schemes which invariably add to the perceptual data some elements of coordination due to the action of the subject. While a scheme of action always implies a perceptual aspect, this aspect can be considered as a signal; in themselves signals have meaning only relative to the schemes on which they depend.

By virtue of the signaling function, a characteristic especially of visual perception is to constantly explore the sector of the surrounding environment that is accessible to it. Field effects of centrations are therefore, above all, the limiting case of a subject's accommodations to an ensemble of chance events; these accommodations make contact between schemes of assimilation and perceptual data. From this viewpoint the chance encounters and automatic couplings express a characteristic of all accommodations. In fact, an accommodation implies an unexpected encounter with a reality that cannot be immediately assimilated or is merely in the process of being assimilated. So-called primary reactions (primary not because they are more primitive but because they are less complex and change little with age) are relatively constant during development because they are not the marching army of progressive constructions of schemes, but the accommodations that are at the forefront and always proceed in the same manner in the presence of chance events while expecting or anticipating a more complete assimilation. One is therefore justified in comparing this state of affairs of primary perceptual encounters with what was said above in connection with the "pure" associations that are also the limit of a simple stochastic process.

(2) An accommodation is always the accommodation of a scheme of assimilation. The point where accommodative chance encounters join the schemes is precisely the action of centration, insofar as it is an act of the subject which provokes the "encounters" by making contact with reality. In fact, the act of centration already confers a pre-schematic unity on the ensemble of encounters and on the resulting automatic couplings within the field of centration.

This unity by itself is noteworthy insofar as it introduces a spatial continuity in data that are essentially discontinuous. This discontinuity of the perceptual data is here not predicated upon our own sketch of perceptual encounters which is merely intended as a model. Nonetheless, the remarkable experiments of the English physicist R. W. Ditchburn on the disappearance of perceived figures (with a less rapid extinction of the part of the figure on which attention is focused), when the small movements of the eyeball are neutralized, afford some measure of likelihood for the model of a discontinuous regard. However, the lack of a continuum referred to above lies in the physical and physiological material, the material from which the perceived figure and the nervous system is constructed.

Moreover, with one centration, we perceive not only a continuum but we perceive it in three dimensions, organized in a topological and measurable fashion. . . .

From the most elementary field effects of centration there intervenes a topological organization of space, an organization that is more primitive than the metric structure (Euclidian or not). This organization introduces into the perceived elements not only relations of a continuum but also of proximity and separation, of edges and relative positions to edges, etc. In this topological domain it is again difficult to accept the notion of a pure registration without a schematization due to the activities of the subject.

(3) One can therefore distinguish, from the viewpoint of assimilation, two kinds of field effects within a single centration:

(a) The (dynamic) effects on a level prior to centration, linked to encounters and automatic couplings. The functioning of these effects ensures the accommodation of the schemes of centration to the exterior data.

(b) The (static or dynamic) effects linked to centration itself. They refer to spatial (figure, etc.) or general qualitative characteristics (color, etc.). As an illustration of a spatial character directly perceived in a single centration recall the "good" or bad forms, figure-ground relations, figure-edge relations (as Rubin showed, the edge belongs perceptually to the figure, not to the ground), the screen effect of Michotte (an object half hidden by a screen does not appear shortened, but as partly situated "behind" the screen), etc.

We propose that all the (b) effects partake of schemes and demonstrate the presence of active assimilation right in the centration. One could therefore speak of primary schemes which would be identical with the familiar "Gestalt" laws. However, the psychological notion of Gestalt, or rather the usual psychological interpretation given to this notion, is by no means identical with our notion of scheme. Koehler considers the Gestalt as a product of an immediate formation or reformation (after the manner of the surface of a liquid which finds its horizontal "form" whenever it is poured from one container into another). For us the scheme is the product of assimilating activities as well as the instrument of subsequent assimilations, hence it is essentially a generalizing instrument as opposed to the immediate and discontinuous "re-formations." It remains to provide some evidence for the schemes which we attribute by hypothesis to the primary structuring described in (b). . . .

(*p. 93*) In conclusion, neither perception nor association leads to a direct contact between a subject and an object which are exterior to each other, as if knowledge were a mere registration; in both cases objectivity is constructed progressively from the indissociable interaction of assimilation and accommodation.

The final selection summarizes the three main points of this study. All three are implied in the general statement that schemes participate at all levels of knowing and that there is no knowledge that is merely a passive registration or reading of data given in the external environment.

(*pp. 93-94*) The aim of this study was threefold. (1) The first task was to show that logic does not constitute a form that is afterwards imposed upon a preexisting content. There exist structurings or constructions of forms at all levels, even if they remain only minimally differentiated from their content: through their growing complexity these forms lead stage by stage to the particular kind of structures which one calls logic, but without any radical discontinuity between the later and the early preparatory forms. (2) To justify this viewpoint it remained to demonstrate that there does not in fact exist a "preexisting content." In other words, the "reading off" of experience is not a mere reading, but an introduction of active schemes into the experience to be read which makes this reading possible in the first place. In fact, the schematization required for this reading seems to be the proper function of prelogical and logical structures in the activities of the subject. The subject employs these structures insofar as he needs readings that are increasingly more precise, up to those which are required for scientific thought. The activity of schemes is already found at all levels (naturally less decisively at the more elementary levels) through the assimilating activity of the subject: the activity consists in incorporating data, from the moment they are given—hence without a prior perception of preexisting data—to schemes established previously or in the process of being differentiated. These schemes alone permit the organism to attribute to the data the status of an object of knowledge. (3) In a reciprocal manner one has to show that from the very beginning this mental assimilation involves some inferential mechanisms. Their function is to ensure the assimilative incorporation. (These inferential mechanisms therefore play the same role as the physico-chemical transformations that produce the incorporation into the organism of substances or energies drawn from the environment during the process of physiological assimilation. Inferences are described in terms of implication proper to the mental life, in distinction from physical transformations that take place in terms of causality proper to physical regularities.) While the inferences are at first inductive or probabilistic, they can lead to the deductive inferences characteristic of logical structures.

# 8

# *memory*

The meaning of the term "memory" can be as general and broad as learning in the widest sense. Every conceivable aspect of learning could be theoretically explained as a direct effect of memory. Memory itself is often thought of as some special ability whose function is to store and retain knowledge for future use. In addition, special conditions or causes for memory are postulated, all lying outside the sphere of knowing proper, as if knowledge by itself never carried sufficient raison d'etre that it be retained.

Piaget insists on clearing up the terminology here and in so doing reveals his biological orientation. We shall here anticipate some points of the more detailed discussion in Chapter 11 concerning the manner in which knowledge about the outside world enters the organism. As K. Lorenz succinctly puts it, knowledge enters the organism in two ways, either by evolutionary means, through the species, or developmentally, through the individual. Knowledge acquired in the course of evolution can be called biological memory or memory of the genes. This is nothing else but

the structures of the organism's exchange with the environment, transmitted directly through the hereditary action of the genes. It suffices
to refer here to the signalling behavior of the bees which implicitly
depends on an astonishing amount of knowledge about sun movements and transpositions of angles, all of which is implied in the total,
adaptive behavior sequence. In this connection Piaget emphasizes two
basic points. First, there obviously must be some correspondence between the structure of behavior and the physiological structure of
the genes that transmit this behavior. Second, behavioral structure and
memory are really one and the same thing; the adequate functioning
of a structure is its own reason for becoming active in biologically
appropriate situations and requires no additional factor of memory
that would explain the continuation of its functioning.

Piaget reasons similarly regarding memory and nonhereditary structures that are acquired in individual development. At all levels, for
Piaget, knowing is identical with active generalizable structures,
whether these are schemes of external coordinating actions or structures of internal reversible operations. Consider the reproductive or
functional assimilation of the beginning sensory-motor period which
is an active manifestation of an elementary scheme and corresponds
functionally to the play activity of the preoperational period. In play
a child represents his structures of knowing in a symbolic medium.
When a child is asked: "How much is 3 + 4?" and he hesitates or
murmurs "I forgot," it is immediately obvious that his operational
structure of the number system is not yet established. To know that
3 + 4 = 7 is considered a feat of memory only where the appropriate
knowledge is lacking. The operational structures of an adult such as
numbers, spatial coordinates, notions of time, are not memorized but
are simply there and available on appropriate occasions. We do not
"remember" that the distance London—Paris equals the distance Paris
—London, we simply "know" it. If the word "memory" is used with
regard to these activities, it is what Piaget calls "general memory,"
built into the nature of a behavioral structure.

Yet there is no denying a different kind of memory, a specific
memory in the strict sense. For example, we recall that Paris is the
capital of France, we recognize a familiar face among others, we reproduce the correct sequence of certain dance steps. In all these cases
it is traditional to define memory as an internal habit or association,
the strength of which is said to be dependent largely upon recency,

frequency of exposure or exercise, contiguity, and associated reward. Memory behavior is thought to consist thus essentially in comparing an internal image with a present perception or in shaping present behavior according to an internal image. In a somewhat more sophisticated form, in which words may substitute for images, many theories of learning continue to schematize the functioning of memory in this manner. With such a framework the nature of images plays a crucial role. If images are but traces of a given perception, Piaget argues, the reason why one and not another is memorized must be looked for in some additional factor apart from retention. But if, after Piaget, images are an internal prolongation of an accommodative imitation, part of a knowing activity that confers meaning, then the basic reason for the conservation of an image is found in that knowing activity, whatever other special reasons may cause it to be recalled at a certain moment.

In short, Piaget, having rejected a copy or representation theory of perception, rejects equally and for similar reasons a copy theory of memory. He puts memory, even in the strict sense, within the totality of intellectual activities, as he has done with perception and symbolic functioning before. In particular, he denies that recognition memory requires by itself the presence of an internal image. For him recognition is an intrinsic part of every sensory-motor habit. He considers it unnecessary and unscientific to postulate the presence of an image in the baby's mind as if without an image the baby could not recognize a nipple momentarily lost from sight, nor welcome the face of his mother as familiar. In those cases Piaget speaks of perceptual indices or signals that elicit a meaningful reaction from corresponding sensory-motor schemes which confer signification on these sensorial inputs. As in all other sensory-motor knowing, recognition occurs in the act of reacting meaningfully to a given object and requires no representational presence of any sort. For Piaget, infants of the sensory-motor period are incapable of representational production and can have no mental images as we understand the term.

There remains the question whether memory is to be equated with the image. Here too, according to Piaget, semantic clarifications are in order. The most specific meaning of the term "memory" is the evocation or recall of events as particularized at a certain time in the past. My general knowledge or recollection that Geneva borders the lake of the same name is a different memory behavior from the specific image of the city with the cathedral in the background and the fountain on the lake, an image which I relate to a visit to Piaget's Institute at a definite time of my past. The general recollection may or may not be accompanied by images; as a memory type it stands midway between the general knowledge of numbers where the use of the term "memory" is hardly appropriate and the specific memory image of the lake of Geneva.

In connection with this example concerning the memory image of a quite specific event that took place at a certain past time, Piaget asks the following pertinent question: Is this memory nothing but the visual image, and if so, is it alone the figurative knowledge conveyed by the image that determines memory? To give another example, is the specific image of the schoolhouse of your childhood all that constitutes your memory of this place? If Piaget can show that operative-structural elements are at work in these situations that most specifically exemplify memory, it is then easier to understand how memory and operativity relate in less distinctly mnemonic situations.

From what has been said above concerning figurative knowledge in general and mental image in particular, one can surmise that Piaget does not exempt memory from operative control. The following discussion on memory and operation is based largely on Piaget's comprehensive book on memory which he only recently completed. Some sections of the book are translated in the Reading section following this chapter and provide both the original reference and further elucidations on the points mentioned in the text.

The memory image of a specific perception does have a particular figurative element, but operativity surrounds the memory image on all sides. This fact becomes clear when the operative schemes underlying the image are listed. First, there are the assimilating schemes to coordinate the original sensory input in the form of perceptual activities; then there is object formation, the formation of a perceptual event "out there," which makes possible an operational and not merely a sensory-motor perception. Moreover, knowing and identifying an event as such-and-such is obviously an instance of classificatory organization. Continuing in this line, we recall that the formation of a symbolic image presupposes an imitative movement that is internalized and receives signification through the identical operation that conferred intelligent meaning on the original perception. So much for the bare image.

What does memory add in terms of operative structures? As Bartlett[1] has shown, any specific memory is dependent on and placed within an intricate network of innumerable behavioral schemes of knowing. A few of these structuring activities go by the name of mnemonic devices. The interplay of these schemes allows one to place the event in time and to recognize it as a particular instance of one's own experience among other instances. By a similar approach to memory Piaget finally defines memory in the strict sense without bringing in a mental image at all, even though it may be psychologically experienced. Yet Piaget emphasizes the particular, figurative elements of knowledge that are made present again in memory as they were originally present in perception.

Piaget would say that the specific function of memory in the strict sense consists in the evocation of a particular past: this evocation is specifically related to the accommodative activity of knowing focused on the figural aspect of a particular event and temporally located at a certain point in time. He would contend that the memory image of Geneva and its lake is but a symbolic manifestation of a whole series of knowing structures that all bear on the known event within a certain past. Thus, the memory image, no less than perception or the symbol, is in essential dependence on operative structures. The borderline between memory and knowing is not sharp, but while the image is perhaps dispensable for memory, knowing must always be there. Thus we can recall that Bogota is the capital of Colombia without knowing the particular time in the past when we learned this fact. Moreover, not having seen the city, no visual image may accompany this recall.

Within such a theoretical framework, Piaget and his associates investigated the functioning of memory. He reports the following experiment, which illustrates well the separate contributions of the figurative and the operative component in memory. Children of six and seven years were presented with a simple picture showing the outline of a decanter, in Geneva a familiar item on the dinner table; the decanter was drawn as tilted to the right and half filled with wine, colored in deep red over the entire lower part of the bottle. In other words, the drawing depicted a phenomenon which children up to eight or nine years of age rarely are able to draw correctly. However,

[1] F. C. Bartlett, *Remembering* (London: Cambridge University Press, 1932).

this time they did not regard a real tilted bottle but the picture of this event, with the horizontal level of the red wine sharply contrasting against the empty upper part of the bottle. Without any difficulty the children recognized the drawing for what it was and were asked to copy it. They succeeded very well in copying the picture. An hour later they were called back to draw from memory what they had seen before. A majority again drew the wine level correctly. When they returned a week later, they still remembered that the drawing had pictured a tilted decanter and red wine. Only this time they were no longer drawing a horizontal level of the fluid, instead they indicated the usual oblique level or other wrong positions of the liquid.

What happened here seems fairly clear. In the original situation the figural aspect of the perceived drawing was sufficiently strong so that the children copied it correctly. An hour later the figurative knowledge still prevailed in the memory image and dominated their drawing. After a week, however, the figurative knowledge became weaker and the operative knowledge became dominant. Now they remembered in the drawing of the half-filled decanter no longer what they had seen but what they had comprehended when seeing. According to their stage of comprehension the children drew a tilted decanter half filled with red wine.

While this experiment demonstrated a memory change due to the fading of an initially strong figurative component, there are other experiments such as the copying of a graduated steplike series of lines of decreasing length, where a different development in memory change with time was observed. After the lapse of one week, some children who were apparently close to but had not yet reached the operational structure of seriation drew an irregular series. When they were asked six months later to draw from memory what they had initially seen, the reproductive drawing showed a distinct improvement. Apparently during those six months the operational structure of seriation had been established. In both cases these children drew not merely what they had seen but what they knew; in the latter case, as their operative knowledge improved, so also did their memory performance.

Piaget makes here the additional observation that the drawing from memory of a steplike series of lines is in close correspondence to what the children do if they are required to reconstruct a series by arranging sticks of varying length. In fact, reconstruction constitutes for

Piaget an important type of memory, midway between recognitive and evocative memory. Reconstructive memory is a kind of evocation in action. With reference to figurative aspects he assigns different bases to each of the three types of memory; perceptual for recognition, imitative for reconstruction, and imaginal or linguistic for evocation. One recognizes that these bases follow the familiar genetic order of the three figurative instruments, perception, imitation, and mental image. Piaget postulates accordingly a similar genetic derivation for the three types of memory.

With a considerable number of experiments relating memory performance of different types to operational situations, Piaget provides empirical evidence for the theoretical position of memory within his theory of intelligence. At times he considers the figurative aspect as essential for all types of memory in the strict sense, as opposed to memory in the general sense which includes everything that one knows. Since this particular formulation of Piaget seems to stress too strongly the imagined configuration it is perhaps more appropriate to conclude with Piaget that memory in the strict sense implies an accommodative activity directed towards specific features of a singular event in the past.

General memory conservation is involved in every kind of knowing activity, including memory in the strict sense. Therefore the conservation aspect of memory in the strict sense is closely related to operativity, hence to action schemes. There is no hard-and-fast line between memory in the strict and in the general sense. As a consequence, memory performance, being in no case a direct copy of a passively received perception, depends most on operative schemes and can be expected to show corresponding changes as these schemes develop or change in importance. In short, while memory in the strict sense is a figuratively oriented knowledge, it is like all other kinds of knowing, embedded in and dominated by a converging network of operative schemes. With memory also, as with images, language and perception, figurative knowledge is as good as the operative knowledge on which it is based.

# Reading 7

# Memory
# and Intelligence

### The operative and the figurative aspect in memory

For Piaget memory in the wide sense is identical with the organization inherent in any scheme. He calls memory of this kind conservation and considers it part of the operative action aspect of a scheme. In this sense it is related to the assimilative, i.e., the incorporating and generalizing, activity that transforms a reality state into an object of knowledge. However, when memory is considered in the strict sense it is more related to the accommodative activity that modifies or applies a general scheme to a particular object.

An accommodation is indissociably linked to an assimilation and vice versa. The level of accommodation corresponds to the level of assimilative schemes to which accommodation is linked. Thus there are perceptual, sensory-motor and representational accommodations. When Piaget writes of a representational accommodation, the word "representational" is to be taken in the wide sense as being identical with "operational." Such an accommodation can, of course, include a figurative representation in the strict sense, as in a mental image, but it need not.

It is pointed out that accommodation is the starting point for all figurative knowledge beginning with the earliest perceptual reactions. In active imitation the specialized function of accommodation is manifest in a kind of representation in external acts. When this imitation is internalized, it becomes the basis of representation proper in the symbolic (or as Piaget calls it, the semiotic) function.

[1] Jean Piaget, B. Inhelder, and H. Sinclair, *Mémoire et intelligence* (Paris: Presses Universitaires de France, 1968) pp. 27-29, 475-478, 480-481. Excerpted and translated from manuscript by Hans G. Furth, by permission of the publishers.

155

Where should one look for the area of contact between conservation of schemes that belong to the operative aspect of action or intelligence and the figurative elements of perception (recognition) or the memory image (evocation) characteristic of memory in the strict sense? It should be in the connections between the schematizing assimilation and the various forms of accommodation of the same schemes to the assimilated objects; objects belonging to the present in many forms of cognitive adaptations or belonging to the past in memory.

Every scheme is the result of an assimilative activity; its function is to incorporate the new to the familiar, to reproduce and, sooner or later, to generalize that which has been discovered. Assimilation therefore necessarily gives its form to the schemes; schemes are the structural results of the functioning of assimilation. Here there is a circle that can be compared to judgments and concepts on the operational level, insofar as judgments and concepts are particular instances of intelligent assimilation and schemes respectively.

But every scheme of assimilation must be accommodated to the objects to which it is applied. Otherwise the assimilation would be deforming or centered on the affectivity of the self, as is the case in symbolic play in which reality is modified according to the arbitrary desire of the moment. Naturally one can have perceptual-motor or representational accommodations. However, there is no assimilation without an accommodation and conversely, no accommodation without an assimilation. This throws some light on the indissociable union of recognition and memory images with schemes of assimilation.

In fact, accommodation is at the starting point of the figurative aspect of knowledge. At the level of perception, perceptual schemes are controlled by assimilation in their general direction of identification and comparison. These schemes are accommodative insofar as it is a question of exploring the perceived configuration, of following the outlines and articulations of a figure, etc. At the level of action in general, accommodation remains equilibrated with assimilation (as it does on the perceptual level) when there is adaptation to novel situations and intelligent comparison. But accommodation can dominate and seek its own interest: in this case it is oriented towards imitation (while primacy of assimilation leads in the direction of play, as mentioned above). This imitation is already active in a general sense in the perceptual exploration that follows the outlines of a figure. But the development of imitation as a particular specialized, sensory-motor or sensory-tonic function leads to a kind of representation in external acts that increasingly corresponds to exterior models, well before the formation of the semiotic function. This imitation, once it is capable of functioning in a deferred and internalized manner, is the source not only of the mental image but very probably of the semiotic function in general, insofar as the semiotic function implies a differentiation between signifier and significate.

What is the relation between the general conservation of schemes and the particular conservation of memory in the strict sense? Since there is an indefinite variety of specific situations to which accommodations correspond, are there as many assimilatory schemes? Piaget answers that accommodations and assimilations cannot be compared in this manner. In fact, he adds, while there are assimilative schemes—and every scheme is an assimilative scheme, i.e., it derives from assimilations and seeks to incorporate material—one cannot speak of accommodative schemes. The product or the direction of assimilative activity is within, i.e., it is identical with the scheme; the product or the direction of an accommodation is, however, towards the outside. This product of an accommodation at best can be called a schema, i.e., something that is figural or particular. Note again the difference between the two words schema and scheme, a difference which so far has been ignored in English translations of Piaget. A *scheme* is inherently linked to other schemes in hierarchical divisions and subdivisions of generality. Not so accommodative *schemas* that are only what they are in the here-and-now dimension.

Schemes range from the most general to the least general or unique. Object permanency is an example of a most general scheme, while a singular scheme would be an object referred to by a unique term or name—"Spot, my neighbor's dog" or "the particular book named *Biologie et Connaissance*." An act of knowledge based on a singular scheme is nothing else but an act of identification corresponding to the stage of intelligence in general. Identification is obviously not a primitive, static act of simply knowing what is there.

It is at this point that the contact occurs between the general aspect, characteristic of assimilation and operativity and the particular aspect, characteristic of accommodation and figurative knowing. A singular scheme of knowing is the operative side of the coin, the figurative side of which can be a particular figurative schema, manifested in a specific image, a proper name, or a memory image in the strict sense. As a consequence, one can expect that an act of memory will not only depend on particular figural aspects of the given situation but will reveal the stage of the operative structure on which it equally depends.

However, memory in the strict sense is based on the use of figurative elements, perceptual for recognition and imaginal for evocation, as well as imitative in the strict sense for "reconstructions" which we place midway between recognition and evocation. It is obvious that memory depends essentially on an accommodation that is more or less differentiated and individualized vis-à-vis the models that have to be recognized or recovered; consequently it also depends on an assimiliation to schemes, since each accommodation is linked to an assimilation.

In this connection a problem arises which is not special to memory but is already found in the case of imitation—which can be considered a special variety of reconstructive memory. Since there is an indefinite diversity of accommodations as sources of memory images or recognition, are there as many corresponding schemes of assimilation? In fact, there do not exist accommodative schemes, only schemas, since a scheme is the result of an assimilation. Assimiliation, just as much as the resulting scheme, is directed towards the generalizable; while accommodation and particularly the memory image that derives from accommodation are directed towards the singular and unique. Precisely to the extent that accommodation becomes particular it is a source of figurative elements. Schemes, on account of their general character, are typically found in some hierarchical ordering, the more general containing subschemes and so on down to singular schemes (i.e., schemes with a unique term). The specific mode of assimilation of singular schemes is identification.

Accommodation, on the contrary, can be more or less detailed or exact or remain global, but there is no ordering. It is therefore not contradictory to see in memory in the strict sense the result of differentiated and individual accommodations and to consider the conservation of memories as necessarily linked to schemes of assimilation. This hypothesis is not simply a tautology that identifies conservation and assimilation—this would not explain anything—but, in fact, it leads to the proposition that the conservation of an element as an individualized subscheme is a function of the conservation of increasingly more general schemes of which it is a part and often even of the system in its totality. This is precisely the hypothesis we want to test. Is memory linked, under different forms, to schemes of actions and operations? And, if so, can the influence of these schemes be observed in the memory behavior of the subject according to his operative level?

## The nature and levels of memory

Piaget first emphasizes again that every general assimilation is accommodated to a particular content. Memory in the strict sense requires detailed and differentiated accommodations. He considers three levels of memory, each one corresponding to different accommodative instruments: (1) recognitive memory, based on perceptual schemes; (2) reconstructive memory, based on imitation, and (3) evocative memory, based on the image.

Piaget considers the problem of memory as related to the general problem of intelligence in its operative and figurative aspect. He seems to take the meaning of the word figurative in a wider sense than usual, in fact co-extensive with accommodative. For he concludes that since assimilation and accommodation are inextricably linked, any knowledge contains some concomitant figurative aspect. This is an illustration of Piaget's inexact use of words, which makes the reading of his works doubly difficult. Taken literally, the sentence "Understanding of the present..." means that there is no thinking without either perception, imitation, or images; an extreme position that Piaget does not hold. Thus one has to interpret the sentence from a developmental standpoint to the effect that all knowledge is based on and incorporates in a new manner experiences that were once figural. Or it may merely mean that any concrete understanding of a situation must somehow be communicated to the mind of the person and this can only be done through perception or symbols, both of which have figural aspects.

In general, a scheme is an instrument of assimilation, hence of generalization, and it therefore intervenes in every problem of intelligence, indeed in every sensory-motor and practical adaptation. But each scheme must accommodate itself to the given situation so that its exercise implies an equilibration between assimilation and accommodation. Accommodation, when it predominates and becomes an end in itself, leads to an imitation which is a more or less pure accommodation to an object or to a process that serves as an exterior model to the imitative action. Imitation that is internalized and capable of activating various degrees of sensorial re-afferences is the source of images.

One can therefore understand that intelligence centers on schemes as instruments of assimilation insofar as it deals with the knowledge of present or future, and particularly when problems to be solved concern generalizable anticipations or operational transformations. In contrast, knowledge of the past is particularized and minimally inferable due to its inextricable mixture of fortuitous successions together with sequences that are lawfully linked to individualized objects or events. Knowledge of the past needs a much more solid base of accommodations that are uniquely determined by real events. Therefore memory in the large sense generally makes use of schemes of all sorts, but memory in the strict sense requires a large number of differentiated accommodations. These are found in perceptual schemes as instruments of recognition, in imitations as source of reconstructions, and starting from a certain level of development, in internalized imitations or images as instruments of evocation. However, we are here dealing with a general process which is found in all forms of knowledge. Understanding of the present and the future requires not only operative elements as sources of structurings and transformations, but also the constant collaboration of figurative elements (from perception to the image by way of imitation) as sources of representation in the narrow sense. In the case of knowledge of the past or memory, the figurative elements are no longer pliable at will (if they are changed at will this leads to deformations or errors) since the past has passed and cannot be transformed. This explains the fundamental and privileged role of figurative factors in what we have called memory in the strict sense.

> Memory is seen as differing from intelligence in general not because of a special figural content but because of a judgment bearing on a particular past. A memory act is described by Piaget as a convergent activity of specialized accommodations. The finer and the more detailed the accommodations are, the better the memory. Yet there is the problem of "false" memories. This of itself indicates to Piaget the fact that accommodations must always be seen as related to schemes that range from singular to more general schemes. It is by reference to the assimilative schemes that some critical control of understanding can be exercised toward the figurative content. In itself the figurative content is beyond critique, it is simply what it is.

However, if a recognition is different from perception, a memory reconstruction different from an imitation, and a memory image different from a representational image, this is not, as we have seen, by virtue of their figural properties or some peculiar quality of their content, but on account of a judgment that attaches one but not the other to the past. This localization in time therefore depends essentially on the context, i.e., on the problems and consequently on the functions fulfilled by the perceptions, images, and schemes in the activity of the subject. From such a viewpoint there does not exist any fixed boundary between the mnemonic act and the act of intelligence in general, rather a series of mobile and interchangeable boundaries. All intelligence partakes of memory, if one takes memory in the wide sense; without memory there would not be any comprehension of the present nor even any new invention. But memory in the strict sense is differentiated to a greater extent the more specialized the manner in which schemes are accommodated. This accommodation is directed to the objects, the momentary states and events belonging to a lived-through and past experience. Therefore both the sentiment of personal identity and reference to the past seem to belong mainly to the figurative aspect of memory rather than to its operative aspect. And this is why one could define memory in the strict sense in terms of the figurative aspect of the conservation of schemes. But this figurative aspect derives from the imitative accommodation of schemes, especially from their differentiation as a function of the unmodifiable and specific character of the data from the past. Consequently only the internal system in its entirety, rather than memory content, can furnish the small measure of critical control necessary for the localization and retracing of past events.

Piaget asks how the three levels of memory—recognition, reconstruction, and evocation—fit in with developmental stages. In particular, how are the operative schemes that control the various kinds of memory interrelated? Piaget shows that the structures of intelligence characteristic of the three main developmental stages are finally incorporated into a higher synthesis and he relates these stage-specific structures to the three levels of memory. He calls these manifestations of stages "types of memory organization." What is interesting is a progression of types on all three levels. That is, recognition is not first perfect and then followed by the development of reconstruction with evocation finally going through the same stages. Rather, there is a simultaneous development on all three levels; yet this development is uneven and, depending on the task, shows some discrepancy or *décalage*.

Hence our final problem relative to the unity of such a system. If every figurative memory, including rote memory, is definitely based upon schemes of varying degrees of differentiation, must one admit that similar schemes intervene in memories as diverse as recognition, reconstruction, and evocation? Or is there an irreducible plurality or, instead, an orderly progression? Even in that form of memory most bound to original models, namely, rote memory of nonsense, one observes that the groupings of sounds or visual forms are subordinated to spatio-temporal relations that involve schemes of proximity, hierarchical ordering, and sequencing.

This problem of unity or heterogeneity in memory is here raised in a general manner in terms which are closely linked to the problems of the unity of intelligence. The question concerns the hierarchical levels in development as well as the relation of the figurative to the operative. As for the developmental levels, one knows that intelligence is manifest during its development in three successive forms that correspond in the mature individual to the three levels coexisting in the hierarchy of behavior: a sensory-motor stage, a representational stage resulting in concrete operations, and a stage of propositional or formal operations. While each of these stages is characterized by its proper structure through which each stage is enriched relative to earlier stages, there is yet a remarkable functional unity. Earlier stages prepare and become incorporated in later stages; later stages begin to reconstruct earlier stages by means of new instruments and then go beyond the earlier stages and generalize and enrich them. Thus the same partial structure, e.g., the group of displacements, is found again under analogous but more and more general forms at the sensory-motor, the concrete, and the formal stage.

In memory one also finds successive levels which are somewhat different from the preceding. They can, however, be situated in the preceding model without too much difficulty. These three levels are recognition, which at first belongs to the sensory-motor stage; secondly, reconstruction, which marks the transition from the sensory-motor to the representational stages; and finally, evocation, which corresponds to the representational, preoperational, and operational levels of intelligence. One can observe in nearly all chapters of this book transformations of memory that go hand in hand with the acquisition of concrete operations. In Chapter X it was shown that the formal structure of a combinatory arrangement is not held in memory until the adequate stage of intelligence is reached (11-12 years). The problem is, therefore, exactly as for intelligence, to establish whether there is a functional unity with incorporation of earlier structures or whether there is heterogeneity between the levels of recognition, reconstruction, and evocation. This is, in the final analysis, the problem of the relation between the figurative aspects of memory (perception, imitation, images) and the operative aspect (schemes). Is there an interdependence or a radical separation between them?

It is essential to bear in mind that in the different levels of memory, including recognition, one invariably finds schemes, and that for each of these levels there is a successive age-determined order of developmental stages. We referred to these as stages or types of memory organization. What varies from level to level is a different rate of development in one level relative to other levels, but not in the types of memory organization (from distorted to more adequate). In particular, one does not encounter in our experiments, as could have been possible, immediate and entirely exact (100% of trials) successes with recognition on those tasks on which age-determined specific stages in reconstruction and evocation were observed. These two facts, a general presence of schemes and a similar successive order of memory types, in spite of the differing ages of success, already argue in favor of a general unity of functioning. But this is not sufficient as an argument, since memories that are similar in their figural form could be based on different schemes. Without doubt, however, a perceptive or sensory-motor scheme of recognition is different from a representational scheme of evocation. It therefore remains to clarify the relations between the schemes.

In conclusion, the schemes of memory are viewed as identical to the general operative schemes of intelligence. The increase in accommodative power corresponds to an increase in assimilative schemes. The difference between memory in the wide sense (e.g., understanding of logical connections) and in the narrow sense (e.g., rote memory of an arbitrary character) is somewhat blurred by the fact that all figurative knowledge is part of and controlled by some system of operative schemes.

In short, a certain unity in the memory processes seems to exist. The schemes of recognition prepare the schemes of reconstruction and of evocation, even though the latter have an increasing capacity for accommodation, hence of figurative power. In recognition, the model is present and perceptible; the role of memory is merely to discriminate the particular model as having been previously perceived in contrast to other models. The relative unity of imitative and finally figurative accommodation with schematizing assimilation in each case explains the faithfulness or distortion of memory. Thus, in the final analysis, there is no essential difference between rote memory and logical memory; in fact, logical memory provides evidence for the indissociable general relation between memory and intelligence.

# V

## Biology
## and
## Knowledge

# 9

# *a biological approach to intelligence*[1]

A natural scientist who investigates a living organ asks himself two vital questions, namely, *what* is the function of the organ within the greater totality of the organism, and *how* does it function. The first question relates to the biological purpose of an organ. The function of the human hand is to grasp and to manipulate objects in contrast to the human foot which obviously serves a different biological function. It stands to reason that a general knowledge of the specific function of an organ will direct future investigations into more fruitful channels than a haphazard search for possibly relevant data. However, in itself a right perspective is perhaps a necessary but not a sufficient precondition for a successful scientific investigation. Scientific understanding and explanation is found only in an adequate answer to the second question.

When Piaget, in his search for an empirical approach to the

[1] This and the following two chapters lean heavily on the works of K. Lorenz (particularly the works listed in the bibliography). Some of Lorenz's ideas have been liberally adapted to the present purpose. Arianne Etienne's helpful comments and discussion on these topics is here gratefully recorded.

167

study of intelligence, adopted the biological model of adaptation, he followed a tradition that some fifty years ago was stronger both in Europe and in America than it is now. For Piaget, however, adaptation is connected in a special manner with intelligence. While it is common to say that intelligence leads to adaptation, Piaget looked for the function of intelligence not in any particular adaptive behavior that resulted from intelligence but in the general process of adaptation itself. The present chapter will first discuss biological adaptation and the manner in which Piaget considered it in relation to the function of intelligence. We shall subsequently see how this view oriented him towards a solution of the second, more essential question, leading to an understanding and explanation of intellectual processes.

Adaptation is an all-pervading biological phenomenon. An organism is adapted when it functions in interaction with its external environment in such a manner that the functioning enhances the biological well-being of the organism. In the history of the biological species, a history that reaches back billions of years, this well-being is manifested by the sheer existence of a living species. The fact that lions live testifies to their successful adaptation, while the untold number of extinct species reminds us that adaptation is not a static, fortuitous state of affairs that can be taken for granted.

The great number of regulatory principles that contribute to the successful living of an organism can readily be illustrated by the fact of homeostasis. A living body keeps a balanced internal environment, in terms of temperature, chemical properties, distribution of oxygen, hormonal distribution, etc. This balance is due to a complex system of interlocking regulatory reactions. A breakdown in any one of its multiple components would make life impossible. In other words, the odds that all things should work harmoniously toward the well-being of an organism are exceedingly small. It is only *post facto*, in retrospective history, that things look easy and appear to proceed with an almost automatic necessity. At the time of the giant dinosaurs, mammals were an insignificant branch of the animal kingdom and no amount of scientific observation and experimentation conducted at that time could have come up with convincing evidence that in a genealogically short time the functioning of the dinosaurs would no longer be adaptive and consequently they would become extinct while the mammals would rise to unprecedented biological success. Looking back, however, we can perhaps give a reasonable explanation for this

individual.[2] In other words, a scientist is able to discover lawful relations between organism and environment by focusing on the adaptive function of behavior in terms of the organism.

For Piaget, behavior or action is always understood as adaptive, not just any external observable movement. In fact, Piaget commonly employs the more specific word *conduite* (conduct) which is better translated as "a specific manner or form of human activity, including external behavior" rather than simply as behavior. Moreover there is the implication, lacking in the word "behavior," of the greater totality within which the specific form of activity is manifest. Only if a certain action has a general adaptive aspect can one term that action intelligent. Hence one should look for the most relevant aspect of intelligence not in the external action itself, but in the general, functional coordination or rules that govern such action.

Lorenz suggests that no animal below man is capable of driving a nail straight into a piece of wood. Such an action is certainly not an ultimate test of intelligence and would perhaps not be suspected of having anything to do with intelligence until one realizes that it is not because of lack of strength, of inability to hold or swing a hammer, or of lack of interest, that primates as well as young children cannot perform this task. What is lacking are the rules of coordination that govern the strokes which compensate for each slight deviation from the vertical. Lower organisms do not have the capacity for this elementary degree of learned skill which can be called "control of an action pattern by continuous compensatory movements." Intelligence is found, thus, not in the activity as such, but in the rule which implicitly governs this activity.

This example can give us a glimpse of the adaptation of human intelligence which is characterized by the fact that it is not tied to specific acts. What we have described is really nothing but a simple prerequisite for the use of any tool. While there is a lot of coordinating and compensating action that is rigidly built into innate specific behavior patterns, and while there is a bare beginning only of nonspecificity in animals, human intelligence can be typically regarded as the organ of nonspecific adaptation.

---

[2] Concerning the meaning and use of "behavior" in contemporary American psychology, the reader is urged to glance at definitions of this word in current textbooks and dictionaries of psychology. They all come down to "anything observable that the organism does" without reference to the relevant biological matrix.

Furthermore, intelligent behavior is not in itself tied to an explicit or reflective knowledge nor to a verbal expression or comprehension. We can turn the assumed implicit knowledge into explicit expression by imagining that an eight-year-old boy stands in front of a plank into which a three-inch nail has been driven about halfway so that it turns a little towards the right. The boy with a hammer in his hand, about to swing it on the head of the nail, is interrupted and asked: "How are you aiming at the nail to make it go down straight?" He may respond by saying that he will aim at the nail somewhat from the right so that while driving it down he at the same time corrects the deviation from the vertical. This reply expresses intelligent thinking which in this instance is no longer merely manifest in the external action. Yet essentially there need be no difference between the coordinating rule which guided the external use of a tool and that which was adequately expressed in verbal form. In both cases the general coordination is the essential aspect of intelligent functioning.

As Piaget set out to probe into intelligent behavior, he did not look for isolated elements of actions, performance of this or that skill, part knowledge of a certain word, or reflective verbal expressions. Rather he focused on discovering the rules that coordinate behavior, and he hypothesized that adult intelligence develops from the practical coordinations of infancy. With this in mind, he began systematically to observe his own three children from the youngest age upwards, and he has continued to make critical observations of children to this day. He has collected literally hundreds of natural observations and developed his theory in detail only after a broad harvest of empirical data. In this manner he became familiar with the natural manifestation of the budding intelligence. He gathered a host of relevant empirical observations that can delight any person interested in the life of children.

Like Darwin or Freud before him, he systematized his empirical observations. Focusing on the rules of coordinating actions, Piaget discovered structures and continuities of structures where others saw nothing but preintellectual and rather inconsequential childish activities or at best a sequential accumulation of elements of knowledge. Just like the two scientists before him, Piaget's investigations were guided by a developmental direction towards the terminal state; for Darwin this was the present biological species; for Freud, the adult neurotic; for Piaget, the implicit norms of adult or scientific logical intelligence.

Having focused on the structuring function of intelligence as related to the internal organization manifest in all living adaptation, Piaget next set out to explain how intelligence functions. Guided by his evolutionary hypothesis, he came to follow an exceedingly simple and straightforward working procedure. While we do not know exactly what adult intelligence is, Piaget argued, we know sufficiently some of the normative principles that characterize its adult state. He then attempted to find out how mature intelligence emerged in the natural life history of a person. In particular he searched for the earliest manifestations or traces of intelligence to see whether with advancing age a continuous increasing adaptation reveals intelligently structured behavior. As he traced the growth of intelligence, Piaget found that the observations at the earlier level helped him to understand more clearly the nature of intelligence at a later level.

On this point Piaget's distrust of defining adult intelligence in terms of introspective and subjective predilections stands in marked contrast to those who implicitly accept so-called common sense notions of intelligence. Due to man's psychic complexities, his self-reflective consciousness, his susceptibility to given social, cultural or personally motivated norms, it is exceedingly risky to rely on personal introspection for an answer to the nature of knowledge or intelligence. Aside from these problems, the final state of a process is frequently an unsuitable point from which to start the investigation of the living process. Intelligence is all-pervasive in adult life and participates in all the different facets of a person's behavior. Where shall one look for the guiding cue that will help analyse such a tremendously variegated and apparently loosely organized behavioral system?

Through his developmental approach Piaget tried to overcome the two above-mentioned difficulties. First, children's intellectual life is less complex and more homogeneous, hence also more easy to comprehend than an adult's manifestation of intelligence. More importantly, to Piaget the process of the developing intelligence seemed closely related to the essential nature of intelligence itself. As a consequence, Piaget could now see a given state of intelligence as the end product of a gradual development. This dynamic view is quite a different thing from merely observing the final state in itself. If intelligence is a terminal state towards which earlier manifestations of knowing tend, Piaget could formulate an internally consistent natural history of biological human intelligence. The task now becomes one of analysing the direction of the living development from states of less knowledge to states of more knowledge. This procedure—in analogy with the best tradition of evolutionary science—may prove to be as close as psychology can come to a "causal" explanation of intelligence.

# 10
# *adaptation*
# *and knowledge*

The view that regards intelligence as an organ of certain kinds of behavior patterns within the living organism is perhaps an unusual one; yet even in this connection, the terminology is still too close to the notion of a faculty or a capacity that has a reality of its own separate from its functioning. The ear, for instance, is a separate organ which is different from the action of hearing. Not so with the notion of intelligence. Here the function and the capacity are literally identical. Intelligence is not a thing which causes intelligent behavior; it is intelligent behavior in its active structure and essential aspect, which we for the sake of verbal economy call intelligence.

There is no need to belabor the fact that misinterpretation of verbal labels has caused and continually causes pseudo-problems. This is particularly the case in the psychological and social sciences that deal with phenomena in which verbalized assumptions, transmitted through one's culture, play a preponderant part. One can stress the fact that progress in these sciences requires nothing as much as clearing up the confusion of unanalysed verbal assumptions to which we are all heir. It is a helpful exercise to translate internally the word "intelligence" into an expanded formula: "the sum total of behavior patterns or coordinations as they are manifest in behavior which we call intelligent." If the reader suspects that the foregoing is an empty definition merely saying that "intelligence is . . . behavior we call intelligent," he has misunderstood my intention. This is not a definition at all; it is the expansion of the short-cut term intelligence into a verbal formulation that exposes the fact that intelligence by itself has no existence and is not an explanatory variable for intelligent behavior.

If one considers intelligence a way of behaving and not, properly speaking, a separate biological organ, one appreciates the importance of placing behavior under the general law of biological evolution and adaptation. It is obvious that whatever special laws human behavior is subject to, it cannot escape the encompassing laws of all living beings. Indeed these laws seem to provide the most valuable base from which to proceed to further specialized analysis. In addition, they offer the most secure approach to avoid being led astray by the overlay of cultural verbiage and uncritically accepted assumptions.

The term "adaptation" introduces at once the fruitful notion that organism and environment are two interlocking systems. One must not imagine that there is a living organism on the one hand and a given environment on the other and that somehow these two things adapt to each other. Such a separation is contrary to the meaning of biological adaptation. Rather, where there is a living organism it is bound to be already adapted to its environment, at least in a certain measure, otherwise it would not be living. Adaptation means literally that the effective environment of an organism is as much related to the organism as the organism to its environment. The fundamental biological unit is the organism within its environment. To us, as adults, this unit seems neatly divided into two separate components, because we have learned—thanks to our intelligence—to regard the environment and our own person as separate objects of knowledge. But this is a specialized achievement of our intelligence, namely, the construction of an object of knowledge. To the infant or to the animal organism such distinctions are not given. A biologically valid analysis of knowledge must start with the primitive organismic-environmental matrix from which the knower-known relation emerges.

To analyse knowing behavior within this adaptive unit, Piaget recognizes two directed activities, one that goes from the environment to the organism, the other from the organism to the environment. Assimilation refers to the organism-inward direction, accommodation to the organism-outward direction. These activities must not be treated as separate pieces of behavior: they are two partial aspects or phases of any one adaptive behavior pattern.

Assimilation and accommodation can be observed already at the mechanical or chemical level but they take on a fuller meaning with regard to living behavior. Here assimilation implies a living structure to which an environmental element is assimilated, a structure which in turn accommodates to the given element. In this process we see the beginning of a dialectic exchange between organism and environment. If we consider learning in the most general sense as a characteristic phenomenon of human intelligence, we notice that the basic capacity for modification is potentially present within this living exchange.

To illustrate the use of the assimilation-accommodation paradigm for our understanding of human knowledge, think of a one-year-old child who is taken on a visit near an airport; the weather is cloudy and one can hear the roar of the planes before one can see them land or take off. (1) The baby, used to all kinds of loud noises, may take no notice at all of the roar, or (2) he may well be fascinated by the unusual noise without connecting it with the planes which cannot readily be seen, or finally (3) he may already have learned the association of planes and roar and make the inference from the noise to its cause with or without being asked or prompted.

In the first instance (1) the baby is unaffected by the noise, that is, as far as the child is concerned, this roar is not part of the environment to which he responds. The reasons for not responding can be manifold. Quite obviously no person can respond to all features of an environmental situation. Selective attention is necessary and typical at any age level. For that particular baby the roar of the planes may be just like the noise of bypassing cars and trucks to which he does not habitually respond. It is of no potential interest to him and consequently there is no act of knowing, recognizing, or even paying attention.

In the second instance (2) the roar is noticed and it is listened to as some unusual noise. The baby attributes some meaning to the sensory impression. As observers we could perhaps label this meaning as "bypassing noise." The sound of this roar is somewhat unusual and different from what hitherto belonged to the category of "bypassing noise." While the roar of the plane is assimilated to "bypassing noise," this assimilation calls for an accommodation of the meaning to the new unusual instance. Thus the child is led to give the noise the more adequate meaning exemplified in the third illustration. Here (3) the child's responding to bypassing noise is already more adequately differentiated into a noise emanating from the street and another caused by airplanes. As every car owner knows, such successive differentiation of attending to motor noises may continue to that level where an expert will know the type of car and the general condition of a particular motor just from listening to the engine's performance.

This example is meant to illustrate the two following points: Whenever we speak of knowing or identifying, even at the most primitive levels, there corresponds to this act of knowing (1) an internal subjective structure that confers meaning, and (2) at the same time a particular instance to which the structure is applied. In connection with the organism, the word structure can frequently be interchanged with such words as rule, pattern, or coordination. Structure, however, has the advantage of focusing on the organizational, systematic character of intelligent and preintelligent knowing. Just as the organism is a living biological system, the organism's intelligence is also a living organized subsystem.

Note also, that insofar as knowledge is a system it is also replicable. The internal structure corresponding to the identification of "noise" is not simply geared to this or that noise. Since "noise" in our example is a generalizable structure, it can subsume a great variety of instances and serve as that to which these instances are assimilated. At a more advanced level, one may identify a particular structure of knowing with the term "concept" and say that an instance is recognized as belonging to that concept. In particular, assimilation, the movement from outside to within, can be regarded as similar to what is meant by the word "comprehension." We have above employed the word "meaning" which in this connection implies nothing more than the fact of some adaptive, i.e., meaningful responding. Piaget habitually asserts that assimilation confers signification or meaning to an encounter which, psychologically speaking, could not take place unless the event were assimilated to a subjective organization.

The word "structure" refers here to the internal organization that becomes manifest in the particular behavior of listening to and identifying a specific noise. Structure implies the presence of elements and their overall interrelation and coordination within the organization. The word "scheme" is on a more specific level in Piaget's vocabulary and expresses the generalizable coordinating aspect of a specific action of knowing. Thus in our example we can speak of a scheme of "recognizing bypassing noise" or a scheme of "recognizing airplane roar." Schemes express the organizational or structural aspect of the action. A scheme is unthinkable in isolation; schemes are always sub-parts of greater, coordinating structures. In the given example, over-riding coordinating structures can be assumed to be eye-ear coordina-tion, the tendency to search for the cause of a noise, not to mention the general ability to hear, i.e., to discriminate between noises. None of these abilities, it must be remembered, is simply given at birth; all represent intellectual achievements of some sort, and all are differ-ent manifestations of the overall structure which is being constructed and which in its later phase we clearly recognize as intelligence.

To forestall misunderstandings in connection with the words "struc-ture" and "scheme" it may be worthwhile to return again to the question about the reality status of schemes and structures. The struc-tures we are here discussing are not simply the structures of the central nervous system nor any other physiological structures. Piaget certainly does not deny that the brain is vitally related to intelligent behavior, but he is intent on analysing intelligence on the level of behavior. He uses words like "internal structures or schemes" be-cause intelligence is identical with that type of behavior that consists in the organizing and constructing of rules, patterns, and principles. If the functioning of intelligence shows structures, intelligence must also be said to be structured. Or to use the suggested expansion of the word, a "structure of intelligence" is identical with the "structure of the sum total of behavior coordinations as they are manifest in be-havior which we call intelligent." Such reminders may appear trivial or pedantic unless we realize that it needs a constant effort on our part not to be deceived by our use of language. When Piaget, in analysing intelligence, refers to assimilation of internal structures, he is not philosophizing nor physiologizing but simply psychologizing, that is, analysing behavior in terms of basic biological activities.

The second general point in the assimilation-accommodation model relates to the more difficult notion of accommodation and to the con-tent or object of knowing. Whereas assimilation is likened to the comprehension of a given event in terms of a generalized scheme or concept, accommodation is related to the application of a given scheme in terms of a particular instance. At the earlier levels of intelligence the accommodative function is almost entirely equated with adaptive perception, in the sense of seeing, hearing, and touching things as they "really" are. Piaget has coined the term "figurative" for this phenomenon, since in the physical world it is the configuration, the outlines or *Gestalten*, which are the chief carriers of perceptive information.

Nevertheless, as our example illustrates, and as Piaget never tires of reiterating, knowledge of a particular event requires an assimilation to schemes. Sensory stimulation as such is not knowledge and does not lead to knowledge unless there is a structured scheme prepared to assimilate it and accommodate to it. The baby in the first instance was not open to the "figurative" aspect of the roar because the minimum prerequisite schemes were not available or not yet constructed. No amount of merely exposing this infant to this noise would change the situation unless with growing age the infant developed adequate schemes to assimilate such an event. This is a difficult and unaccustomed notion, quite contrary, in fact, to our traditional belief. Perception is here proposed not as something that is simply given, as the elements from which further intellectual progress is built up. Rather it is seen as the product of an accommodative action, it is an accommodative response to the perceptual configuration which is necessarily correlative to an assimilative activity of comprehension. In this connection one can grasp the meaning of the statement that just as in development the internal structure of intelligence is built up, so also meaningful aspects of the physical environment are constructed by this growing intelligence.

This opening up to or construction of the known environment is clearly demonstrated in the third illustration in which the child identifies the noise as the roar of an airplane. In this case the accommodative disequilibrium between the perceived noise and the assimilative scheme of noise became great enough to result in a more adequate knowledge. In such an instance the meaning of accommodation is most readily comprehended, since as a result of the accommodative pull of adaptation an initial more general scheme of bypassing noise is more finely differentiated into "noise from the street" and "noise from the airplane," at the same time as the general scheme of bypassing noise becomes more adequately coordinated and anchored in new experiences.

Piaget, as has been shown, employs the assimilation-accommodation paradigm throughout all the manifestations of knowing activities. With increasing adaptation in mental development the undifferentiated matrix of organism-in-environment becomes structured into organism-knows-environment. The structure that is thus built up is intelligence, considered as the general framework within which we know the world. The process of knowing has two directions, one ingoing and assimilating the object of knowledge to familiar internal structures, the other outgoing and accommodating an internal scheme to particular instances.

Those who know the history of philosophical thinking will notice that the old problem of universal knowledge, of universals and particulars, of general rules and concrete instances, is rearing its head in the guise of these two aspects of any act of knowing. Assimilation recalls the general aspect, accommodation the particular here and now. Assimilation demonstrates that knowledge is indeed a construction, an active transformation of the environment in terms of the knower's general structures. The application of the general structure to an individual instance—without which knowledge would be an empty affair not oriented towards reality—is implied by the accommodative activity of intelligent adaptation.

With Piaget the problem of universals has changed from a philosophical battle of words and uncritical opinions to a critical theorizing on the solid basis of empirical observation. Here we are at the heart of Piaget's efforts. If, as he claims, the methods of natural science, through controlled observations and critical experimentation, can give a reasonable answer to the question as to the nature of intelligent knowledge, then the entire branch of epistemology that has been considered to be the prerogative of philosophers becomes accessible to natural science. The question ceases to be philosophical and becomes a scientific problem.

# 11
# *knowledge in evolution*

The reader knows that Piaget's quest is for a theory of intelligence in the sense of knowledge in general. Thus Piaget is not primarily concerned with the particular fact that some child knows or does not know that Bern is the capital of Switzerland, a knowledge that no general reasoning could have provided; but Piaget cares about the capacity to understand the terms of the question, that is, the child's ability to comprehend what is meant by geographical terms like country and administrative notions like capital. A moment's thought suffices to convince the reader that the second ability is the prerequisite general knowledge on which understanding of any particular knowledge is based. Or to borrow from examples mentioned before, Piaget asks about the general ability to coordinate the use of tools in an anticipatory and compensatory fashion or about the child's general search for reasonable causes of heard noises.

In all these instances it is the generalized aspect of knowledge that is Piaget's concern. In this sense, generalized knowledge and intelligence are strictly identical. The sentence

"Jane knows the rules of multiplication" and "Jane has the intellectual structure which enables her to succeed on all kinds of multiplication tasks" have identical meaning, although in the usual context the first sentence refers definitely to an actual behavior while the second could simply mean that Jane could understand multiplication if she were appropriately exposed to it.

Piaget, as was said before, approached the task of investigating the nature of knowledge by asking the question: How does this knowledge come about? By what type of knowledge is a given structure of intelligence historically prepared? How far back can it be traced? It is this procedure which enabled him to change philosophical speculations or unsatisfactory psychological part solutions into fruitful scientific questions.

Let us briefly sketch once more the traditional view of knowledge as conceived by an intelligent adult in our society. For him knowledge begins with sensation and perception of things as they are. Perception reads off what is given to the senses according to this typical copy-theory of knowledge. Perceptual and motor knowledge is constructed according to principles of association and conditioning. Images are considered to be internal traces of perception, just fainter and less detailed. Intellectual or "abstract" knowledge starts from a perceptual concrete basis of imposing a logical representational structure on perceptual knowledge. Where does this logical structure come from? For some, it is an innate higher principle that is ineffective during early childhood; for others logical rational knowledge is qualitatively not different from perceptual knowledge. Logic is simply the manifestation of generalized rule learning that is similar to habit learning and conditioning and is the direct effect of a greater amount of practice, a greater number of elements to be associated, and a more complexly interconnected network of associations and associative chains. For many the socialized language, the child's mother tongue, is the main determining prerequisite to change concrete to abstract knowledge.

It is easy to see why a scientist with such an implicit or explicit view on the nature of knowledge would see no need for a special theory of knowing, in fact the acquisition of what is called intelligence would be assumed to follow along the same lines as perceptual-motor habits. In short, the object of knowledge could be said to lie out there; we learn to read off what is useful and rewarding to our life by conditioning, association, and internal representation.

Such a position treats a biological phenomenon, a living function, in a mechanical fashion that perhaps once was popular in scientific circles but is no longer accepted in biology or even in theoretical physics. Moreover, Piaget insists, the underlying philosophy of this position violates flagrantly a hallmark of scientific methodology. For this copy-theory of knowledge only lives by the grace of philosophical positivist postulates which arbitrarily limit the object and procedure of science.

Why is this view on the nature of intelligence so popular if it is based on weak arguments? This question has been raised already in Reading 3 by discussing in a summary fashion the history of Western thought and of philosophical theories of knowledge. Without doubt, the philosophical views of any period constitute an over-reaction against abuses and misapplication of previous opposing views. Positivism, with its dogmatic assertion that only things that are observable and measurable are fit topics for scientific study, is still reacting against a view that imposed religious and outmoded social-cultural norms on scientific thinking. As is commonly the case, the new view tends to see itself as simple, obvious truth.

Piaget's answer to the positivist view, as to other theoretical approaches regarding the nature of knowledge, is not a philosophical polemic but the scientist's challenge. He might well say: "Let the facts answer." In his critical treatment of major topics he provides us with hundreds of relevant observations on such phenomena as logical thinking, perception, imitation, images and physical causality, and he consistently discusses general theoretical issues from different, including traditionally held views. In the final analysis it is the observed facts which make certain theoretical views more adequate than others.

Among these facts are the findings of biology and evolutionary theory on the topic of knowledge. That Piaget himself considered the biological perspective as basic to his theory of knowledge is attested to by his own words in the preface and in the subsequent reading section, as well as in his autobiographical note. What follows is but the barest sketch of a general survey of knowledge from a biological-evolutionary viewpoint. It is based predominantly on the work of K. Lorenz and is an attempt on my part to relate the thinking of Lorenz to Piaget's theory of knowledge. While I naturally take into account Piaget's exposition in his own book on the relation of biology and knowledge, I am of the opinion that the biological facts on which Lorenz bases his theoretical views are of more immediate concern to the psychologist than those which Piaget selects in his recent book. Piaget's biological discussion, as can be seen from Reading 8, stays throughout on a fairly theoretical level. The comparative observations of ethologists regarding the spontaneous knowing behavior of animals, on the other hand, seem to be a more direct parallel to Piaget's own sampling of developmental observations in humans.

Animals can be said to know a great many things, as for instance, the location of the nest, the coming of the cold season, the specific signals that communicate help needed or coming, strategies for attack or defense. The word "knowledge" in this connection means that the animal habitually acts in an adaptive, functional fashion and that environmental and social information is utilized within coordinated actions. Nearly all of these actions are quite typical and characteristic for a given species. The science that investigates behavior of animals should have been a branch of psychology, namely comparative psychology. For reasons that have been touched upon in connection with its basically unbiological orientation, modern scientific psychology was not particularly interested in the natural behavior of animals. Zoologists have relatively recently begun to take an interest and have established the science of ethology that deals explicitly with the behavior patterns of species in their natural habitat.

Two features were observed that provided the impetus for a scientific analysis of the otherwise vague and not easily definable description of animal behavior as instinctual. It was noticed that larger behavior sequences such as feeding, fighting, courting, or food seeking were typically made up of action patterns that could be considered building blocks of these larger units. These actions were rigid in the sense of being the same for all animals of a species and not modifiable by special training or circumstances, and they constituted coordinating movements both in themselves and in coordination with larger behavior sequences. These units were called fixed action patterns or instinctual coordinated movements.

A second, even more surprising discovery concerned the specific sensory cues which trigger off specific action patterns. On the basis of these observations it was hypothesized that built into the action patterns are internal cues which correspond to distinct neuro-sensory messages. Once these messages enter the organism the action pattern follows in a regular, automatic fashion. Because of this regulating property, ethologists speak of an innate releasing mechanism. While its sensory-neural characteristics are still largely obscure, the specific environmental stimulus which is the external counterpart of the internal cue can be investigated by behavioral experiments.

Consider the question how a fish like the stickleback knows which fish to chase away from his own territory. Since there is no need to fear the competition of other species who feed on different material available within the environment, the fish must only recognize other fish of his own species. The stickleback possesses a very characteristic red spot on his belly and thus it is not surprising that this red spot has become the exterior cue which sets the innate releasing mechanism for aggressive behavior patterns in motion. It can be shown that any slow moving body with a red spot on its lower part will be attacked, whether or not it is another stickleback or just a decoy that shows this peculiar red spot on its lower front side. In this way it can be convincingly established that the fish in question does not "recognize," in the human sense of the term, the object of his aggression as a fish. The fish merely reacts in a rigid manner to a built-in signal, a cue pattern, with the result that in the natural order of things the signal-action relation "works."

The ethologist Lorenz asks the additional pertinent question: How did the knowledge about the lower-red signal enter the organism of the stickleback? Where did it learn that this is a distinct and nearly always effective cue for triggering aggressive behavior against an intruding individual of its own species? The traditional answer of "instinct" is a purely negative reminder that the fish did not learn this signal through imitation, conditioning, or trial-and-error learning. The behavior is innate, built into the organism. Should we then say that something is known that has never been learned? Far from it, says Lorenz, who sees in every adaptive behavior and every adaptive organ a built-in knowledge concerning some environmental data. What is called instinctual, or more strictly innate, knowledge refers to learning that took place during the millennia of biological evolution, as distinct from individual learning, with which this term is usually associated.

In this evolutionary perspective the terms instinctual and innate take on a scientifically respectable meaning and lose the negative role of being a cloak for ignorance. Moreover, individual learning can now be seen to be a special case of biological learning that is at the core of the living process of evolution. Piaget would not reject the notion of evolutionary learning, he merely considers environmental pressures and chance genetic mutations in themselves insufficient causes. As mentioned briefly before and as will be outlined in greater detail in the following section on equilibration, he postulates the functioning of a regulating and organizing factor within evolutionary and individual development. This self-regulating factor is basic to Piaget's view. It is presupposed in any particular learning, whether individual or phylogenetic.

In most cases, particularly on the lower level of the animal kingdom, the innate coordinating movements are quite rigidly built into the biological system so that hardly any variability is left for further modification. Such rigidity does not preclude a high degree of complexity, even social interactions and communications. Take for example the marvelous system by which bees communicate to other bees the location of a promising field for honey. Their signaling behavior has been carefully investigated so that we can form a fairly complete picture of some of the significant cues. The signaling bees accomplish their task by noting the direction of the honey field in relation to the actual position of the sun. Back at the hive they perform a figure-eight shaped dance on the vertical comb. A vertical upward dance-axis indicates the direction to the sun, a downward dance-axis a direction away from the sun. The angle of deviation, left or right, from the vertical dance-axis corresponds to a similar angle of deviation from the direction of the sun. Equally noteworthy is the ability of the bees to compute the actual location of the sun. They can do this even though the sun is covered by clouds so long as a small part of the sky is visible.

These complex social behavior patterns indicate an extreme form of evolutionary development where capacity for individual learning hardly applies. However, one can follow a gradual emergence of modifiability in those behavior patterns that become fixed only after a first trial which supplies the organism with a bit of knowledge that was not built into it. An interesting instance is provided by a family of fish, cichlids, who use the position of the sun for purposes of orientation in their habitat. Those kinds of cichlids that only swim in the northern hemisphere have built into their orientation mechanism the knowledge that the sun, being always north of the equator, moves in a left-right direction. There is, however, another kind of cichlid found both north and south of the equator. These fish fix their orientation mechanism only after a first contact with the sun has informed them whether their living space is north or south. Facing towards the sun a left-right moving would indicate north, a right-left moving sun would indicate south. The northern type of fish are never able to adapt their orientation mechanism to a southern sun, but their equatorial cousins are given, by evolution, one bit of freedom to make an individual experience from which to compute their position according to a left-right or right-left movement of the sun. Once the fish have learned this bit of knowledge, their orientation mechanism is fixed and does not seem to be any longer modifiable.

Pursuing the line of evolutionary development along an increased liberation from rigid, automatic behavior, we are led to the mammals, and within that group, to the primate apes. In mammals especially, one observes that behavior patterns are not simply given at birth. Moreover, the patterns are unspecific and not triggered by a single sensory cue. Individual periods of development and acquisition of mature behavior become typical, even though mature behavior is still highly similar for all members of a species. Concerning the locus where modifiability occurs, Lorenz mentions a significant difference between the evolutionarily highest branches and lower ones. In lower animals it is predominantly on the receptor side that learning takes place. Animals learn to distinguish relevant cues, learn to aim better at objects which they approach, or acquire necessary information to complete an inbuilt behavior pattern. Even where they seem to acquire new sequences of movements, these sequences are found to be made up of separate fixed elements of movement that are only poorly coordinated. However, freedom to acquire new motor patterns is characteristic of the highest mammals, as is witnessed by the development of that part of the brain which controls voluntary movements.

The direction of this development seems of importance for a basic understanding of human intelligence. One notices that lower down on the scale of evolution animal behavior is rigidly fixed in its adaptation. Above this level there is increased modifiability in the form of greater responsiveness towards the environment on the receptor side, and finally there emerges the capacity to move freely and to act on and manipulate things of the environment. The most conspicuous witness to an unspecific motor capacity is the human hand, foreshadowed by the grasping hand of primates. The grasping hand has evolved in connection with the habitat of the monkeys. With life in the trees, a rigid motor pattern could not serve the biological need for jumping freely from branch to branch. Likewise free orientation in space, already developed to a degree in lower branches of the mammalian group, gives the primates a sensory-motor coordination which we can admire in the circus or zoo.

Most significant of all for human intelligence, primates begin to use their grasping hands for the sake of manipulation and exploration. In fact, in all higher vertebrates one can already observe an attitude towards new objects that can only be called curiosity. Lorenz reports that a young raven will systematically explore any new objects by means of behavior patterns adapted for feeding. The remarkable fact, however, is that the animal is at the moment not at all hungry; one can aptly describe the raven's behavior by saying that he wants to know "theoretically" whether the thing is edible. Compared to lower behavior sequences in evolution where immediate physiological needs dominate all actions, behavior of curiosity and exploration shows a split between action and immediate need. This decentration from immediacy in its different forms is a prerequisite for human knowledge, as many psychologists have pointed out. Lorenz reminds us that the things explored or manipulated by the animal are certainly stored within the organism, since they are put to functional use when future occasions arise.

The manipulatory hand becomes the organ *par excellence* which allows primates to grasp and touch a thing from various angles even if for no other functional purpose than to get the feel of it. By acting on and manipulating objects, the animals highest on the evolutionary scale learn to know things in a manner which strikingly resembles the earliest manifestations of intelligence in humans. Indeed, we can see that some of the evolutionary stages sketched above have been replicated in Piaget's description of the growing human intelligence.

From the foregoing samples of comparative observations one can perhaps envisage that the main direction of growth during evolutionary history is in that function which in man will be called intelligence. On first impulse one might consider knowledge that is innately built into the organism as of a different, lower kind from knowledge that is individually acquired. This distinction appears based on the sharp traditional separation between innate and learned. However, as we have seen in the cichlids, learned behavior can be as rigid, as stereotyped as inborn action patterns. Second, the general capacity for learning cannot but be innate and itself determines the range and the kind of possible acquisition. Third, as Lorenz has pointed out so forcefully, whatever is innate has itself been learned or acquired by the species during evolutionary development. Reconsidering these three points, one realizes that along the continuum from innate to learned behavior one still has not discovered the vital direction of intelligence.

Nor can we expect to find the main trend by merely adding up, if it were possible, the amount of specific environmental and social knowledge which a given species, e.g., the bee, has available. It is not the amount of particular knowledge as such, nor the way it entered the organism—innately or acquired—which seems to point towards intelligence.

Instead, a more fruitful theoretical viewpoint for the emergence of intelligence is the degree of specificity and immediacy of general behavior patterns. Piaget speaks in this connection of a growing dissociation between form and content, form being the generalizable inner aspect of behavior and content its particular situational manifestation. When an action pattern is rigidly triggered off by one stimulus cue, a cue which the animal has no power to examine for its veracity, we have a highly specific cue-action relation. To say that the stickleback "knows" the intruder is obviously only a way of expressing that the animal reacts specifically and immediately to the intruder who provides the releasing cue. Compare this completely automatic reaction with the manner in which a cat reacts to a mouse. Here we have much more justification in saying that the cat recognizes or knows the presence of a mouse. Depending on the cat's physiological condition, it may engage in a variety of aggressive reactions that may or may not lead to the consummatory killing. Moreover, a cat will only react to a specific perceptual configuration, not merely to one isolated cue. A toy mouse that is made to imitate movements will not be reacted to in the same rigid fashion as if it were a real mouse. The cat will soon learn to modify its reactions according to whether the object is living or merely a toy. As distinguished from the specific reaction mechanisms of lower animals, the cat shows by its behavior that is "knows" the difference between a decoy and the real thing.

Parallel with the development towards less specific stimulus-reactions is the emergence of exploratory behavior, the kind of activity that does not serve any immediate physiological need. This behavior indicates a transition between a reaction to an environmental event as fulfilling a present physiological need and responding to the environment as providing potentially useful knowledge. To use familiar examples, one can place the curiosity behavior of the higher mammals somewhere between the reflex movement of the eyes that turn in the direction of a sudden loud noise and the comprehension of relative probabilities.

Notice also that the two characteristic trends are related and mutually imply each other. Where all action is within a rigid behavior-signal relation, biological adaptation can take care of only the most pressing immediate physiological needs. In such a situation an organism, strictly speaking, cannot make an error, nor has evolution given it the opportunity for making one; it has provided it with all the information is needs to know in order to live. When the coordinating movements lose the fixed relation to a single exterior cue, the possible alternatives of external accommodation increase. At the same time there needs to be a more highly structured capacity to assimilate a variety of potentially adaptive events of the environment. The less specific, or in other words, the more general the coordinations become, the greater also is the biological need to accommodate in a less immediate fashion to the environmental events that are being explored.

A highly specific fixed action pattern cannot afford not to engage immediately the whole organism in the outgoing reaction: a stickleback that would not immediately chase away its intruder would lose its territory and means of subsistence. On the other hand, a highly unspecific action pattern cannot afford to engage its total organism in immediate accommodative reactions, otherwise any slight error in assimilating environmental information could have fatal consequences for the animal. Trial and error in behavior—or a slow period of development—can only be permitted when immediate vital needs are not in danger. If the young raven were actually to feed on everything to which he applies the coordinated movements of feeding, he would soon die of indigestion.

For the raven, coordinating feeding movements are largely innate but considerable freedom is left regarding the final objects of eating, the specific foods, their location, size, etc. As a consequence evolution utilizes the movements of feeding not merely for the consummatory ingestion but also for the purpose of making the raven familiar with things, only some of which become real objects of feeding. In the meantime, these things are to the raven ... what? Should one or should one not say, objects of knowing?

Whatever the exact status of exploratory behavior on the continuum from reflex reaction to reflective intellectual knowing, we are here without doubt in the presence of intelligence in the making. Moreover, we observe that motor actions on things are the source of knowledge. The general biological organization manifest in the physiological organism, in innate activities tied to receptor organs, in motor learning and in knowing behavior, forms the basis of a continuum in which we can with Lorenz or Piaget envisage certain significant trends. While conclusive empirical data are far from adequate, the theoretical importance of situating intellectual knowledge in an adequate biological-evolutionary framework can hardly be exaggerated. The following reading provides an example of Piaget's own way of putting his main theoretical concepts within a wider biological setting.

# Reading 8

# Biology
# and Knowledge[1]

This is the final section of a comprehensive book in which Piaget explicitly gives a broad biological basis for his entire theory of knowledge. In the preceding section Piaget outlines the place of knowledge within a theoretical evolutionary perspective. He considers that a biological organization as an "open system" is subject to the vicissitudes of the surrounding environment. While it has an inherent tendency to extend itself into the environment, at the same time it must tend to close the system in order to conserve its own organization. External behavior in general is seen as fulfilling this double function with, however, only incomplete success. Knowing is a further step in this evolutionary direction. With its tendency towards reversible regulations and towards a stable equilibrium, knowledge can eventually attain what external behavior could not do. Knowledge can extend itself to an indefinite variety of situations, to the entire universe and all potential, thinkable situations and yet conserve the stability of its structure through complete compensation. The reason for this lies in the dissociation between the general forms of knowledge and the particular content to which the forms are applied. This dissociation, slowly prepared for in evolutionary history, implies for men the possibility as well as the necessity of social interaction. The human subject who is the carrier of knowledge is therefore not an isolated individual. The biological intelligence which Piaget explores in the "epistemic" subject is as much a social as an individual intelligence.

Continuing in this perspective Piaget asks in subsection I the old philosophical question: Where should we look for truth? His answer, as a scientist, is to look into the biological organization, which includes within its own nature the tendency to go beyond itself.

[1] Jean Piaget, *Biologie et connaissance* (Paris: Gallimard, 1967), pp. 413-423. Translated by Hans G. Furth, by permission of the publishers.

## 23. *Organic regulations and cognitive regulations*

This collective surpassing of forms already constructed, beginning with the biological organization, puts in a proper perspective the conclusions which we must now draw from the whole series of our analyses. It remains to justify the hypothesis that cognitive functions are a specialized organ for regulating exchanges with the external environment and that they yet derive their instruments from general forms of biological organization.

I. LIFE AND TRUTH. One could say that the necessity of a differentiated organ is obvious since it is characteristic of knowledge to attain truth, while the characteristic of life is only the search for continued life. But while one does not know exactly what life consists of one knows even less what is understood by cognitive "truth." In general, one agrees to see in truth something other than a simple copy conforming to the real for the good reason that such a copy is impossible. In fact, only the copy would furnish the knowledge of the model to be copied and yet that knowledge would in turn be necessary for the copy! Nonetheless the attempt to follow the copy theory has resulted in a simple phenomenalism in which the subjectivity of the self constantly interferes with perceptual data. Such a situation by itself demonstrates an inextricable mesh between subject and object.

If truth is not a copy, it is then an organization of the real. But an organization on the part of what kind of subject? If it is only the human subject, this case, with only minimal gain, would risk the enlargement of egocentrism into anthropocentrism which at the same time would be sociocentrism. Consequently all philosophers seriously concerned with the absolute have recourse to a transcendent subject that goes beyond man and particularly beyond "nature." They place truth beyond spatio-temporal and physical contingencies and make "nature" intelligible in a timeless or eternal perspective. But the question arises whether it is possible to jump over one's own shadow to attain the "subject" in itself without it remaining in spite of all "human, all too human" as Nietzsche said. Unfortunately, from Plato to Husserl, the transcendent subject has constantly changed its appearance, without any other progress except that due to the sciences themselves, hence to the real model and not the transcendent model.

Our intention is therefore not to flee from nature which no one can escape but to understand it more deeply step by step with the efforts of science. In spite of what philosophers may say, nature is still far from having disclosed its secrets. It may be worthwhile, before placing the absolute in the clouds, to look into the interior of things. Moreover, if truth is an organization of the real, the preliminary question concerns the understanding of how an organization is organized. This is a biological question. In other words, since the epistemological problem is to know how science is possible, one should exhaust the resources of the immanent organization before taking recourse to a transcendent organization.

However, if truth is not egocentric and should not be anthropocentric either, must one reduce it to a biocentric organization? From the fact that truth goes beyond man, must one look for it in protozoa, termites, or chimpanzees? It would be an impoverished result to define truth as only that which all living beings, including man, have in common in their vision of the world. But if it is characteristic of life constantly to evolve further and if one looks for the secret of the rational organization in the biological organization *including its evolving*, the method then consists in trying to understand knowledge by its own construction. This is reasonable since knowledge is *essentially a construction.*

In subsection II, Piaget describes the triple deficiencies of the organism with regard to (1) its extension into the environment, (2) its maintenance or conservation, (3) its regulation. The reason for these deficiencies is linked with (1) the hereditary mechanisms tied to genetic recombinations and (2) the phenotypic, i.e., individual, interactions with the environment that follow a rigidly built-in reaction norm. Behavior can be viewed as partly compensating for these deficiencies by a "functional" extension of organic forms. The regulations of the assimilative and accommodative activities of behavior emerge as cognitive functions.

II. THE DEFICIENCIES OF THE ORGANISM. This evolving appears to us from a cognitive viewpoint inherent in the biological organization and is therefore essential as a primary datum. An organization involves a system of exchanges with the environment; it tends therefore to extend itself to the totality of the environment yet with only limited success; hence we can see the role of knowledge which is capable of functionally assimilating the entire universe without staying limited to physiological, material assimilations. Biological organization also creates forms and tends to conserve them with complete stability, again with only limited success; hence we can see the role of knowledge which extends material forms into forms of actions or operations; as these forms are dissociated from contents they are capable of conservation in their diverse applications. Finally, this biological organization is a source of homeostasis at all levels, and possesses regulations that ensure equilibrium by quasi-reversible mechanisms. This equilibrium remains fragile, however, and only resists the surrounding irreversibility by momentary stabilizations. Thus evolution appears like a series of disequilibria and re-equilibrations that tends toward an unattainable goal of integrated construction and reversible mobility. Only the cognitive mechanisms are able to realize this goal by integrating the regulation in their construction in the form of "operations."

In short, the need for differentiated organs that regulate exchanges with the external environment results from the deficiencies of the biological organization to realize its own program written in the laws of its organization. The program involves two points. (1) The organization has genetic mechanisms which construct and not merely transmit. But the modes of construction as far as is known, namely recombinations of genes, comprise only a limited sector of construction. This limitation is due to the requirements of a hereditary programming which is restricted for two reasons. First, it does not harmonize construction and conservation in one coherent dynamism (this is done by knowledge) and secondly, it does not possess sufficiently flexible information about the environment. (2) The phenotypes actualize in a particular manner the interaction with the environment and are distributed along reaction norms which are themselves limited. Moreover, each individual actualization remains limited and without influence on the total system, since there are no social or exterior interactions such as are possible only to man in his cognitive exchanges. The only influence on the total system is the genetic recombinations with the above-mentioned limitations.

This double deficiency of organisms in their material exchanges with the environment is in part compensated by the construction of behavior. Behavior emerges from the biological organization as an extension of its internal program. In effect, behavior is nothing else but the organization of life, applied and generalized to an enlarged sector of exchanges with the environment. The exchanges become functional as distinct from the material and energy exchanges which the physiological organization already takes care of; "functional" implies that one deals with actions and forms (or schemes of action) which extend organic forms. These new exchanges, as all others, consist in accommodations to the environment, taking account of its events and its temporal succession and above all in assimilations that utilize the environment. These assimilations frequently impose forms on the environment by the construction and arrangement of objects to suit the needs of the organism.

This behavior, like all organization, involves regulations. Their function is to control accommodations and constructive assimilations on the basis of results of actions or anticipations through which the organism can foresee favorable events or obstacles and ensure the required compensations. These regulations, differentiated from internal regulations of the organism (since it is now a question of behavior), are the cognitive functions. The problem is to understand how regulations can go beyond the organic regulations to the point of accomplishing the internal program of the biological organization without being limited by the mentioned deficiencies.

In subsection III, Piaget first provides a quick glance at the evolution of cognitive functions from early levels in which they are hardly differentiated from organic functions to the final stage of scientific, objective knowledge in its twin forms of experiential knowledge and logical knowledge that involves logical necessity.

Piaget proceeds to clarify the nature of instinctual knowledge, the type of knowledge that is tied to organic hereditary programming but yet carries in it the seed of its final transformation. Possibilities for change are foreshadowed in certain behavioral adaptations of instinct that point toward further evolutionary progress in cognitive regulations.

III. INSTINCT, LEARNING AND LOGICO-MATHEMATICAL STRUCTURES. The fundamental facts in this regard are as follows. Cognitive regulations begin by using only the instruments which served organic adaptation in general, i.e., heredity with its limited variations and phenotypic accommodations: such regulations are the hereditary forms of knowledge and in particular the instincts. But then the same deficiencies which were observed in the initial organization and which the new stage of behavior corrects to only a limited degree are found at this level of innate knowledge: hence in the superior stages of evolution a final breakup leads to a dissociation of instinct according to its two components of internal organization and phenotypic accommodation. As a result, and by complementary reconstructions in two opposed directions—and not, as one has seen, from the dissociation itself—there emerge both logico-mathematical structures and experiential knowledge, as yet undifferentiated in the practical intelligence of the anthropoids (who are geometricians as well as technicians) and in the technical intelligence at the beginning of humanity.

The three fundamental types of knowledge are: innate know-how, the prototype of which is instinct; knowledge of the physical world which extends learning as a function of environmental data; and logico-mathematical knowledge. The relation between the first and latter two types of knowledge appears essential for comprehending how the superior forms of knowledge are, in fact, an organ for regulating exchanges. Therefore we elaborate this point as a fitting conclusion.

Instinct undoubtedly involves certain cognitive regulations: as evidence, for example, there is the system of feedbacks constituted by the "stigmergies" of Grassé. [Stigmergies are a type of hereditary and behavioral regulation in termite colonies.] But these regulations stay limited and rigid, precisely because they take place in a frame of hereditary programming and because a programmed regulation is not able to make new discoveries. It does happen that an animal succeeds in dealing with some unforeseen situations by means of readjustments that foreshadow intelligence. We have seen previously that the coordinations of schemes produced in those situations can be compared to the innate coordinations of the instinctual cycle that concerns the species and not the individual. Here is an interesting indication of the possible parentage of functioning between instinct and intelligence in spite of characteristic differences on epigenetic and phenotypic levels. Yet these phenotypic extensions of the instinct remain quite restricted and do not correct the systematic deficiency. Evidently a form of knowledge that remains tied only to the instruments of organic adaptation, even with some faint indications of cognitive regulations, scarcely advances in the direction of the achievements which intelligence must bring to life.

Although the area of learning proper, going beyond the innate, may well begin at the level of protozoa, it enlarges only very slowly up to the cerebralization of the higher vertebrates. This area, apart from some significant exceptions noted already at the level of insects, shows no systematic new start before the primates.

> As Piaget points out in subsection IV, a new type of knowing appears only quite late in evolutionary history. The mechanisms of instinctual behavior finally burst and give way to new constructions; the two essential components of instinct are taken over by the new type of knowing while the central part of hereditary programming that dominated all instinct disappears. The two components are (1) the general organized functioning that regulates instinct from within and (2) the extension of the organization in external encounters. Analogously, the new knowing turns (1) inward towards its own sources and (2) towards acquisition and learning from its interaction with the external environment. Corresponding new regulations appear that become part of the constructs of knowledge so that regulations are no longer differentiated from the constructs. In mature intelligence all constructs are formed within the framework of general regulations: in other words, all empirical abstractions are carried out under the control of reflective, formal abstraction. Indeed for Piaget, the relation of intelligence to instinct illustrates an essential characteristic of a reflective formal abstraction as a "convergent reconstruction with further evolving."
>
> The new cognitive regulations are flexible in the sense that they

are not tied to specific, innately given information. Knowledge is free to apply itself to any or all particular instances. Moreover, since flexible regulation cannot be programmed within the genotype, a period of active acquisition is required. The higher an organization develops by its own activity the more incomplete are the innate regulations. The utter helplessness of the human newborn is the reverse side of the intellectual mastery which his development achieves.

IV. THE BREAKUP OF INSTINCT. The basic fact of the breakup of instinct, in other words, of the nearly total disappearance in anthropoids and in man of a cognitive organization that was predominate during the entire evolution of animal behavior is itself highly significant. This is not, as one says quite commonly, because a new mode of knowledge, namely, intelligence considered as a whole, replaces the now extinguished mode. Much more profoundly, significance lies in the fact that a form of knowledge until now nearly organic extends into new forms of regulations. While this new mode of knowledge takes the place of the former, it does not properly speaking replace instinct. Rather, the change involves the dissociation and utilization of its components in two complementary directions.

What disappears with the breakup of instinct is the hereditary programming in favor of two kinds of new cognitive self-regulations, which are flexible and constructive. One might say, this is a replacement, indeed a total change. But one forgets two essential factors. Instincts do not consist exclusively of hereditary programming. As Viaud expresses it so well, such a concept views instinct at its extreme limit. On the one hand, instinct derives its programming and particularly its "logic" from an organized functioning which is implicit in the most general forms of biological organization. On the other hand, instinct extends this programming in individual or phenotypic actions that involve a considerable margin of accommodation and even of assimilation that is partly learned and in certain cases quasi-intelligent.

With the dissolution of instinctual behavior, what disappears is only the central or middle part, i.e., the programmed regulations, while the other two realities remain: the sources of organization and the results of individual or phenotypic adjustment. Intelligence inherits therefore what belongs to instinct while rejecting the method of programmed regulation in favor of constructive self-regulation. That which intelligence retains makes it possible to branch out in the two complementary directions, interiorization towards the inner sources and exteriorization towards learned or even experimentally controlled adjustments.

A preliminary condition for this double progress is of course the construction of a new mode of regulations. These regulations, from now on flexible and no longer programmed, start by the usual interplay of corrections based on the results of actions and of anticipations. Tied to the construction of schemes of assimilation and the coordination of schemes, the regulations tend by a combination of proactive and retroactive effects in the direction of the operations themselves. In this manner they become precorrective rather than corrective regulations. Moreover, inverse operations ensure a complete and not merely approximate reversibility.

These novel regulations are a differentiated organ for deductive verification as well as for construction. Thanks to them, intelligence manifests itself simultaneously in the two above-mentioned directions of reflective interiorization and experimental exteriorization. One can understand that this double direction does not simply divide up the remaining functions of the instinct, namely, its function as a source of organization and its outgoing explorations and individual experimentations. As the work of intelligence consists in going deeper into the sources and in extending the explorations, it makes new constructions of two types. One type is the operational schemes that derive from reflecting abstraction and focus on the necessary conditions of general coordinations of action; the other type assimilates experiential data to these operational schemes. In this way these two processes extend the former components of instinctual tendencies.

After the breakup of instinct, a new cognitive evolution begins. In fact it is a beginning again from zero, since the innate programming of the instinct has disappeared. Although the cerebral nervous system as well as intelligence insofar as it is a capacity to learn and to discover is hereditary, the activity that has to be accomplished is henceforth phenotypic. Just because this intellectual development begins from zero, one does not readily relate it to biological organization and especially to the constructions of the instinct in spite of their importance. Intelligence provides an apt example of what we have called "convergent reconstructions with further evolving." In the case of human knowledge this reconstruction appears complete to such a degree that hardly one theoretician of logico-mathematical knowledge has thought to search for an explanation in the indispensable framework of biological organization. It is only quite recently that mechano-physiology has shown the interrelation of logic, cybernetic models, and the functioning of the brain and that McCulloch has spoken of a "logic of neurons."

> In subsection V Piaget links the presence of an interindividual system of exchanges to operational objective knowledge. This provides a partial answer to a criticism often heard that Piaget neglects the role of society. His answer is indicated in this section when he asserts that biological intelligence in the case of man includes man in his social aspect.

V. KNOWLEDGE AND SOCIETY. Such a complete reconstruction is possible only because intelligence gives up the instinctual cycle that transcends the individual in order to rely on interindividual and social interactions. There does not seem to be any discontinuity in this regard since even chimpanzees work only in social groups. This direction towards social interaction takes place at the same time as intelligence loses the support furnished by hereditary programming and proceeds in the direction of constructed and phenotypic regulations.

From a cognitive viewpoint, as already mentioned, the social group plays here the same role as does "population" from a genetic and consequently an instinctual viewpoint. In this sense society is the supreme unity and the individual succeeds with his discoveries and intellectual constructions only insofar as he himself is the place of collective interactions. The level and the value of these interactions depend naturally on the society as a whole. The great man who seems to launch new movements is but a point of intersection or of synthesis, of ideas that were elaborated by continuous cooperation. Even if he is opposed to current opinions he responds to underlying needs which he himself has not created. This is why the social milieu effectively fulfills for intelligence that function which in evolution is carried out by the genetic recombinations of the total population, or in instincts by the species-specific cycle.

In a sense the modes of transmission and interaction in a society are external and educative as opposed to the hereditary transmissions or combinations. Nonetheless society is still a product of life. The "collective representations," to quote Durkheim, presuppose the existence of a nervous system in the members of the group. Therefore the important question is not to weigh the relative merits of the individual and the group (a problem that is analogous to the chicken and the egg); it is rather to distinguish the logic found in individual reflection and in cooperative efforts from the errors or insanities that occur in collective opinion or in the individual conscience. In spite of Tarde there are not two kinds of logic, one belonging to the group, the other to the individual: there is only one way in which to coordinate the actions A and B according to relations of class ordering and serial ordering. It makes no difference whether these are actions or distinct individuals, some of A, others of B, or whether they are of the same individual who certainly did not discover them by himself since he is part of the whole society. In this sense cognitive regulations or operations are identical in a single brain and in a system of cooperations (is not this the meaning of the word "cooperation"?).

The final subsection VI, besides some personal remarks that may be typical for a French-speaking author but that seem inappropriate to an English-speaking audience—many adjectives and insinuations have been softened here by the translator—ends with a strong plea

for the continuance of scientific epistemology. This is not a senti-
mental wish on Piaget's part. It is the serious concern of a scientist
who has not been inclined to or not been able to build a school as
Freud did, who has not a large number of pupils and who is not
generally recognized for what he is. Piaget's work and his Center of
Genetic Epistemology have yet to make their full revolutionary impact in the world of philosophy, epistemology, biology, mathematics,
the theory of science, and last, but not least, psychology.

VI. CONCLUSIONS. In general we believe that we have verified the two
hypotheses that formed the main theme directing this work: the hypothesis
that cognitive functions extend organic regulations and that they are a
differentiated organ regulating exchanges with the external environment.
This organ is only partially differentiated at the level of innate knowledge,
but it becomes more and more so with the logico-mathematical structures
as well as the exchanges inherent in all experience (including social
experience).

These are perhaps rather obvious hypotheses. But it seems necessary
to stress and deepen them, all the more because, curiously enough, some
specialists in epistemology and especially in mathematics forget too
readily the biological perspective, and biologists as a rule fail to see the
relevance of such questions as why mathematics is so well adapted to
physical reality.

The entire book may have all sorts of deficiencies. There is perhaps a
lack of strict proofs, and propositions are advanced which are based on
facts but go beyond them. Nevertheless we have thought it useful to write
this essay because the kind of collaboration between biologists, psychologists, and epistemologists needed for the above proofs hardly exists and
is highly desirable. Only through an interdisciplinary effort is scientific
epistemology possible and this cooperation is still much too infrequent for
the problems at hand. We have attempted to set forth the ideas contained
in this volume in the hope of encouraging this cooperation.

# VI
# Development
# and
# Learning

# 12
# *equilibration and development*

Piaget's view on intelligence, as sketched in the previous chapters, has a biological depth and a structural unity that reaches from the first spontaneous glimmer of a living organism to the threshold of critical reflection. Human intelligence, for all its uniqueness, is seen as the end manifestation—and who would dare to say the final end?—of a biological process that spans the billions of years of evolutionary history, the thousands of years of human civilization, and the sixteen odd years of individual development. How can Piaget be so bold as to consider all past history a mere prelude to the capacity for logical thinking within an adolescent of today? Perhaps also there are other aspects of human life that could be as well or better singled out as the "purpose" of life in general.

This objection derives from two basic misunderstandings, one about the nature of adaptive development, the other about intelligence. First, from a biological viewpoint there is no such thing as an outside purpose that pulls or directs a given adaptation. In all life processes the motive force, the activity and the goal are but three aspects of the same process. If adult intelligence is viewed as the end of a process of development, one should not consider that intelligence is a purpose outside the process, but that it is an integral part of the process, subsuming earlier manifestations in a higher synthesis.

Second, as Reading 8 demonstrates, Piaget proposes not only that the internal organization in living beings lies at the root of all development, but he considers adult intelligence as deriving directly from this internal organization. According to him the structural aspects of life become explicit in the form of knowing behavior. In fact knowledge for Piaget is the structural aspect of psychological life while the dynamic aspect is termed *affectivity*. Under this heading would fall what is usually discussed as motivation, emotions, or personality.

What Piaget calls general intelligence thus extends as far and as wide as human knowing in general under its millions of manifestations. It is present in all behavior, as is motivation. There is no intelligent act without an aspect of motivation, and there is no motivated act without structuring intelligence at work. If Piaget focuses his research on the logical, critical use of intelligence, this is because he considers that in logical thinking the organization of behavior can be observed in its purest and most developed form. At the same time, Piaget points out that intelligent or preintelligent regulations to a greater or lesser degree structure all forms of behavior.

As Piaget recognizes an internal principle of organization that determines all living processes or changes, so also he postulates the functioning of a self-regulating mechanism that governs the development of intelligence within the individual. Piaget's concept of this regulating mechanism falls within the more general trend in evolution that leads from reflex action to less immediate and less specific reactions. This trend, outlined in the previous chapter, is also manifest in the development of human intelligence. There it takes on a special form which Piaget calls *equilibration*. It is conceived as the factor that internally structures the developing intelligence. It provides the self-regulation by which intelligence develops in adapting to external and internal changes. Equilibration coordinates the various forces that come from physiological maturation and from the physical or social environment and that bear on the growing intelligence.

Piaget insists on the factor of equilibration partly because he needs a unifying principle of development and cannot accept other factors as that principle. On a more profound level, he finds internal regulations present in living organizations at all levels of evolution and development and in all living forms of an organ or of behavior. Does this imply that the presence of other factors is superfluous so that intelligence would by its own force develop even out of contact with an environment? Piaget does not take such a patently absurd position. If botanists describe the internal mechanism by which a plant grows and lives, do they thereby suggest that environmental circumstances are of no import? Piaget, by stressing the biological roots and principles of human intelligence, does not reduce interaction with a normal environment to an unnecessary luxury. On the contrary, his constructivist theory of intelligence precludes the contradictory notion that a person can construct his known environment without experiencing it. It follows that for Piaget physiological factors of maturation, physical objects in the world, and the social environment are absolutely necessary for normal growth. The entire accommodative activity of the knowing person is directed to the environmentally given, the objective situation. Environmental factors are the medium in which intelligence works and with which it interacts; it is therefore influenced by the constraints of this medium.

However, in connection with factors contributing to the growth of intelligence, Piaget suggests that we should not only or primarily think of such causal factors as the heat that causes water to evaporate. If only this kind of causal influence were at work, the addition of equilibration as another causal factor would be redundant. Piaget contends that no living structure can be adequately explained in physico-causal terms alone, and this is even truer of the structure of mature intelligence. A logical conclusion is not the physical effect of the premises nor does $2 + 7$ "cause" 9. It is at a level of structural implication that intelligence grows and lives and finds its most adequate explanation. Implication is a relation of logical necessity proper to intelligence and consciousness which cannot be reduced to the lawful relations of causality typical of physical manifestations.

Piaget considers the concept of equilibration particularly appropriate for two specific reasons. He relates equilibration to implication as an intrinsic form of causality within a total organization and to the lawfulness peculiar to dynamic systems as they are studied in cybernetics. Piaget likes to draw a parallel between probability laws of equilibration and the transition from unpredictable or less predictable

responses of preoperational children to the highly predictable and ultimately logically necessary responses of strict implication. In this light
the development of intelligence appears to an observer as a coordinated sequence of behavior such that a present stage of development
is most likely, considering the immediately previous one, even though
the intrinsic probability of its occurrence, considered from levels far
removed, appears only small. For Piaget the concept of equilibration
makes comprehensible why, in retrospect, alternatives or degrees of
freedom for further evolution or development are progressively reduced with succeeding stages.

Piaget illustrates this idea by the preoperational child who observes
the pouring of a liquid from a wide into a narrow beaker. The child's
judgment concerning the quantity of liquid is at first unpredictable.
The probability that he pays attention to the height or the width is
about equal. When operational reversibility is approached, the child
may first be inclined to follow a single rule, for example, focusing on
the dimension of height; but this strategy is beginning to break down
because of the child's inability to neglect other dimensions altogether.
At this time the child will increasingly pay attention to different views
of the same event and will more often than not know that a one-sided
view is wrong because he realizes that there is another view; yet he
will not know how to correlate these views within a stable system.
From this transitional level the next step in behavior becomes comprehensible: the child will pay attention to both dimensions and use their
inverse changes to argue for compensation. Yet when the perceptual
discrepancy becomes too large, that is, when the column of water appears disproportionately high, he will relapse into the former strategy.
Following this the final step in achieving conservation of quantity becomes likely, and the child's facility in full reversibility makes his
correct response certain.

Piaget also has great faith in cybernetics,[1] which he considers the
science of organizational laws within a total system. He is hopeful
that his own logical formulations of intellectual development will
prove to be related to general laws concerning open systems such as
are found in biology generally. If this is the case, some of the less com-

----

[1] On cybernetics, see S. Papert's section "Épistémologie de la cybernétique" in
J. Piaget, *Logique et connaissance scientifique* [Encyclopédie de la Pléiade, Vol. 22]
(Paris: Gallimard, 1967). This volume is Piaget's recent updating of his favorite
interest, a scientific epistemology. About half of the 1300 pages is from Piaget's own
pen; the rest is written by collaborators.

prehensible attributes attached to intrinsic self-regulatory equilibration may yet be clarified. Among these attributes can be mentioned formal abstraction, progressive interiorization conceived as dissociation of a general form from its particular content, or the apparent "finality" of evolution and development. These notions are now receiving scientific respectability since feedback circuits, content-free operations, and self-organizing systems have become familiar terms in cybernetics and computer-based simulations of intelligence.

By his concept of equilibration Piaget makes explicit his biological view of intelligence, a view he thinks has not been sufficiently stressed by scientists and experts concerned with intelligence in the theoretical or applied sciences. The evolutionary trend towards a lesser degree of immediacy and specificity in behavior becomes in intellectual development a process of increased reflection, a turning inwards or an interiorization of action that changes coordinated external actions into systems of interior, reversible operations. Equilibration can be viewed as a compensatory response to these biological trends, or better as guiding and regulating this trend towards the building up of more advanced structures. In both Reading 8 and Reading 9, Piaget relates the concepts of interiorization and equilibration when he considers equilibration as the inner regulating factor which in development leads to an increasing dissociation of the general forms of structured behavior from particular content. He believes that the first task of those who wish to understand or control intelligence is an adequate analysis of the development and organization of the general forms implied by every kind of intelligent activity.

As in evolution, so in individual development it is clear that at more advanced stages there is more knowledge or better adaptation than at earlier stages. This poses a problem for our scientific understanding and must be faced squarely. With regard to the development of the structures of intelligence two views are current. The structures can be considered to come primarily from outside, having been learned through contact with the physical world or with the linguistic society. Alternatively they can be considered innate; the gradual manifestation of intelligence would be the gradual activation of these structures which in turn determine behavior the way in which an architect by means of a blueprint controls the building of a house. The first view is rejected by Piaget as contrary to his empirical observations, which give evidence of a slow development of active construction and elaboration. The second opinion is equally unacceptable since the end product to be explained is already posited as the source of explanation at the beginning. Piaget chooses a third way. In so doing he refuses to follow the empiricist's model of a genesis without inner structure or the idealist's theory of a structure without genesis.

It was before intimated that intelligence for Piaget is not just any bit of particular knowledge or particular skill. It is that aspect of behavior which brings order, lawfulness, purpose, meaning, or as he prefers to say, structure into behavior. Individual development is itself a process of structure or structuring and is encompassed by Piaget's concept of intelligence. Consequently the question about factors contributing to the development of intelligence takes on a different light. As was said above, the activity and the end result are but partial aspects of the same process. Whatever is intrinsic to intelligence is also intrinsic to development. Piaget chooses equilibration as the notion of intelligence that approaches most closely the descriptive character of a living self-regulatory process. Equilibration maintains the organization of reciprocal assimilation and accommodation and compensates for internal and external imbalances and in so doing reaches beyond itself to more advanced structures of organization.

For Piaget, development is not seen as something apart that causes intelligence, nor as something given that is recopied bit by bit. Intelligence in development is to Piaget an intrinsic aspect of intelligence. For some students of Piaget, the notion of a self-regulating process of equilibration is likened to propositions that purport to explain anger by the irascible appetite or reading difficulties by an incapacity to transform visually perceived symbols into auditory images. Piaget's use of the term equilibration is then seen as no more than an empty play on words. However, there is this difference between Piaget's approach to development and the reasoning behind the aforementioned propositions. Anger or reading are partial abilities, skills or attitudes that do not carry by themselves the wherewithal of organic development and consequently need an "exterior" contribution for their development. In this respect, the relation of general intelligence and development is unique: both phenomena, intelligence and development, are aspects or manifestations of identical regulations and structures. Piaget attributes as much structure to development as he attributes to intelligence itself.

In addition to these general theoretical considerations in support of equilibration, Piaget points to the actual functioning of intelligence, which reflects at all levels the working of equilibration. There is the sensory-motor period with its gradual building up of coordinating structures for practical behavior including perceptual schemes vis-à-vis things in the environment. Perception is described as the product of a balanced process including centration on the one hand, with the senses focusing on a given point of the sensory field, and on the other hand decentration which comes about through coordinating movements guided by perceptual schemes. Perception illustrates thus an elementary state of perceptual equilibration where regulating activities tend to compensate for the deforming effects of single centrations. Likewise increasing adaptation of sensory-motor actions can be viewed in the light of equilibration. Repeated exercise of assimilating activity leads to finer differentiations, through which in turn superior accommodations are possible. An infant who has acquired the ability to follow with his eyes the outline of a visual object has thereby a better equilibration between assimilation and accommodation than if he were merely able to focus randomly on various points of that object.

With the close of the sensory-motor period we witness the emergence of the first invariant, the formation of the permanent object. An invariant is like a point in a gravitational field around which actual and potential acts of knowing stand in equilibrium. It is the basis for the relative stability in a structure of knowing. Thus the permanent object is the end product of increasingly complex motor and perceptual coordinations and the foundation upon which future equilibria are constructed. Yet this tendency towards wider and more stable equilibria seems to bring about a long period that is characterized by disequilibrium. This period before the establishment of reversible operations includes the preoperational activities and the blossoming of the symbolic function.

Object permanency, the knowledge that something exists outside of and apart from the acting self, is in one way the crowning end product of a previous period in which the object was merged with subjective activity. On the other hand, object permanency leaves the child in a situation where he has to regain at the level of objectivity what he had previously achieved at the level of external, practical actions. The notions that he forms as a function of object permanency seem to aggravate the situation at first: while object formation enables him to "think" of something, it does not by itself give him the means to comprehend the object. The collective symbols of language can play a similarly disconcerting role. The misapplication of words by small children is proverbial and follows from their unstable schemes of thinking. Consequently this is a period of great disequilibrium.

To illustrate a preoperational child's thinking, here is an example on the estimation of distance. Piaget shows the child a board on which there are two small trees. The child is asked how long the distance is from one tree to another tree. Whatever he answers is acceptable, for instance "pretty far." Whereupon a screen is put between the trees and the child is asked whether now the trees are "less pretty far" or "more pretty far" or "just as pretty far" as before. The child says invariably that they are now nearer to each other. The basis for the answer of the child was provided by a little girl who volunteered the information that if there were a little hole in the wall the distance would remain equal. Taking his clue from this little girl, Piaget substituted a screen in which was built a little window. Sure enough, the distance between the trees changed now with the opening and closing of the window.

Besides providing a glimpse into Piaget's "clinical method," this example shows that for the preoperational child distance and length are unstable notions. "Far" is for the child a subjective notion related to his own actions in traversing the distance. As the child finds things that fill the interval, a distance is judged shorter than the same distance with no objects in between. What the child lacks are the invariants of length measurement in terms of which he can overcome the deforming centration on his own action. These invariants are the points of stability that characterize systems of reversible operations and usher in the second great period of equilibration, the stage of concrete operational intelligence to which the foregoing was a period of slow preparation.

The preoperational child lives in his own world, especially during play activity, unaware of the disequilibrium that objectively exists between his own notions and the real world that he will come to know. Piaget indicates this disequilibrium when he states that, in play, assimilation to the self prevails over accommodation to the real world, while in other types of children's behavior an adequate operative assimilation is lacking in figurative and imitative accommodation. These types of behaving demonstrate that the child does not have the need for the assimilation-accommodation equilibration of mature intelligence. The child and nature take their time.

The logical thinking of the concrete operational child emerges around six or seven years as the second stage of equilibration. The manifest criterion for the full operational structure is observed in Piaget's well-known tasks of "conservation." A judgment or notion of conservation is identical with what was before called an invariant and makes manifest the most characteristic new attribute of the child's structure of knowing, reversibility. The common feature of all conservation tasks is the external change or transformation in a certain aspect of a physical object to which the child's judgment is directed. Some of the invariants were mentioned before, as for instance, distance, length, class, series, and number. Many more can be readily imagined and have in fact been investigated by Piaget and his associates. The best known conservation tasks deal with quantity in three conditions: substance, weight, and volume. A child is shown two identical balls of clay. He is to pretend that they represent dough or bread and he is asked one of three questions: whether they are the same amount to eat, or whether they weigh the same, or whether they take an equal amount of space when put under water. After the child's judgment of equality, one of the balls is transformed—in the child's presence—into different shapes. The child is then asked the corresponding question as above; whether the two pieces of bread are the same, or one is more or less than the other.

To understand Piaget's terms we must distinguish the external transformation and the external instability of the physical attribute from the internal processes of thinking. Piaget contends that a correct judgment of conservation is the result of a compensating transformation. In this case the reversible operation of intelligence must be applied to the given problem of quantity. The failure of the preoperational child is attributed to the child's assimilating the problem to his own subjective action of handling the clay. A subjective action is, however, on a different plane from the objective impersonal transformation that alone determines a logical judgment. Interestingly these children in general do not "see" external changes as transformations that lead from one state to another but focus, as was mentioned in connection with the mental image, on the static figural aspect of the end result. Thus perception of the external transformation follows the ability to construct internal transformation through compensatory reversibility.

In connection with the above problem this thinking transformation is expressed in words like, "This bread is longer but thinner" or "One could press it back into the first shape." Notice also that recognition of an external instability is present only for those whose structure of intelligence, while not in reversible equilibration, is yet sufficiently receptive to the need for stability. These are children who are in the transitional stages from irreversible preoperations to reversible operations. Here one can observe in a dramatic manner the groping towards compensating mechanisms. Such transitional periods are important occasions of seeing equilibration at work. As Inhelder mentions in Reading 1, an extended series of learning studies is now in progress at Piaget's Institute, the explicit purpose of which is to gain a clearer insight into these transitional changes of operative intelligence.

How does operational conservation differ from the preoperational judgment of identity? What is the relation between the first invariant, object formation, and the first conservations of reversible operations? All schemes of knowing have a transformational aspect by which a neutral event is transformed into a psychological stimulus or an object of knowledge. Knowledge in the full sense of intelligence can be said to begin with the first invariant. The invariant of the object, itself the product of action coordinations, makes it possible to reconstruct things on a new plane, the plane of operational knowing in distinction from practical knowing. Each operational transformation is thus more than a mere corresponding reaction to an external event, an external trend towards balance, such as the lowering of one arm on a balance in correspondence with the raising of the other arm. It is both a transformation and a reconstruction on a higher level through which the external state is understood for what it is. Piaget points out that an operation of transformation must leave at least one aspect unchanged, otherwise there would be no internal possibility of reversibility but simply the substitution of one state for another state. Even at the preoperational level there is at least one invariant point in terms of which the things or events of sensory-motor reactions are reconstructed on the level of operativity. This is the product of object formation, the invariant of the known, permanent thing. At the operational level proper, the invariant relative to reversible transformation is the structure of conservation.

The difference between the early invariant of the permanent object and the later invariants of the conservation experiments corresponds therefore to the different systems of intelligence that produced the invariants. A true notion of conservation is a construction that rests on a fully reversible system of knowing. Actually it is the system as a whole that is conserved, and the thinking activity of conservation implies this system. Earlier instances of permanence lack the characteristic of conservation precisely because they lack the equilibrated organization of the intelligent activity with regard to the given problem. At the preoperational period, thinking activity is still too much tied to the symbolic representations of sensory-motor actions that focus on the personal, figurative, static aspect of the activity rather than on the transforming, coordinating action aspect. Symbol-dominated thinking cannot produce a stable system because its focus is the shifting subjectivity of the child's own actions.

A four-year-old child may give the impression of being able to comprehend the identity of a class, for instance, the class of the inhabitants of Geneva. This identity response is not the product of a conserving structure of classification, but a statement that simply dissociates the characteristic of living in Geneva from other characteristics. Asked whether there would still be people that live in Geneva if all Swiss people would go to live in another country, the Genevan child will answer "Yes" according to his subjectively oriented representations. Moreover, it is easy to train some animals to react in a similar manner to a common feature of different physical objects disregarding other irrelevant features. And any kind of perceptual recognition which is part of sensory-motor activity likewise implies an early kind of identity response. Thus it is demonstrated that identity responses do not even require the level of object formation.

The various identity responses of the sensory-motor stage, of the symbolic-oriented object formation stage, and of the operational conservation stage show a superficial similarity of forms of behavior that imply different levels of internal organizations. Each succeeding stage constitutes what Piaget calls a "reflection" on the preceding level. It is by formal or, as Piaget terms it, "reflecting" abstraction that intelligence builds on a new plane of a more stable equilibration the invariant notions that form the framework of logical thinking. Thus a trained animal gives a color response as a function of an unstable exterior schedule of physiological rewards. A preoperational child, in a so-called concept formation experiment, succeeds in responding to the relevant attribute as a function of a more stable internal knowledge of color. Yet compared to the operational period the younger child is still centered on his own action towards the color and does not regard the color attribute in an objective fashion which permits him to see it as a reversible attribute within the classes of other possible attributes.

Logical structures, as formalized in mathematical and symbolic language, are for Piaget more than a mere luxury of model building. In spite of the relative arbitrariness of logical systems—and Piaget admits that other types of logical models could be envisaged—he insists that logic is not something that is added to natural thought like the frosting on a cake. When Piaget asserts that logic mirrors thought, this correspondence is not like the inside of the frosting that is shaped according to the outside of the cake.

Reflect for a moment on the nature of logic and compare it with the nature of intelligence that Piaget has laid bare. By his study of children's thinking Piaget discovered the operational nature of the structures towards which intelligence tends in spontaneous development. These structures are characterized by an increasing equilibration through which the parts of the system relate to each other and as a whole maintain their organization in the face of interior and exterior changes. Logic is but the formalization of an equilibrated structure. Consequently, says Piaget, a structure of intelligence is inevitably a structure that can be formalized as a logical system.

Piaget's logical analysis of operational structures is therefore not an *a priori* imposition of a finished norm on human thinking nor is it a mathematical model that somehow fits the case. Far from imposing ready-made formalizations on thinking Piaget discovered logical structures that had not been considered before and for which he had to work out new formalizations. This is not surprising, since logicians in general are only interested in the perfect finished product, not the imperfect structures of the developing intelligence.

The relation of logic to intelligence is for Piaget based on a necessary internal correspondence between an intelligence that from its first beginnings tends towards a natural logic and is able at the same time to reflect on its own logic in a formal fashion. In logic, Piaget sees reversible operations in their purest forms, the final stage of the most primitive coordination as observed in adaptive exterior actions. The continuum that had its beginning in adaptive motor functions leads through formal, reflecting abstraction in its purest *natural* form to the operational thinking of the adult scientist and in its purest *formal* form to mathematico-logical systems.

Piaget's concern for a description of natural intelligence in terms of a formal system of logic is thus the necessary consequence of his insight into the operational nature of intelligence. Yet he is criticized by logician and psychologist alike for constructing logical models that are not sophisticated enough for the one, or too far removed from real thinking for the other. To both he can say that he only builds the model to fit the case of the developing intelligence; he is neither out to invent a new logical system nor to shape human intelligence according to a specific model. If this is granted, one should be able to consider Piaget's logical constructions as noteworthy attempts at formalizing the common properties of a great variety of thinking activity.

Piaget, as was mentioned before, distinguishes three main stages of intellectual development, each characteristic of relatively stable structures of knowing behavior. The sensory-motor stage as outlined in Chapter 3 is limited to a practical equilibration in terms of adaptive mean-end relations, including sequencing in time and coordinating in space. Object formation ushers in the second period, the period of intelligence proper, of internal operations. We observe now on the plane of operations a gradual process of structuring directed not merely toward reacting to things, but toward knowing things.

In this development a first level is reached at the age of six or seven with such structures as classification, seriation, number, and space. Piaget asks what the common characteristics are of these systems. Having observed that these logical systems imply more general superstructures, he was the first to formalize the latter into systems which he called "groupings." This stage is therefore the relative end result of the long period of preparation between the ages of two and seven.

Piaget refers to this period as the stage of concrete operations and contrasts it with a final stage of equilibration, the period of formal operations which become apparent from age twelve onward. The most characteristic aspect of concrete operations are the two groupings that allow the child to make reversible operations within each system but do not provide the means of coordinating the systems with each other. On the one hand, there is the grouping of hierarchical classes, on the other hand the grouping of relations. The child's thinking is capable of constructing objects and their classes and relations, but it is focused on the things themselves or on their symbolic representations. In other words, the figurative content of the child's thinking, although it no longer dominates his operational activity, sets a limit to its application.

At the formal operational stage thinking moves one further step away from figurative content. It becomes capable of reflecting upon its own operations and can therefore reason on the basis of the operational relations themselves regardless of content. This is the sense in which Piaget considers that formal operations are operations of the second order. The focus of formal thinking is no longer the real known object but the logically possible in which the real is recognized as one among many possibilities. Formal operational activity is a kind of thinking about thinking which permits one to examine critically the thinking process itself and to see the possibilities of different combinations from those that are existing or proposed. On the basis of formal operational structures hypotheses can be formulated. Strict logical deductions and scientific thinking based on experimental verification become possible. At this stage it is possible to construct a logical superstructure that can unify the two separate groupings of the concrete-operational stage. The formerly limited logical systems of classes and relations are now subsumed under a logic of propositions. This logic appears in the form of a logical group in which the two kinds of inversion that were separated before are synthesized into one system. The characteristic inversion in a class system is the negation or absence, while inversion in a system of relations is by reciprocity, the inverse of "A greater than B" being "B greater than A." These two forms of reversibility are both integral members of the propositional group in which Piaget sees the culmination of the entire process of equilibration.

The main characteristics of the concrete operational "groupings" as well as of the formal operational "groups" have been discussed and illustrated by Inhelder in Reading 1. It remains only to add that Piaget's formalization of logical structures should not be considered as a final, definitive word. Piaget and his associates are currently engaged in closer examination of logical structures at more primitive levels, such as the functions of the preoperational period, briefly mentioned on p. 97. Moreover, more work is being done towards elucidating in a formalized manner the typical changes from concrete to formal operational structures.

The concept of equilibration implies not only a constant development from less to more stable stages of equilibration but precludes the notion of a static beginning or end product. Although the formal operational stage is considered a final one in terms of structural changes, it is conceived of as a dynamic equilibration that is wide open to limitless elaborations and particular applications.[2]

[2] It is not unusual for readers to find the concept of equilibration difficult to understand. This may be due to our ingrained tendency to look for external or mechanistic causes of developmental processes. For example, one of the prime sources for this chapter, *Discussions on Child Development*, Vol. IV, edited by Tanner and Inhelder, includes a series of discussions by Piaget on development and learning. Although the audience was sympathetic, Piaget was forced to admit at the close of the meetings that the notion of equilibration was still mysterious and largely incomprehensible to many.

# 13

# learning
# and
# intelligence

In psychology two great schools of thinking are traditionally concerned with learning. One focuses on the learning process, the other on the capacity to learn. Each school makes use of specialized procedures and reflects different preoccupations. The first school includes a great variety of learning theories, derived from the strict behavioristic tendency, the other school emphasizes tests and measurements and standardization of individual differences. For historical reasons these two branches of psychological inquiry are only superficially related to each other. One might expect that those who are concerned with learning would give serious thought to the capacity to learn and that those who test growth in performance of the child would be interested in relating their analysis of performance to the essential process that enables the child to attain an age-determined level of intelligence.

Against this background Piaget's biological theory of intelligence presents itself as a unified approach to intelligence and learning. Here, the notion of learning is placed within a framework that recognizes the nature of intelligence. As with

220

the notion of "memory," Piaget first insists on semantic clarifications, and is at once confronted with theoretical issues. The old schools of psychology contrasted learning with maturation and defined them in an exclusive fashion, whence the notorious nature-nurture controversy regarding intelligence. More cautious modern scholars no longer make a clear distinction between these two terms or at least insist that in real life there is a constant interaction between the two processes.

However, this interaction is not a real issue since it is agreed that *in concreto* the unity of the behaving person necessarily includes all possible aspects into which any past or future psychologist divides the behavioral totality. What is questioned by Piaget is the tacit implication that behavioral changes can only be either maturational or learning processes. The underlying theoretical assumption of this dichotomy is that all learning is basically a learning of things that are given in the environment.

Piaget explicitly restricts the notion of learning to an acquisition of new knowledge that derives primarily from contact with the physical or social environment. He opposes it on the one hand to maturation which is based on physiological processes; on the other hand and most importantly he differentiates it from the acquisition of general knowledge or intelligence which he defines as the slowly developing sum total of action coordinations available to an organism at a given stage. This general knowledge, Piaget contends, is not just given, to be taken from a tree or a book; it is actively constructed by the person who in constructing this knowledge lives the process of his development.

It will be recalled that Piaget set out initially to investigate not learning as such, but the growth of intelligence. His first contact with psychology came in connection with the testing of general intelligence in the tradition of Binet. Thus he did not decide *a priori* to differentiate the process of intelligent development from special learning processes. He observed children's learning with the purpose of obtaining an answer to the fundamental question: What is the nature of the intelligence that enables a child to learn a certain fact? How does his intelligence develop? Following the model of biological adaptation, Piaget came to see in the functional coordination of adaptive action the source of all intelligence.

Piaget calls equilibration the essential factor at work in the process of the growing intelligence. Previous chapters have attempted to describe the process of equilibration as it underlies the development of operative intelligence. The crucial point for our present discussion is Piaget's discovery that intelligence has its own laws of internal growth and that its successive acquisitions are not merely drawn by cumulative addition from the child's physical or social environment. Coordinations, behavior patterns, action schemes, operative structures are but different names for the continuous, functionally identical nature of intelligence. These things, Piaget has shown, are not given anywhere in the environment. They are essentially properties of the world of adaptive knowing and cannot be reduced to relations between physical stimuli and particular motor responses.

The growth of knowing structures can be called learning, but this is for Piaget a different kind of learning than what we commonly mean by learning. We learn that Bern is the capital of Switzerland, but do we *learn* that tomorrow what is called today will be yesterday? To be sure, we learn the vocabulary, but the comprehension of temporal succession is never taught or learned in the same manner as the name of a capital city. And as with temporal, so also with spatial understanding: No mere learning in the strict sense of the term will bring the preoperational child to understand the notion of what a country is or the notion of a capital city.

The learning of Bern as the capital of Switzerland seems incomparably less important than the capacity to understand what the terms mean. Or rather, these are not things that can be compared with each other. It is like asking what is more important for sustaining life, food or the earth? If we speak of meaningful learning it is obvious that some general comprehension is the indispensable prerequisite for the learning of any particular fact.

It is significant that traditional psychology has no proper word for this general knowledge, nor a proper term for the process by which it develops. We do have the word "intelligence" and it is quite appropriate to the occasion. However, in its everyday use, which is not far from the scientific or philosophical use, the word "intelligence" has most undesirable overtones that range from a peculiar faculty of the soul to an inborn hereditary-determined special disposition. General opinion has taken the lower stages of the child's developing intelligence for granted, or rather has never seen a connection between early motor activity and abstract logical reasoning.

For millennia, philosophers have been busy analysing what they considered the essential features of intelligence by means of a procedure that is now rightly regarded as highly suspect: the use of their own intelligence was both the primary means and the primary object which they studied. Two characteristics of this "common sense" notion of intelligence should be singled out: first, the notion that intelligence is some specific quality of the human person as a special creation or capacity and consequently not inherently connected with manifestations of knowing as observed in animals or young children; second, the related notion of an inborn, static thing that is somehow there and becomes manifest as children gradually lay off childish ways, like layers of curtains that are successively withdrawn to let the picture be seen in its uncovered beauty.

It is not surprising that behavioral scientists could do nothing with this philosophical notion of intelligence and at first neglected its investigation altogether in favor of studying events that can be more easily observed and controlled, e.g., the memorizing of words or the training of a particular skill. All these behavioral changes come under the general heading of learning. Gradually, a working hypothesis became general to the effect that any change in behavior, any new acquisition of skill or knowledge, is simply the product of learning, its interaction with physiological maturation being understood. Insofar as one can observe a change in intellectual function, this, too, is considered to be learning like everything else.

Today a person concerned about intelligence finds that common sense leaves him an unsatisfactory intermediate view between two incompatible extremes. One extreme is the behaviorist's identification of intelligence with something learned, much as one learns such facts as the length of the longest bridge in the world in feet. The other extreme is a philosophical conception of a special, innate quality that makes us distinct from lower animals, a quality present in individually different "amounts" within us. If one is inclined to worry about this disagreement at all, the constant use of intelligence tests with their exact numbers and correlations will usually alleviate one's rising intellectual uneasiness.

There is strong reason to feel uneasy about the behavioristic hypothesis that learning principles can explain human intelligence. Learning principles were principally derived from observation of semi-starved animals, in an artificial, that is, ecologically invalid situation. What one should object to here, as Lorenz suggests, is not the irrelevance of the study of animals for the study of humans, but rather the artificiality of a situation that does not permit the animal to show its inherent repertory of behavior patterns. Consequently such isolated experimental situations, contrived to tell us something about learning principles, reveal precious little about the biological knowledge of the animal that is being tested. They certainly tell us very little about human intelligence, unless one assumes gratuitously that whatever learning principles are discovered in this experimental situation are an integral part of human intelligent behavior.

The basic assumption which pervades the thinking of behavioral science on intelligence is left unchallenged primarily because the alternate view of intelligence, as expounded on the philosophical side, is equally distasteful. There is no serious bit of evidence that a child "learns" general intelligent knowledge in the way in which behaviorists explain the acquisition of a new response in an animal experiment. As a matter of fact, most behaviorists will have nothing to do with intelligence and make no statements about it of any kind. Yet the deadlock between gratuitous assumptions of a mechanistic-positivist science and unscientific philosophical speculations is not solved by the use of intelligence tests. These can be employed more or less usefully according to practical circumstances, but it is vain to look to them for a deeper understanding of the nature of human intelligence.

Piaget charted his course in full view of the twin forces which claimed the domain of intelligence as their own. He recognized the deceptions of philosophy as well as the deceiving dogmatism of a positivist-mechanistic science, all the more deceiving when it uncritically claims that it is nothing but science and in no way takes any philosophical position. When Piaget states that the evolution of intelligent behavior does not come about primarily from learning what the environment has supplied, he is not philosophizing in the manner in which Kant proposed innate categories of understanding. Where the philosopher questioned his own understanding, Piaget observed on many occasions how a child behaved in situations that required some degree of intellectual understanding. For instance, how does a child acquire the judgment of conservation of quantity? Why does it take a child about five years after the acquisition of the needed vocabulary to recognize that the amount of water poured from a wide into a narrow container has not changed? All he has to say is "same," a simple word that he uses frequently. Yet one will not find a single two-year-, three-year-, or four-year-old, and hardly a five-year-old who will not deny that the two containers have the same amount. After eight years of age there will not be many who will not immediately, as a matter of course, assert equality.

Piaget infers from such observations that a correct response requires the structure of operational quantification which develops according to an internal regulation of equilibration around the age of six or seven. If the acquisition of this structure were a question of mere learning in the strict sense any three-year-old could quickly be taught to give the right answer. With hardly a need for reward one can teach a three-year-old child that Bern is the capital of Switzerland so that henceforth he can pass any oral exam on this particular question. Piaget thinks that no manner of reward, no manner of experience will teach the same three-year-old to give a generalizable appropriate answer in the quantity-transformation situation.

Notice the paradox. No specialized experience is needed to acquire conservation judgment of quantity, but no special experience suffices to teach it before the appropriate biological time. On the other hand, special teaching is required to learn the name of Switzerland's capital and this learning experience is as necessary for the twelve-year-old as for the three-year-old, and, moreover, it works in both cases if they are sufficiently motivated. Piaget's theory seems to have a firm observational basis when he points out the difference between these two acquisitions, the one due to learning and depending on a particular bit of knowledge which must be provided by the environment, the other due to equilibration depending on no *particular* bit of environmental information but simply on normal living and biological time. The word "particular" is emphasized to stress the difference between a uniquely given and the normal, general environment. This latter is nothing else but the corresponding environmental side of the general knowledge that develops from the original organism-environment matrix.

But if we grant this, are we not implicitly accepting the view that intellectual capacities are innately given and have no relation to lower-order experience? By no means. Intelligence for Piaget does not start with the seven-year-old who understands the equality of the transformed quantity. If Piaget merely pointed out these two contrasting observations—a seven-year-old's correct judgment of quantity and a three-year-old's faulty judgment in contrast to both children's learning the name of a city—our understanding concerning intelligence and learning would not have appreciably increased.

As pointed out before, Piaget conceived of intelligence as the adaptive action of a biological organism, and he observed a wide range of natural behavior that falls under the notion of intelligence. Piaget does not simply state that operational intelligence appears at such-and-such age and not earlier. His concern is to provide biological reasons why it should be so and to demonstrate how this intelligence is being built up by successive equilibration. Even before any factual results, the functioning of intelligence and the development of intelligence are, for Piaget, identical phenomena. As a consequence, the conception of an innate, non-developing intelligence would be a contradiction in terms.

To most psychological scientists Piaget is too much of a philosopher, while to most philosophers he is too much of an observer who ties everything down to biological behavior and strips the intellect of its proper height and freedom. The latter think that by denying the innateness of the higher intellectual categories and relating them to lower-order behavior patterns, Piaget posits the source of all knowledge in the physical or social environment. In other words, philosophers blame him for doing the very thing which psychologists blame him for not doing.

The gist of Piaget's criticism [1] of contemporary philosophical thinkers who follow the tradition of psychologizing philosophers is their uncritical treatment of psychological facts and their claim of a para-scientific or suprascientific evidence. He implies that their "facts" are supported only by philosophical intuition without being subject to the usual critical scrutiny of scientific inquiry. In turn, philosophers criticize Piaget and call him a positivist when he asserts that intellectual knowledge has its root in the biological organism. His critics seem to have misunderstood the concept of a biological organism and misinterpret Piaget's position as if he asserted that all knowledge derives

---

[1] This paragraph, as well as other points in this chapter, is based on *Sagesse et illusion de la philosophie*, Piaget's quasi-autobiographical book. Since the concept of learning is basic to the prevailing empiricist atmosphere of much psychological thinking, it seemed appropriate to discuss here in some detail the empiricist-positivist position on learning and the idealist-mentalist position. Even though the latter view is largely irrelevant to English-speaking psychologists, it is almost impossible to comprehend Piaget's own presentation if not seen in opposition to both of these philosophical schools.

from the environment. In fact, Piaget strongly denies this—and for that he is damned by psychologists. Piaget rejects with equal vigor the contention that intellectual knowledge requires a special, supra-scientific cause—and for that he is condemned by many philosophers. Yet these same philosophers are quite willing to admit that some knowledge has its adequate cause in the environment. In their view, so-called lower knowledge, perception, instincts, habits are more or less copies or imprints that environmental events make on the senses or the muscles. True intellectual activity then takes off from these elementary bases to soar in abstract heights of its own. This view appears much more "positivistic" than Piaget's. Philosophers merely exclude intellectual knowledge as being environmentally derived. For Piaget, however, there is no knowledge whatsoever, from the most concrete reflex to the most abstract reflection, that is *merely* derived from environmental experience.

Does this imply that Piaget denies the necessity of any environmental experience and does this not do away with the usual concept of learning altogether? We must avoid going from one extreme to the other. Piaget distinguishes action-derived knowledge from environmentally derived knowledge. He sees in action-derived knowledge the essence of biological intelligence which is basic to any knowing. However, it is quite obvious that environmentally derived knowledge exists; but each and every kind of environmentally derived knowledge presupposes the framework of some previous action-derived knowledge. Thus a three-year-old child can learn the name of a capital because he has already reached the intellectual stage that makes him capable of learning names.

In every learning situation, according to Piaget, one can theoretically distinguish an operative action aspect and a figurative learning aspect. The operative aspect provides the basic condition for, and the particular manner of, learning a particular piece of knowledge. The educated person's knowledge of Switzerland's capital is not identical with the child's knowledge, quite apart from other learned knowledge that makes the adult knowledge richer. Rather the adult's knowledge of the general concepts *country* and *capital* imply a large component of operative understanding of which the three-year-old just is not capable.

In this connection Piaget can cite numerous experiments. These studies indicate that learning an identical external task differs according to the inner operative structures. Searching for the right combinations of movements that bring about a desired result must be a different process in an adolescent who comprehends the combinatorial properties of possible events, in a ten-year-old who follows a single system, or in a five-year-old who tries to remember the points according to a subjective perceptual image. Yet all three can succeed in discovering the right external solution. The internal action structure has to be carefully inferred from the external performance. In Piaget's theory, a tally of success or failure or of time taken to reach success is hardly an adequate measure for the purpose of clarifying the underlying structure.

Piaget suggests that a model of intelligence that starts with a ready-made organism and a ready-made environment is hard put to explain why any environmental stimulation should ever be welcomed. It is no wonder that learning theories focus on the need for externally imported motivation in order to connect the organism and the essentially unrelated environmental event. From Piaget's biological outlook, it makes no sense to speak of an environmental event unless there is an organism capable of responding to it. That is, the internal scheme of the organism corresponds to the aspect of the environment towards which the organism reacts or adapts in a meaningful manner. Moreover, a scheme always includes, besides the structuring aspect of knowing, a dynamic aspect of affect. Every knowing scheme wants to function. Growth of knowledge is not entirely dependent on motivation from outside the scheme, since the existence of a scheme is intrinsically geared towards its proper environmental object.

The more primitive a scheme the more undifferentiated is its object, and hence we observe the primitive tendency of generalizing assimilation. A baby's scheme of grasping is indiscriminately applied to anything his hands can get a hold on. Notice again that Piaget starts with different assumptions on learning than more traditional opinion. While others have to explain why a scheme functions at all and particularly why it generalizes to other objects, Piaget postulates the existence of these two tendencies as inherent in a living scheme, and his concern is how schemes become stabilized, not in a static-mechanistic sense, but in the sense of a living system that internally compensates and anticipates variations to which a scheme may have to accommodate.

Consider with Piaget the function of an early sensory-motor

scheme with its inherent drive to assimilate all events to it. With respect to this scheme, the world of the baby can be said to be divided into things that can be assimilated and things that cannot be assimilated. Are these the only alternatives? Biological evolution has provided a third way between success and failure by means of an extension of the accommodative activity of adaptive behavior. In accommodating to some particular variation that is new, the feedback from the new accommodation to the scheme can result in a differentiation of the scheme which then begins to function as a new scheme.

Piaget expresses himself at times as if every accommodation to a novel facet of the environment resulted in a new scheme. But he certainly does not mean to exclude the possibility of the accommodation of a scheme—and every accommodation implies some sense of novelty—which does not result in a new scheme. There are no *a priori* rules for judging the extent of the modification requisite for calling the result a new scheme. True, new schemes arise on the occasion of active accommodation to new environmental aspects. However, every scheme has an assimilative and accommodative activity, and yet not every active accommodation leads to a new structure.

In the first part of the sensory-motor period the new variations are fortuitously imposed from outside, but with progressive and reciprocal structuring of schemes a novel and most important characteristic of knowing behavior appears. Newness, first imposed from outside, becomes now "interesting" in itself and is searched for as possible means to specific ends. Schemes multiply by differentiation vis-à-vis environmental events as well as by reciprocal assimilation. Reciprocal assimilation is but a manifestation of the generalizing tendency of each scheme so that, for example, touched objects become an occasion for the active scheme of seeing and vice versa. Differentiation of new schemes proceeds within what Piaget calls the "optimal zone of interest," that is, in those areas of new variations that are not too distant to be simply rejected, yet not too near to appear simply as variations of the old scheme. With development of more general schemes, these zones of interest become wider and one observes a clear need for exploration and knowing that finds its own satisfaction with no need for external reinforcement, not even that of achieving a practical goal.

Thus far we have described the development of new sensory-motor schemes. Is this learning in the strict sense, is it developmental equilibration, or is it both? The subsequent Reading 9 illustrates how Piaget analyses this question and considers the possible alternatives. In the case of acquiring a new sensory-motor scheme, we can recall Piaget's definition of learning as the acquisition of new behavior derived primarily from the environmental event. This definition apparently fits accommodation in the restricted sense in that it involves a kind of imprint from an object that possesses an initially unwanted newness, yet leads to new behavior on the part of the baby. However, this is not the whole story, and it would seem that both accommodative learning in the strict sense and development are involved.

Let us take the example of a baby who learns to hold and use a spoon. Piaget reminds us that there is no accommodation without a scheme and that consequently a first attempt at using a spoon presupposes a variety of well-established schemes of holding, viewing, and moving the thing that is held to reach a desired goal. These and other schemes provide the conditions of any possible learning and only because the new movement can be assimilated to these old schemes does the acquisition of new variation enter into the zone of optimal interest. Granting then these preconditions, two questions remain: (1) is the specifically *new* combination of using a spoon the result of learning from external experience alone?, and if so, (2) could one not say the same of the previous schemes until one reaches back to the first schemes? With regard to this last point, Piaget is quite explicit: learning, like any other process in biology, never starts from zero. As far back in development as one goes there will always be an assimilating scheme which itself resulted from the differentiation of an earlier scheme and so on. Concerning the first question, the answer is bound to be somewhat arbitrary since no hard-and-fast criterion exists for defining and enumerating all separate schemes. However, a scheme is a generalizable aspect of behavior patterns and on the sensory-motor level can aptly be called a practical concept. The generalizable aspect itself is never entirely learned in the sense of a physical abstraction from the object but includes a formal, reflecting abstraction from the adaptive activity itself. It follows, therefore, that every learning situation includes at least assimilative activity of previous schemes as a condition for learning and, insofar as new learning involves new structures of coordinations, these, too, are not merely taken from the external environment. The reader will have noticed the similarity of our present discussion on learning in the strict sense and the remarks on memory in the strict sense discussed in Chapter 8.

One reason why accommodation during the sensory-motor period leads to new schemes is the fact that all schemes are more or less tied to a particular content. Hence any new content is liable to break the old scheme and lead to a new structuring of schemes. This exemplifies what Piaget means by lack of stability. For an internal scheme the only way to acquire stability would be to include a whole range of variations as internally anticipated within the scheme. In this manner an accommodation to a specific variation would not lead to the breakup of the old scheme or the establishment of a new scheme. Such stability is characteristic of operational structures. While some internal regulations of anticipation are observable at more primitive levels, as for example, in the perceptual recognition of the whole from a given part, the first operational stability is only achieved with the formation of the first invariant, the permanent object.

In object formation, this construct of the transition from sensory-motor to operational intelligence, a generalizable coordination has for the first time become dissociated from a specific content. Knowing behavior has reached a new equilibration in which a construct of knowledge, the known object, can function without being tied to the child's own action or to a particular content. It is self-sustaining. Any variations in content not only do not disturb it but serve to strengthen it. This illustrates Piaget's notion of stability or equilibrated intelligence, at least in its first and most primitive manifestation. Starting at this period the child's behavior changes from a person who knows what to do to a person who knows that he knows.

From where does the child's knowledge of the object derive? Why is it that a child begins to behave towards things with an implicit belief in their permanency and stability? Is such knowledge learned? Or, if not learned in the sense of coming from the physical or social environment, is it innate, at least in the sense that it was learned by the human species during evolution? We know that Piaget rejects the notion that operativity derives from events in the environment as firmly as he rejects the notion that it is innately built into our hereditary structure. The reason why it takes children so long to recognize simple logical rules is precisely that these rules are not "out there," but must be constructed from the activity of the child himself. This construction is not something that the species is programmed to do; rather, each individual must go through the development.

What is transmitted through the genes can never go beyond sensory-motor intelligence because gene-transmitted structures are tied to specific organs and are therefore inseparably linked to the organs and the sensory content to which they selectively respond. Stable operative knowledge is predicated upon an increased freedom of schemes from subjective actions and specific content. Such knowledge cannot be handed on through physiological devices. Not by chance is man born more poorly equipped with innate mechanisms than any other living being. This fact enables him to exercise his schemes of adaptive activity with a freedom from the specific and the immediate like no other animal. But at the same time it forces each individual to go through the process of development. The child's activity serves him both as a source of further progress and as an obstacle to overcome.

Activity is a source and condition of progress since all knowledge is derived from adaptive activity; thus, for intelligence, to act is to live. Intelligence is the organ that structures itself in functioning. Through reflecting formal abstractions sensory-motor intelligence feeds back into its own structure the accommodating coordinations by which it grows. As the internal sensory-motor schemes become numerous and intercoordinated, they become capable of generating the beginning of the operational stage within which the first invariant object occurs.

At the same time the subject's own activity is an obstacle to be overcome. There is the whole preoperational period that bears witness to the slow progress of operativity and objectivity over subjective deformation. Earlier it was said that Piaget's theory of intelligence not only gives us interesting information as to what a child can or cannot understand at a certain age level, but also supports these findings with reasons drawn from biology. To understand is much more than to transmit outside information. To understand means to restructure the situation and transform a given problem in terms of one's internal equilibrated structure. The structuring of intelligence cannot take place without development, and development needs the environment of space and time. Piaget shows that the time from the end of the sensory-motor stage to the first operations is a period of continual decentration from subjective ego-involved activity and of preparation for logical reversible operations.

With the advent of operational thinking, action schemes are gradually turned into thinking schemes and the great invariants of objective knowledge begin more and more to dominate the child's thinking. These invariants include the permanent object, the self, the other, space, time, class, and causality. The entire structure of thinking takes on the nature of a tightly interrelated and hierarchically ordered network of schemes. Piaget referred to sensory-motor schemes and their assimilations as practical concepts and practical judgments and pointed out that the schemes and assimilations, like concepts and judgments, are but two aspects of the same reality. With even more justification we can consider operational and particularly strictly operational schemes to be logical concepts, and an operational assimilation a logical judgment. Note that the words "concept" and "judgment" do not here include or imply a linguistic expression or any other symbolization. That we have an indefinite multitude of concepts does not mean that they have been singly acquired one by one and are only externally related to each other. On the contrary, learning a concept, that is, understanding a certain phenomenon, invariably implies an indefinite multitude of active schemes, including the most particular that is accommodated to the task at hand, as well as the most general that carries with it logical necessity.

What we call logical necessity is a logical coherence, an implication that one part stands and falls with the whole. Our knowledge that a class can never be smaller in extension than its subclass or that a correct conclusion follows from adequate premises is not fallible as long as it stays on the logical level. Philosophers have long wondered where we acquire our absolute trust in these judgments. Not knowing where they could come from, idealists called the judgments "innate" to connote a radically different, higher type of knowledge. Empiricists preferred to reject the evidence of our convictions and consider them on a par with our empirical knowledge, e.g., that humans have two eyes or that bodies fall to the ground. In other words, they considered that all these convictions derive eventually from the observation of physical facts and are indeed "learned," in the strict sense of the term, and only generalized by a reasonable induction.

For Piaget, however, logical necessity is the internal necessity of an equilibrated system, not the external necessity that we attribute to physical events. Logical necessity cannot be learned in any strict sense of the term but is derived from the developing intelligence itself as it reflects on its own equilibrated working. This reflection is not an introspective activity but a reflecting feedback mentioned before under the term of formal abstraction. This is the essential mechanism of acquisition by which the internal structure at all levels grows. It is a feedback from the accommodating activity of the scheme and not from the physical object on which the scheme acts.

We have seen that for Piaget every kind of learning in the strict sense implies the functioning of assimilating schemes and that the developing network of schemes has no absolute beginning. Consequently, there is no certain scheme at which logical structures begin. For every scheme of a logical form there is a previous scheme that contains this form in an attenuated prelogical manner and so on, *ad infinitum*. If acquisition of new knowledge is the law of development and if all learning in the strict sense is conditioned by logical or prelogical structuring, the basic mechanisms of learning are not different from the equilibration process of the whole developing intelligence. Even learning in the strict sense is, for Piaget, never merely a copy or a mechanical association caused by external factors. The structuring contribution of the assimilating organism enters as a necessary component into every learning situation and explains why no result of learning can be merely a function of factors external to the learning process itself.

# Reading 9

# Learning
## and Knowledge[1]

In this article Piaget is concerned with the concept of learning and its relation to development. He limits the meaning of learning in the strict sense to acquisitions that derive essentially from a particular outside contribution and differentiates it from the process of equilibration which regulates the growth of operative schemes according to contributions internal to the organism. In this sense, the problem of learning with regard to general schemes and operations implies a delicate balance in dividing the internal from the external contributions.

The first selection presents this problem in all its ramifications. The distinction between the form of a scheme and its content is introduced. The particular content is linked to learning, the generalizable form to equilibration. One notices that the accommodative pole of an adaptation seems more closely related to learning, but one must be careful not simply to identify these two notions. Again, if assimilation is closer to the notion of equilibration one should remember that equilibration takes place only between an assimilation and an accommodation.

(*VII, p. 62-63*) The question is whether these structures of schemes or of systems of schemes that prefigure in the most elementary manner classes, inclusions, and groupings, constitute the product or the conditions of learning.... We can now respond without ambiguity, it seems, that

[1] Jean Piaget, "Apprentissage et connaissance" in *Études d'épistémologie génétique* VII, pp. 21-67, and *Études d'épistémologie génétique* X, pp. 159-188 (Paris: Presses Universitaires de France, 1959). Translated by Hans G. Furth, by permission of the publishers.

235

both affirmations are true, for they are not incompatible with each other. A new scheme is the product of learning in the strict sense, insofar as it results from the differentiation of a previous scheme and insofar as this differentiation involves an accommodation that depends on experience. But for this learning to take place there must exist previous schemes that can be differentiated during assimilation of new objects. Moreover, the structure of these schemes and the assimilation, considered strictly as the prerequisite of the structure, are preconditions and not products of learning. In a word, learning relates to the content of the schematism while the generalizable character of its form does not result from learning but is a necessary condition for the functioning of the schemes. Since at the elementary levels form and content remain indissociable, one is ill-advised to set up a list of forms ready-made and attempt to draw a firm line between the preconditions and the results of learning. While admitting that forms are constructed on the occasions when content is enriched, one must not forget that this construction presupposes an activity that has not been learned in the strict sense, but rather is derived from the act of assimilation that produces the schemes.

It is therefore again necessary right from the [earliest] system of schemes, which are partially isomorphic to the logic of classes, to distinguish between learning in the strict sense and in the broad sense. What is learned in the strict sense is the totality of differentiations due to accommodation as the source of new schemes vis-à-vis the increasing diversity of contents. But what is not learned in the strict sense is the assimilative activity with its consequence of an equilibration between assimilation and accommodation. Assimilation is the source of the gradual coherence of schemes and of their organization in equilibrated forms in which one can already discern a sketch of logical classes with inclusion, intersections, and groupings within a totality. The interactions between assimilation and accommodation imply therefore two factors, learning in the strict sense and equilibration. These two factors underlying the functional process in its totality can be called learning in the broad sense and are practically identical with development.

> The second selection is a translation of the conclusion omitting the three final paragraphs and one minor portion of the text. Piaget first lists the four possible relations between learning and equilibration. He then proceeds to point out that some stabilizing factor must be part of any learning theory. Notice the phrase "the compensating effect...of each...regulation is sanctioned by experience." This illustrates the close interaction between the two factors of learning and equilibration as well as the dynamic factor inherent in Piaget's notion of equilibration.

## Learning and equilibration. Epistemological conclusions

(*X, p. 183-187*) . . . In fact, if everything in the acquisition of logical structures is not "learned" (in the strict sense), that which is acquired but not learned in these structures (in which the innate seems to play only a negligible role) can only derive from a process of equilibration. Actually we do not know of any other model distinct from the innate or the learned, and there exists an evident relation between the reversibility of logical operations and the mechanisms of compensation within equilibration.

We never intended to substitute the model of equilibration for that of learning. The only question concerns the relation between them, a relation that could take one of the four following forms: (1) independence is maintained between the two processes; (2) learning is a precondition (necessary but not sufficient) of equilibration, in the sense that the strategies leading to equilibration involve a learning (this would constitute a learning of equilibration); (3) equilibration is a precondition (necessary but not sufficient) of learning in the sense that every learning presupposes the intervention of activities not learned that bring about its equilibration; (4) equilibration and learning are mutually required conditions that in their interaction result in a complete reciprocity.

The results summarized previously can be condensed in the following two propositions: (a) all learning presupposes the utilization of coordinations not learned (or not entirely learned); these coordinations constitute a logic or prelogic on the part of the subject; (b) learning of logical structures supposes the utilization of other preexisting logical or prelogical structures not learned (or not entirely learned). These coordinations that were not learned in the strict sense are the specific domain of equilibration; their development consists in a progressive organization oriented in the direction of an operative reversibility, i.e., compensations that are increasingly more complete. Precisely insofar as they are mechanisms of compensation, coordinations are not learned in the strict sense but derive from the activity of the subject in response to external changes. . . .

If these considerations are well-founded, it follows that the third of the four possible relations between equilibration and learning is true: in fact, every learning presupposes a logic and as this logic derives from a process of equilibration, equilibration is therefore a necessary condition of learning. Actually, all theories of learning must, implicitly or explicitly, take account of the dimension of the equilibration or stabilization of responses. If responses are considered as normally stable, their generalization constitutes a problem. If the theory of conditioning is followed, stabilization is the starting problem, since conditioned behavior is by nature temporary.

However, in the totality of observable situations the factors of learning and equilibration are inextricably meshed because the compensating effect of each operation or of each preoperative regulation is sanctioned by experience. Consequently equilibration may well be a necessary precondition of learning, but it would be futile to look for a corresponding temporal priority.

> The next two paragraphs as well as the last one in this section are devoted to possibilities of isolating the separate contributions of learning and equilibration in a controlled empirical manner. The observation that identical structures are not uniformly applied to different contents points to the necessity of distinguishing between form and content or between equilibration and learning.

Vinh-Bang's paper in Vol. IX opens up a new perspective as to the possible dissociation between the factors of equilibration and learning. In connection with his collaborative effort for some years with B. Inhelder on the standardization of our tests, he points out differences in rate of acquisition for certain tests. In particular there are acquisition convergences toward an identical structure and divergences that demonstrate the disparities in the application of these structures. Vinh-Bang proposes that the processes of development can explain certain aspects of learning while laws of learning cannot explain all development. Learning seems to be in many cases merely the extension to new content matter of structures already formed or in the process of formation (at varied rates). . . . From the viewpoint of equilibration such an analysis may make it possible to dissociate the factor of equilibration from the factor of learning in the strict sense. Certainly in all areas of intelligent behavior, every acquisition that presents an aspect of equilibration involves at the same time a more or less direct element of learning. But one can hope that a study of the hierarchical arrangement of acquisition curves will permit the more effective isolation of factors of internal coherence and structuring *versus* acquisitions as a function of experience.

One can also hope to get some clarification on this point from an analysis of acquisition in the area of perceptions proper. G. Noelting presented a summary on perceptual learning (Vol. VII) in which a subject made successive estimations without being informed of the correctness of his response. This seems to be the case of an acquisition without external reinforcement where equilibration, although in this particular case rather incomplete, was almost entirely active by itself. It is true that this behavior is on a much lower level than intellectual acquisitions proper. Nevertheless it is striking that this kind of learning develops with age and is not simply "anterior" to more complex behavior where the factors [of internal structuring and external acquisition] are meshed. It goes without saying that at genetically elementary levels, as at the level of purely reflex organizations, there is neither learning nor acquisition in the normal sense (as opposed to "exercise of reflexes"). Yet there is already equilibration in the sense of a system of regulations that are in themselves innate.

There follow two paragraphs of general epistemological significance. In the first one Piaget defends his theory of "interactionism" against the philosophical theory of apriorism. He considers, however, that his main opponent is empiricism, which would limit the process of acquisition exclusively to learning in the strict sense.

These indissociable relations between learning and equilibration have an evident epistemological significance. The relations express the circle or spiral that unites without discontinuity the structures which are learned with those which make learning possible. If the structures that make learning possible could be dissociated from those that are learned, this separation would confirm a certain apriorism but since every structure belongs at the same time to the one and the other of these two categories, it seems futile to look for such an *a priori* interpretation on the basis of the lower limits which we recognize for learning in the strict sense. The "objectivism" of Lorenz and Tinbergen attributes to the organism "spontaneous activities" which Goustard invokes in his theoretical note (Article IV of this volume) in order to deny the all-powerful influence of the environment. Even this "objectivism" should not lead to an apriorism properly so called as Lorenz has often underlined.

However, since learning has always been the preferred instrument of empiricism, the preceding discussion can most pertinently serve the argument between empiricism and interactionism. The registration of experiential data has previously been shown to be much more than a mere reading off. Likewise, learning does not appear now to be a process during which the subject's activity is limited to receive or to react automatically to what is received; rather, learning seems to be a complex construction in which what is received from the object and what is contributed by the subject are indivisibly linked.

But everything is not yet said, when one considers that the proper function of learning is to lead to a knowledge of the object. The active contributions of the subject are at first an obstacle to learning and objective knowledge. It is only later that they in fact become a necessary condition of objectivity. One of the essential tasks of epistemology is to show the limit of subjective and objective contributions in their mutual dependence. Therefore this developmental shift or decentration in the nature of the subject's contribution [toward subjectivity or objectivity] is a most revealing indication of the nature of the subject's activities.

# VII
## Summary

# 14

## an
## overview
## of
## seven
## themes

This final section can serve both as a summary and as a place for quick reference concerning the material discussed at greater length throughout the preceding chapters. It is an attempt to present a succinct outline of what I believe to be the main themes in Piaget's theory of intelligence. As such, they are not contrasted with dissenting opinions. They attempt to give a bird's eye view of the depth and the range of the theory and to convey to the reader the unity and coherence on which a fruitful and critical understanding of this theory can be based.

1. BIOLOGICAL BEHAVIORAL UNIT. The starting point concerning intelligence or any other psychological phenomenon is the fact of adaptive, coordinating actions found at all levels along the evolutionary scale. In these actions, one can distinguish two aspects. First, the external process of a particular act involving organs and movements and responding to environmental events; this aspect is called the content of the action. The other aspect is the general form of an action. The notion of form refers to the coordinations, the general-

izable, hence repeatable behavior patterns which become manifest in adaptive actions.

From the evidence that actions are adaptive and repeatable in similar or analogous situations, it follows that these coordinations cannot be considered as being merely external and thus identical with the content. Adaptation implies a meaningful encounter of organism and environment and repeatability insures the conservation or continuation of the adaptive activity. These two features express the relative invariant functioning that remains stable among the differing external manifestations of adaptive actions. Consequently the invariant functioning, that is, the coordination, differs from the coordinated action as does the general form from the particular content or, better, as the inner structure from an external construction.

The coordination thus unites the three basic terms within a biological unit: the organism, the environment, and their interaction. These three terms are indissociable and imply each other. One cannot conceive of an organism unless it finds itself in some meaningful exchange with the environment. Likewise there is no biological environment unless one postulates the presence of an organism that is responsive to, hence adapted to the particular environment. The notion of coordination includes all three terms. In this perspective, the association of organism and environment is an intrinsic one that is not based on externally aroused motivational states. In a similar vein, the active coordinations or behavior patterns do not as such require the impetus of independently caused motivation. The presence of a living coordination is its own reason for functioning, which means maintaining an active organism in adaptive contact with relevant environmental events.

2. BIOLOGICAL ORGANIZATION. A biological phenomenon involves an organization that must be considered as interior to the phenomenon, as the form to a content, or as the coordination to a coordinated act. The notion of biological phenomenon includes the entire range of biological events, in particular, (1) the total living organism as well as subunits within the organism; (2) the physiological as well as the behavioral functioning viewed as active and present; (3) all modifications of behavior within the individual organism (whether considered as development or as learning); and last, but not least, (4) the development of all biological phenomena within evolutionary history. A biological phenomenon is therefore an organized totality which in its genetic dependence and actual functioning manifests an organizational

inner structure. If one views organization in an individual, one can speak of beginnings; but viewed in its general form, no organization has a zero point from which it can definitely be said to begin.

The functioning of an organism vis-à-vis its environment is called behavior. The aspect of behavior which expresses the behavior's dependence on an organizational inner structure is its adaptation. An active adaptation can be considered in two directions. When the organism incorporates environmental data into its own organization, this process is called assimilation. When the organism adapts, modifies, or applies its inner organization to the particular environmental reality, this is referred to as the process of accommodation.

A number of different terms are used as equivalents of the word organization, e.g., inner structure and form. A salient feature of any organization is the interdependence of all its subparts as well as its dependence as a whole on a greater totality. As there is no absolute zero, there is also no isolation of any one part-organization from its encompassing totality.

Another characteristic of a biological organization is the presence of regulating mechanisms at all levels so that the organization tends to conserve itself in a steady state. This conservation of a biological state is not a static but a dynamic, living equilibration; it consists in a compensating balance between subjective organization and objective reality, between ingoing assimilation and outgoing accommodation, between the risk from openness to the environment and the gain expected therefrom. On the level of the internal physiological environment there is homeostasis. On the level of behavior, or the organism's exchange with the external environment, there is equilibration, resulting in developmentally successive regulations that lead from the most primitive knowledge implied in an adaptive action to the general knowledge implied in adult intelligent behavior.

3. INTELLIGENCE. Intelligence is the totality of behavioral coordinations that characterize behavior at a certain stage. Taken in its most general sense and including all pre-forms and forms of intelligence proper (wherever one places the dividing line), intelligence is the behavioral analogue of a biological organ which regulates the organism's behavioral exchange with the environment. This interaction constitutes behavior. All adaptive behavior implies some knowing in the form of at least minimal knowledge concerning the environment.

In distinction to operational intelligence, practical intelligence includes all types of knowing behavior that are intrinsically tied to external actions. Within practical intelligence, one can observe an evolutionary development from specific and immediate behavior re-actions (e.g., instincts) to more general behavior coordinations. This tendency indicates a loosening of the tie between the form of coordi-nations and the content of its external manifestations; however, a true dissociation is realized only in operational intelligence. One can link two more phenomena to this trend. First, the change from behavior patterns that serve immediate vital needs to behavior that is explora-tory or simply curious to know. Second, a change from behavior patterns that are programmed and transmitted through the hereditary genes—in other words, behavior that has been acquired through the process of evolutionary development—to behavior patterns that are acquired in the course of individual development. Together with these trends, one can increasingly distinguish the structural from the dy-namic aspect of behavior. Although these two aspects are *in concreto* always present, one can consider, particularly in humans, the structural aspect alone as directly related to knowing and intelligence; the dy-namic aspect of affectivity covers what is typically called motivation, interest, value, etc.

Evolutionary development proceeds in a manner of an organizing totality, not in the sense of an outside influence or purpose that pulls from ahead, or a drive that pushes from behind, but as a regulating factor that is intrinsic to the unfolding of evolutionary organizations. In a similar manner, individual development proceeds according to an intrinsic, that is, self-regulating factor of equilibration which leads to stage-specific equilibrated states of intelligence. In both cases, in evolu-tion and individual development, the self-regulating factor and the resulting state of intelligence are not two different things but two aspects of an identical biological reality. This is the reason why the regulation of development is the same as the development of regula-tions and why only a developmental approach to the investigation of intelligence is adequate.

Intelligence is the regulating force of a living organization that tends towards a stable equilibration between organism and environ-ment. This tendency finds expression in development. One can dis-tinguish more or less equilibrated stages along the evolutionary con-tinuum as well as in early human development. These stages are characterized by an overall structure within which individual behavior is coordinated so that higher stages incorporate the achieved regulations of a lower stage. However, the stages of practical intelligence lack the complete stability which implies reversible compensation vis-à-vis factors that disturb equilibration.

4. OPERATIONS. As long as acts of knowing are identical with external acting the child is still on the level of practical or sensory-motor intelligence. Development during this stage consists in the increasing structuring of coordinations from reflex activity to a practical knowledge of ends and means as well as of space, time, and causality. The general coordinations are called internal schemes. At the sensory-motor state there is no distinction between the self acting on a thing and the thing to which the self reacts. The increasing complexity and interrelatedness of schemes leads to a first basic invariant, the conservation of the object. Through this intellectual achievement a beginning is made of the dissociation between form and content, between the general scheme and the self-specific action in which it is expressed. The child begins to know that things are "out there" and independent of his own actions. A knowledge that functions by external reacting gives way to a knowledge that simply knows.

A period of gradual development of about five years separates the emergence of the first invariant from the first operations at the ages of six to seven. The first clear separation of form that is free from specific content expresses itself with full reversibility and within an overall structure of intelligence. The first operational structures are called "groupings" and give the child the means to know the world within stable systems of logical classification, seriation, numbers, spatial and temporal coordinates, and causality. These systems permit reversible operations, acts of knowing that can move within the system in reverse directions, e.g., from part to whole or from before to after and vice versa. Thus, through operations an individual can compensate for disturbances and can assimilate the external transformation of a given state (e.g., a semicircle turned into a straight line) into a system of internal transformations which keep the invariant (i.e., the length) constant.

There are two stages of operational intelligence, an earlier one called concrete operational that starts by age six or seven and is further elaborated for another five or six years. The stage of formal operational intelligence is achieved with the emergence of more perfect

structures of intelligence, called "groups," that permit the person systematically to perform operations on operations. In this final stage, a
new freedom from content is obtained in which the person knows
how to apply logical operations not only to concrete situations—the
characteristic of the earlier stage—but also to the systems of logical
operations themselves. This "reflection" provides the basis for seeing
the real as just one of many possibilities and for the forming of scientific hypotheses. At the same time the objective world becomes all the
more stable and objective, as a knowledge of invariants that is free
from any one particular objective experience is achieved. These invariants are experienced as necessary implications of logical thinking.

The equilibration attained in formal operational intelligence is the
culminating achievement of the evolutionary-developmental tendency
towards a knowing system that is fully stabilized, because fully reversible. Moreover, thanks to its capacity to reflect on itself, intelligence remains an essentially open system that can be elaborated and
applied to the indefinite variety of new knowledges that the future
holds in store.

5. FORMAL REFLECTING ABSTRACTION. There is an intrinsic relation between intelligence and formal logic, not in the sense that
logic provides an externally imported norm or model which intelligence has to follow, but insofar as the internal coherence of logic expresses structuring and regulating characteristics of intelligence. A
logic or a prelogic necessarily inheres in a system of regulations. However, while asserting the general requirement that operative intelligence *can* be formalized in a logical system, any one logical system
is in a sense arbitrary and cannot claim to be the final or the only one
possible.

The intrinsic necessity of logical systems is foreshadowed in the
invariants of the preoperational period and in the schemes of the
sensory-motor stage where one can speak of a "practical" logic. In an
evolutionary developmental perspective, one can derive the necessity
of logical implications from the biological organization itself through
formal abstraction.

As schemes are exercised in coordinated actions, they are enriched
by feedback from the actions. This feedback is here called a formal
abstraction in the sense that through it the knowing activity is increasingly interiorized, which in this case means a dissociation of the

*general form* from its *particular content*. It is also referred to as a reflecting abstraction, insofar as a "reflected" structure incorporates structures of lower stages in a higher synthesis, e.g., the operational knowledge of space incorporates, and can reflect on, the sensory-motor knowledge of space. Formal abstraction is thus the primary source of the process of equilibration that constitutes the growth of knowledge and its invariants at all levels. Logical necessity is seen as similar to the necessity intrinsic to the self-regulation of a biological organization.

While formal abstraction constitutes a feedback from the general coordinating activity and leads to general knowledge, physical abstraction is a feedback from the particular object to which the activity is accommodated and leads to the entire range of particular knowledges. Just as there is no assimilation without a corresponding accommodation, formal and physical abstractions are correlated. A physical abstraction is intrinsically linked to a formal abstraction from two points of view. It presupposes an assimilation of a generalized scheme which itself is always the product of a previous formal abstraction; moreover, there is always a concomitant formal abstraction insofar as the physical abstraction involves some generalizable rules or strategies.

If learning is defined as new knowledge derived from experience with particular events, physical abstraction illustrates learning in its dependence on general knowledge realized by means of formal abstraction. According to this definition, the development of general intelligence is not a process of learning, but of equilibration through formal abstraction. This statement does not deny the biological necessity of a physical or social environment but merely specifies the manner in which *general* and *particular* knowledge grows in the person's interaction with the environment.

6. FIGURATIVE KNOWLEDGE AND MEMORY. An accommodated knowledge that is focused on a sensorial content provides by this fact some knowledge about a reality state. Sensory-motor coordinations and operations, on the other hand, transform a state without focusing on the descriptive or figural aspect of the state as such. In this sense one can distinguish figurative knowledge that concerns the external content from operative knowledge that incorporates a state into a system of internal transformations. As with learning, figurative knowing is intrinsically linked to operative knowing.

The most primitive form of figurative knowing is a perceptual accommodation of the senses to external data. Previous to the formation of the permanent object, the percept is not something known apart from the organism's reaction. The meaning of a figurative accommodation is always linked to the scheme that is being accommodated. Consequently, only a sensory-motor scheme rather than the accommodation to external states by itself can explain the knowing of a thing perceived as present.

Closely allied to perception is imitation, that in its primitive and basic form is illustrated above as part of an accommodation resulting in the perception of some object. In a more narrow and developed sense, imitation involves the accommodating, hence not merely passive, copying of external outlines or movements. This imitation expresses or, better, embodies the knowing of the child.

There are three stages of imitation. First sensory-motor imitation which takes place in the physical context of the model only. Second, deferred imitation, characteristic of the transitional period from sensory-motor to preoperational intelligence. It takes place outside the immediate context of the model and hence presupposes object formation. It is most conspicuously observed during symbolic play. A third stage is internalized imitation, that is, an imitation that remains largely covert to an outside observer (although it can be demonstrated by special instruments) but persists as something that the individual himself can experience. Internalized imitation can occur in any sensory modality and constitutes a mental image. It is noted that images are not available to the sensory-motor child.

These three kinds of imitation are the so-called instruments of figurative knowledge: 1. Perception with its concomitant imitative accommodation. 2. Deferred external imitation. 3. Mental image as an internalized imitation.

Memory in the strict sense is the evocation of a past event as belonging to one's past. It is an accommodated knowing, relating a specific event to a particular past. While it may (but need not) involve a figurative image, it certainly requires active operative schemes —correlative to the specific accommodation.

Recognition memory, as distinguished from evocation, has no necessary reference to the past and in itself merely means that a scheme of knowing responds appropriately to the corresponding environmental situation. By itself, recognition does not presuppose an image and is present at the lowest levels of sensory-motor functioning.

Memory in the broad sense includes every kind of available knowledge that has been acquired by the individual or through the evolutionary process. Only in this sense can one speak of memory for general intelligence: the existence of structures of knowing implies by itself their conservation and availability.

7. SYMBOL FUNCTIONING. A symbol is a material event (signifier) that signifies for the person who uses the symbol another event which he knows (significate). It is distinguished from the signal that is for the organism an undifferentiated part stimulus of a global situation. The behavioral reaction is the criterion whether a signifier is a signal or a symbol, that is, whether there is signal or symbol behavior. Signal behavior belongs to sensory-motor adaptation and is characterized by the organism's similar reaction to the signifier and the significate.

Object formation is a chronologically prior precondition of symbol behavior since symbol behavior presupposes knowledge of A, the material event that is the symbol, and knowledge of B, the event that is the significate. The essential symbolic act is: A, recognized as different from B, is used as a material representation in place of B. As a material event, a symbol has a figurative aspect which is derived either from deferred imitation, as in play, or from internalized imitation, as in the mental image or language. As a meaningful representation, a symbol shares the identical operative activity which generated knowledge of B.

Symbolic functioning provides intelligence with the means of representing in a material manner events that are not present to the senses. Since during the entire preoperational period intelligence is dependent on perceptual or representational support, symbolic functioning is essential to the development of intelligence as a whole. Yet it is not an inherent part of operative intelligence. An inadequately controlled dependence of intelligence on symbolic functioning produces deformations in knowledge. Operational intelligence in the strict sense still uses symbols but in a controlled fashion that does not lead to deformation.

A symbol refers directly to an operative knowing: the relation symbol-knowing is the meaning of a symbol. This relation presupposes knowing and does not explain it. An idea or concept as the interior product of knowing is sometimes said to "represent" the known thing and "representational" intelligence is identified with operational intelligence and contrasted with sensory-motor intelligence. However, such use of the word "representational" is misleading since a concept does not *represent*, but *is* the known thing. Note also that the interiorization of a knowing operation is a different process than the internalization of a symbolic instrument.

Operational knowing is not inherently linked to any symbol representation, and this includes language. Language and speech constitute a special symbol system, biologically evolved for social communication and consequently of vital importance for socialization. Language is required and used by the growing child in a manner similar to other symbolic instruments; it is not an indispensable medium for intelligence—the example of deaf children without language who acquire operational intelligence is evidence contrary to such an assumption. However, only a system of language is able to provide the means of communication on which civilization and its transmission is based. The educative influence accumulated by a given civilization seems to constitute the greatest impact, though indirect, of language on intelligence.

# *autobiography*[1]

### JEAN PIAGET

I was born in 1896. My higher education focused on the fields of biology and philosophy, and between 1911 and 1925 I published about 25 studies on terrestrial and aquatic molluscs. This training was extremely useful for my subsequent psychological investigations and formed in me the habit of thinking simultaneously in terms of adaptation to the environment and in terms of an interiorly regulated development on the part of the subject.

While I wanted to devote myself to biology, I had an equal interest in the problems of objective knowledge and in epistemology. My decision to study the development of the cognitive functions in the child was related to my desire to satisfy the two interests in one activity. By considering development as a kind of mental embryogenesis, one could construct a biological theory of knowledge. Thus, various

---

[1] This autobiography was prepared by J. Piaget for the *McGraw-Hill Modern Men of Science*, Volume II, a supplement to the *McGraw-Hill Encyclopedia of Science and Technology*. Reprinted by permission of the McGraw-Hill Book Company.

investigations on children's thinking were published between 1921 and 1967 and others are still forthcoming. At the same time, I did not entirely abandon biological studies and published some research in zoology (1929, 1965) as well as in botany (1966). A synthesis of these various interests has only recently been completed in a volume published by Gallimard entitled *Biologie et connaissance* (1967). There is found a biological theory of knowledge which I had always envisioned.

Let me now describe my work with children in greater detail. Initially in my studies on the formation of intelligence and thinking in children I used predominantly verbal methods. These investigations concerned the relations of language and thinking, reasoning in the child, his representation of the physical world, his moral judgment, and his ideas on physical causality. These five investigations were restricted to verbal questions and answers with no provision for concrete objects which the children could manipulate. Consequently the results of the first works were limited and simply served to pose problems that were new at the time.

However, around the year 1936, after having critically observed day by day the development of my own three children, I was in a position to publish *The Origins of Intelligence in Children, The Reconstruction of Reality in the Child*, and *Play, Dreams and Imitation in Childhood*. In these works I studied for the first time the formation of intelligence and of thinking on the basis of sensory-motor actions. Particularly in the first two volumes I was able to study the psychological problems of thinking formation in an epistemological perspective. By an analysis of the manner in which the notions of the permanent object (until eight or nine months, objects that are hidden behind a screen are not considered to conserve their existence), of space, time, and causal relations are re-established, I could demonstrate that they were not simply the result of perception or experience in the sense in which empiricists use the term. On the contrary, I discovered that a continual organizing activity on the part of the subject was necessary to lead to the formation of these fundamental structures.

Subsequently, as I studied and published with A. Szeminska *The Child's Conception of Number* and with B. Inhelder *Développement de quantités physiques*, I reached a perspective on the development of intelligence that was different from that of my first books. I considered that the central mechanism of intelligence is found in the construction of operations which derive from the general coordinations of actions. The fundamental operations, such as uniting (related to inclusion and classification), seriating (related to order, chaining, and asymmetrical relations), equalizing, putting in correspondence, etc., are actions that are interiorized (in part with the help of language but not deriving from it), reversible (through inversion and reciprocity) and coordinated in wholistic structures. At that time I started to study these structures formally (*Classes, relations et nombres*, 1942, and *Traité de logique*, 1949), and especially also in an experimental manner. From these endeavors stem the above-mentioned books on number and quantity as well as the two books *Le développement de la notion de temps chez l'enfant* and *Les notions de mouvement et de vitesse chez l'enfant*. Then there followed a series of studies together with B. Inhelder, on space, chance, elementary logical structures, and the work published as *The Growth of Logical Thinking from Childhood to Adolescence*. These numerous works, not all of which have appeared in English translations, demonstrate clearly that operational structures are characterized by the forming of notions of conservation (conservation of a whole, of continuous quantity, in concrete material, of length, of surfaces, etc.). The beginnings of such notions can even be observed between four and six years of age at the preoperational stage of thinking.

Moreover, over a long period I studied the development of perception in children (*Les mécanismes perceptifs*, 1961). Then, together with B. Inhelder I published *L'image mentale chez l'enfant* and recently completed a study of memory as it develops between three and four and eleven and twelve years of age. All of these investigations were carried out by constantly relating the particular phenomenon to the formation of intellectual operations.

The third major interest of my career has been epistemology. Philosophical epistemology asks about the nature of knowledge in general. However, because all knowledge is continually evolving and in no branch can be said to be closed, it appeared to me more scientific to reformulate the problem as: "How does knowledge come about?" This question implies an attempt to explain knowledge through its formation and its development. *Introduction a l'épistémologie génétique* which appeared in three volumes in 1950 enlarged upon these notions. Based on these ideas an "International Center of Genetic Epistemology" was created at Geneva together with numerous collaborators and has already published some 22 volumes. Quite recently appeared *Logique et connaissance scientifique* as a volume in the *Encyclopédie de la pléiade* in which present and former members of the Center collaborated in a new presentation of epistemological questions. I consider epistemology as a science distinct from philosophy and upheld this proposition more directly in a small book that caused some lively discussion in Europe. In this book, with the English title *Uses and Abuses of Philosophy*, I suggest that philosophy does not attain a "knowledge" but rather a "wisdom" as long as its investigation does not become dissociated as a specialized science, precisely as is the case with genetic epistemology.

# *bibliography*

Furth, H. G., *Thinking Without Language: Psychological Implications of Deafness.* New York: Free Press, 1966. (Section III)

Inhelder, B., "Operational thought and symbolic imagery," in P. H. Mussen ed., *European Research in Cognitive Development, Monographs of the Society for Research in Child Development.* (1965) No. 100, pp. 4-18. (Chapter 7)

Lorenz, K., "Psychologie und Stammesgeschichte," in *Über tierisches und menschliches Verhalten*, II, pp. 201-54. Munich: Piper, 1965. (Section V)

———, "Phylogenetische Anpassung und adaptive Modifikation des Verhaltens," in *Über tierisches und menschliches Verhalten*, II, pp. 301-58. (Translated as *Evolution and Modification of Behavior.* Chicago: University of Chicago Press, 1965.) (Section V)

Piaget, J., *La formation du symbole chez l'enfant, Imitation, jeu et rêve, image et représentation.* (Neuchâtel: Delachaux et Niestlé, 1946.) (Translation: *Play, Dreams and Imitation in Childhood.* New York: Norton, 1951.) (Chapter 5)

———, "Logique et équilibre dans les comportements du sujet," in *Études d'épistémologie génétique* II, pp. 27-118. Paris: Presses Universitaires de France, 1956. (Chapter 12)

257

Piaget, J., "Assimilation et connaissance," in *Études d'épistémologie génétique* V, pp. 49-108. Paris: Presses Universitaires de France, 1958. Selected excerpts translated in Readings 2 and 6. (Chapters 3 and 7)

———, "Apprentissage et connaissance," in *Études d'épistémologie génétique* VII, pp. 21-67 and *Études d'épistémologie génétique* X, pp. 159-88. Paris: Presses Universitaires de France, 1959. Selected excerpts translated in Reading 9. (Chapter 13)

———, "Épistémologie mathématique et psychologie," Part 2, in *Études d'épistémologie génétique* XIV, pp. 143-332. Paris: Presses Universitaires de France, 1961. (Translated in Beth, E. W. and J. Piaget, *Mathematical Epistemology and Psychology*. Dordrecht, Holland: Reidel, 1966.) (Chapter 12)

———, *Les mécanismes perceptifs: Modèles probabilistes, analyse génétique, relations avec l'intelligence*. Paris: Presses Universitaires de France, 1961. (Translation: *Perceptual Mechanisms*. London: Routledge & Kegan Paul, 1969.) (Chapter 7)

———, "Le langage et les opérations intellectuelles," in *Problèmes de psycho-linguistique*, pp. 51-61. Neuchâtel: Symposium de l'association de psychologie scientifique de langue française, 1962. Paris: Presses Universitaires de France, 1963. Translated here in Reading 5. (Chapter 6)

———, *Sagesse et illusion de la philosophie*. Paris: Presses Universitaires de France, 1965. (Translation in preparation.) (Chapters 1 and 13)

———, *Biologie et connaissance. Essai sur les relations entre les régulations organiques et les processus cognitifs*. Paris: Gallimard, 1967. Final section translated as Reading 8. (Section V)

Piaget, J., and B. Inhelder, *La psychologie de l'enfant*. Collection "Que sais-je." No. 369. Paris: Presses Universitaires de France, 1966. (Translation: *Psychology of the Child*. New York: Basic Books, 1969.) (*Passim*)

———, *L'image mentale chez l'enfant: Étude sur le développement de représentations imagées*. Paris: Presses Universitaires de France, 1966. (Chapter 7)

Piaget, J., B. Inhelder, and H. Sinclair, *Memoire et intelligence*. Paris: Presses Universitaires de France, 1968. Excerpts translated in Reading 7. (Chapter 8)

Sinclair-de Zwart, H., *Langage et opérations: Sous-systèmes linguistiques et opérations concrètes*. Paris: Dunod, 1967. (Chapter 6)

Tanner, J. M., and B. Inhelder (eds.), *Discussions on Child Development* IV. London: Tavistock, 1960. (Chapter 12)

Parentheses denote sections of the book for which the reference was a primary source.

# *glossary*

1. ABSTRACTION, FORMAL, REFLECTING—Feedback from the co-ordinating or operational activities to the interior organization which enables it to "reflect" on the general form of the activities. Formal, reflecting abstraction is the principal source of the growth of intelligence as general, logical knowledge.

2. ABSTRACTION, PHYSICAL—Feedback from the result of actions on physical objects or qualities. Physical abstraction presupposes the framework of formal abstraction and leads to critical, objective knowledge of the physical world.

3. ACCOMMODATION—The outgoing process of an operative action oriented toward some particular reality state. Accommodation applies a general structure to a particular situation; as such, it always contains some element of newness. In a restricted sense, accommodation to a new situation leads to the differentiation of a previous structure and thus the emergence of new structures.

4. ACTION—A functional exchange between a biological organization and the environment that presupposes an internal structure and leads to a structuring of the environment. For Piaget, action is not limited to external action. It is generally synonymous with behavior.

259

5. ADAPTATION—A balanced state of a biological organization within its environment. In behavior, an equilibration between assimilation and accommodation.

6. AFFECTIVITY—The aspect of behavior that has to do with interest, motivation, dynamics, energy. It is indissociably linked to the structural aspect of knowing.

7. ASSIMILATION—The incorporating process of an operative action. A taking in of environmental data, not in a causal, mechanistic sense, but as a function of an internal structure that by its own nature seeks activity through assimilation of potential material from the environment.

8. CENTRATION—In perception, the focusing on a specific part of a stimulus; in general, a subjective focusing on an aspect of a given situation leading to a deformation of objectivity.

9. CONCEPT—In a logical sense, a mental construct of the generalizable aspect of a known thing; it has an intension (or comprehension) answering the question, "What is its essence?" and an extension answering the question as to which things are exemplars of the concept. In a psychological sense, a concept is identical with an individual's internal structure or scheme and corresponds to the level of that structure (e.g., "practical" concept). In its verbal manifestations, concept is a verbalized expression of a logical concept together with its verbalized comprehension; however, verbalization is extrinsic to the logical concept as such.

10. CONCRETE OPERATION—Characteristic of the first stage of operational intelligence. A concrete operation implies underlying general systems or "groupings" such as classification, seriation, number. Its applicability is limited to objects considered as real (concrete).

11. CONSERVATION—The maintenance of a structure as invariant during physical changes of some aspects. The stability of an objective attribute is never simply given, it is constructed by the living organization. Conservation therefore implies an internal system of regulations that can compensate internally for external changes.

12. COORDINATION—The functional adaptation or the unifying form of the elements of an action, particularly of an external action though not limited to it; implies an active internal structure.

13. EMPIRICISM—A philosophical opinion that holds that all knowledge including necessary logical truth has its adequate and sufficient cause in information that derives ultimately from the senses; it assumes that objectivity is simply "out there" and veridically given.

14. EPISTEMOLOGY—The theoretical science concerning the nature of knowledge, in particular of scientific knowledge and of necessary logical truth; usually considered a branch of philosophical inquiry. For Piaget, epistemology is a problem open to scientific, particularly psychological, investigation.

15. EQUILIBRATION—The internal regulatory factor underlying a biological organization; it is manifested in all life, particularly in the development and activity of intelligence. Intelligence makes explicit the regulations inherent in an organization. As a process, it is the regulatory factor that unifies evolution and development; as a state (an equilibrium), it is a continuously changing balancing of active compensations.

16. FIELD EFFECTS—Perceptual phenomena occurring during a single centration of the sense organ. They can be considered as the momentary limit of perceptual activities.

17. FIGURATIVE KNOWLEDGE—Knowledge that focuses on the external, figural aspect of an event in a static manner, closely tied to a particular accommodation as illustrated in perception, imitation, image, memory. Figurative knowledge is conceivable only within a framework of operative knowing.

18. FORMAL OPERATION—Typically manifested in propositional thinking and a combinatory system that considers the real as one among other hypothetical possibilities. Formal operations are characteristic of the second and final stage of operational intelligence which "reflects" on concrete operations through the elaboration of formal "group" structures.

19. IMAGE—The internal representation of an external event. The image is one of the products of the symbolic function, hence of intelligence in its total functioning; it is not a mere trace from passive perception.

20. IMITATION—The figurative correspondence of motor activity to an external event. Imitation has three stages: (1) sensory-motor imitation, identical with perceptual accommodation, (2) deferred imitation (gesture) in the absence of the model, the beginning of symbol formation, (3) internalized imitation, the image.

21. INNATE—Present at birth or conception. "Innate" is frequently opposed to "learned," yet evolutionary learning is as true a learning as developmental acquisition. Innate behavior patterns are called instincts.

22. INTELLIGENCE—In the wide sense, the totality of possible coordinations that structure the behavior of an organism. Intelligence considered as a totality characterizes a given stage and is derived from the actual coordinations of a previous stage through formal reflecting abstraction. In a narrower sense, it is limited to operational intelligence, including sometimes the later stages of the sensory-motor period.

23. INTERIORIZATION—The eventual dissociation between the general form of a coordination and the particular content of an external action. Interiorization leads from "practical" to operational intelligence and is the precondition for objective knowledge as well as for symbolic representation.

24. INTERNALIZATION—The eventual diminution of external movements that become covert and sketchy, illustrated in imitation and language. Internalization leads to internal symbols; to be differentiated from interiorization. Piaget commonly uses the one French word *intériorisation* for both interiorization and internalization. English writers use both words interchangeably while meaning internalization.

25. KNOWLEDGE—The structuring of behavior as interchange between organism and environment. Behavior at every level implies a certain amount of knowledge on the part of the organism concerning the environment. General objective knowledge is identical with intelligence.

26. LANGUAGE—The natural spoken (and heard) symbol system of communication typical of a society. One of the manifestations of symbol functioning. Language is acquired and used like other symbol behavior and chiefly influences intelligence indirectly through the social, educative impact of society.

27. LEARNING—In the strict sense, acquisition of knowledge due to some particular information provided by the environment. Learning is inconceivable without a theoretically prior interior structure of equilibration which provides the capacity to learn and the structuring of the learning process; in the wide sense, it includes both factors.

28. LOGIC—As a formalized system, can be employed to describe the structuring spontaneously manifest in intelligent behavior. The internal consistency and necessity of logical judgments command our intellectual assent. There is a continuous genetic relation between mature logical forms and prelogical structures of early behavior.

29. LOGICAL POSITIVISM—A philosophical opinion that holds that logic and abstract intelligence are heavily dependent on the correct formali-

zation and use of language. Logical positivism is a modification of empiricism, which emphasizes language as the source of logical intelligence.

30.  MATURATION—Biological changes as a function of increasing age in the anatomical and physiological system, insofar as they determine behavioral development.

31.  MEMORY—In the strict sense, active knowledge that refers to a particular past; image evocation and recognition do not by themselves imply memory. In the wide sense, memory is the availability of any knowledge and merely expresses the fact that the conservation of a scheme is identical with the functioning of the scheme.

32.  OBJECT FORMATION—The scheme of the permanent object is the first most general invariant that constitutes initial objectivation, the presence of a thing "out there" independent of the child's own actions. The environment does not by itself provide objectively given reality. Object formation stands at the threshold of operational intelligence.

33.  OPERATION—In the strict sense, the characteristic interiorized generalizable action of mature intelligence; an operation implies a structure through which: (1) the resulting "knowing" need not be exteriorized as in sensory-motor intelligence, and (2) an operation is reversible—it can turn in an inverse direction and thus negate its own activity. In the wide sense, operational is here taken to include preoperational but exclude sensory-motor actions.

34.  OPERATIVITY—Contrasted with figurative knowledge it implies the action aspect of intelligence at all periods, including sensory-motor intelligence. Operativity is the essential, generalizable structuring aspect of intelligence insofar as knowing means constructing, transforming, incorporating, etc.

35.  ORGANIZATION—The most general expression of the form of a biological organism, a totality in which elements are related to each other and to the whole, the totality itself being related to a greater totality. The functioning of the organism gives content to the organization. All biological phenomena including intelligence and evolution find their basic explanation in the biological organization. An organization has intrinsic regulatory mechanisms.

36.  PERCEPTION—A knowing activity that is focused on the immediately given sensory data.

37.  PERCEPTUAL ACTIVITY—Regulations of sense organs during perception; a coordinating of successive centrations. Perceptual activities usu-

ally compensate for the momentary deformations of centration, thus are part of operative, more specifically sensory-motor intelligence.

38. PLAY—As a symbolic instrument, play expresses the knowing of the child who uses things or gestures in a symbolic manner, that is, not adapted to their proper function but assimilated to the child's ego-motivated representational activity.

39. PREOPERATIONAL—Often used to designate the period after the sensory-motor stage but prior to the formation of the first operations in the strict sense. The preoperational period is the preparatory part of the stage of concrete operational intelligence, characterized by the de-forming need for symbolic support, hence egocentrism.

40. REPRESENTATION—In the strict sense, "to represent" means "to make present something not present"; e.g., as in an image or symbolic play. In a somewhat inappropriate and misleading sense, "representational" is attributed to knowledge above the sensory-motor stage, insofar as it is no longer exclusively tied to external acts.

41. REVERSIBILITY—The possibility of performing a given action in a re-versed direction. Its two chief forms are negation (not male=female) and reciprocity (not better=worse). Reversibility is the criterion of an underlying operational structure.

42. SCHEME—The internal general form of a specific knowing activity, frequently, but not exclusively, used for sensory-motor intelligence. The generalizable aspect of coordinating actions that can be applied to analogous situations. Operations are nothing but the most general schemes of operational intelligence. Schemes are coordinated among themselves in higher-order structures or schemes. (Piaget distinguishes scheme from the term "schema," which conveys a representational outline, a figurative model. Schema is related to a figurative accom-modation or symbol; scheme, to operativity.)

43. SENSORY-MOTOR—The characteristic mode of knowledge of the first stage of intelligence in which the form of knowledge is tied to the content of specific sensory input or motoric actions. Also referred to as practical intelligence.

44. SIGN (SIGNIFIER, SIGNIFICATE)—An event that takes the place of another event as evidenced by its behavioral effect. A sign is a signifier and as such indicates another event called a significate. Sign behavior falls into two distinct categories according to whether the organism reacts to the sign as a signal or as a symbol.

45. SIGNAL—A signal is a substitute stimulus to which the organism reacts without differentiating the signifying sign from the significate. Hence,

it is an undifferentiated part of a global situation and the reaction is to the total situation, not to the signal as such. Sensory-motor intelligence corresponds to signal behavior, e.g., in conditioning, perceptual recognition, associative learning. A signal is also called an index.

46. STAGES—Successive developmental periods of intelligence, each one characterized by a relatively stable general structure that incorporates developmentally earlier structures in a higher synthesis. The regular sequence of stage-specific activities is decisive for intellectual development rather than chronological age.

47. STRUCTURE—The general form, the interrelatedness of parts within an organized totality. Structure can often be used interchangeably with organization, system, form, coordination.

48. SYMBOL, SYMBOLIC FUNCTION—A symbol is a sign that is differentiated from its significate. The symbolic function is the person's capacity to construct or produce a symbol for representing that which the person knows and which is not present. Consequently, any symbol, whether produced or comprehended, presupposes the constructive activity of operational thinking and depends on it; in turn, operations do not always require symbols. While a signal signifies the external event in an undifferentiated manner, the symbol signifies ("refers to") the thing-as-known. Piaget restricts the meaning of the word "sign" to linguistic or other conventional symbols and in contrast restricts the word "symbol" to an ego-involved signifier; he has recently renamed the symbolic function as the "semiotic function" in order to indicate that what he calls signs are also included in this function.

49. THINKING—Active intelligence or knowing, usually limited to operational (in the wide sense) activities.

50. TRANSFORMATION—As external transformation, refers to the constantly changing appearance of the physical world. As internal transformation, refers to knowing as constructing invariants through which external changes can be internally compensated for. Operations are internal transformations relative to an invariant and consequently they lead to an objective understanding of physical changes.

# index

Abstract-concrete distinction, 20, 183, 227
Abstraction:
  formal or reflective, 65-66, 75, 94, 197, 200, 214, 234, 248-49
  physical or experiential, 65, 197, 249
  as simple dissociation of external characteristics, 215
Accommodation, 85, 135-36, 145, 180, 245
  and learning, 229-31
Adaptation, 168-71, 176, 244-45
Affectivity, 206, 246 (see also Motivational aspect of behavior)
Affolter, F., 129
Ajuriaguerra, J. de, 129
Apostel, L., 128
Aristotle, 68, 78, 123
Assimilation, 13-14, 44-45, 85, 116, 177-78
  and habits, 29, 53-54
  and learning, 235-36
  and perception, 146-47
Ausubel, D. P., 99, 101

Baldwin, J. M., 46
Bang, Vinh, 25, 238
Bartlett, F. C., 152

Behavior, 170-72, 196, 245
  generalizable aspect as knowledge, 15-16, 56, 190, 244
Berlyne, D. E., 74
Bertalanffy, L. von, 33
Binet, A., 16, 112, 127, 221
Bovet, M., 99
Bruner, J. S., 74, 129
Brunswick, E., 123
Bühler, C., 125

Carnap, R., 123
Centration, perceptual, 144-47 (see also Field effects)
Chomsky, N., 109
Classification, 36-39, 63, 124
Concept, 53, 76-78, 178, 233
Concrete operations, 30-31, 63-64, 125, 213, 217-18
Conservation tasks, 30, 113-14, 125-26, 129, 213-14
Constancies, in perception, 138
Copernicus, N., 7
Cybernetics, 207-8

267

Darwin, C., 4, 7, 169, 172
Deaf people, 105, 119-20, 129
Descartes, R., 69-71, 79
Development (*see also* Intelligence, Learning):
  continuity-discontinuity, 17, 28, 100, 105
  factors contributing to, 33, 122, 127, 206-7, 227, 232
  obstacles to overcome, 50, 98, 211, 232
  stages, 17, 28-29, 161-62, 217, 246-47
Dewey, J., 59
Ditchburn, R. W., 145
Durkheim, E., 201

Education, 7
Egocentric, 112, 117
Einstein, A., 6
Empiricism, 19, 22, 71-72, 81, 233, 239
Epistemology, genetic, 23-24, 181, 202
Equilibration, 33, 187, 206-11, 222, 237-39, 246, 248
Etienne, A., 167
Evolution, 169, 184-92, 246

Field effects, 139-40, 144-47
Figural aspect of an event, 47, 249
Figurative knowing, 47, 58, 86, 103, 135-36, 180, 249 (*see also* Language, Learning, Memory)
  instruments, 141, 250
Form, dissociation from content, 51, 60, 190, 195, 231, 236, 245-48
Formal operations, 31-32, 127-28, 218, 247-48
Freud, S., 5-8, 13, 95, 172
Furth, H. G., 105, 118, 120

Galanter, E., 59, 74
Gestalt theory, 30, 73, 146
Goustard, M., 239
Grasse, P. P., 198
Group *and* Grouping, 26, 127, 217-18, 247-48

Harris, Z., 128
Hjelmslev, L. T., 128
Hume, D., 71
Hunt, J. McV., 103
Husserl, E., 194

Identity judgment, 158, 214-15
Image, symbolic, 90, 140-41
  studies, 142-43
Imitation, symbolic, 49, 212, 250

Inhelder, B., 10, 33, 80, 99, 104, 127, 129, 143, 214, 219
Innate intelligence, theory of, 19, 224-25, 231, 233
Innate knowledge, 186, 197, 224, 231
Innate releasing mechanism, 185
Inner speech, 118
Instinct, 186, 197-200
Instinctual coordinated movement, 185, 187
Intelligence:
  as behavior, 175-76, 245-47
  and development, 18, 173-74, 206, 210, 226, 246
  and evolution, 189-92
  and learning, 222-23
  practical, 51, 60, 230, 247
  tests, 4, 16, 220-23
Interiorization, 58, 61, 76, 78, 101
Internalization, 60, 73, 77-78, 90

James, W., 59

Kant, I., 24, 224
Knowing, Knowledge (*see also* Intelligence):
  structures of, 13, 17, 20-21, 75, 92, 178-79, 245
  as structuring aspect of behavior, 15, 170-72, 210, 246
  theory of:
    Piaget's 20, 75-78, 81, 93-94, 134, 210, 224-26
    traditional, 19, 68-73, 81, 92-93, 133-34, 149-50, 183-84, 209-10, 222-24, 231
Koehler, W., 146

Lamarck, J. B. de M., 169
Language, 108, 252
  and accommodation, 115-16
  acquisition, 114-17
  and assimilation, 116-17
  and classification, 122
  and conservation, 113-14, 129
  figurative aspect, 141
  and logical thinking, 103-105, 108, 119-20, 122-28, 252
  as symbolic function, 90, 109-10, 126
Learning, 220-39, 249
  and development, 33, 235-39
  and evolution, 186
  operative and figurative aspect, 227
  in two senses, 221-22, 236
Leibniz, G. W., 70-71
Locke, J., 71

Logic:
  of action, 47, 51, 125
  of functions, 97, 218
  and intelligence, 18-19, 26, 216-17, 248-49
  and necessity, 233, 248-49
Logical positivism, 75, 123
Lorenz, K., 24, 119, 148, 167, 170, 184, 186, 188-89, 192, 223, 239
Luria, A. R., 130

McCulloch, W. S., 200
Maturation, 19, 33, 207, 221, 223
Memory, 148-63, 250-51
  and accommodation, 156-63
  biological or general, 149
  and image, 150-52
  operative and figurative aspect, 151, 155-58
  studies of, 152-54
Meyer-Taylor, E., 31
Michotte, A., 146
Miller, G. A., 59, 74
Morf, A., 128
Morris, C. W., 123
Motivational aspect of behavior, 5, 15, 53, 95, 206-7, 228, 244 (see also Affectivity)

Nativism, see Innate intelligence
Nietzsche, F., 194
Noelting, G., 238
Nominal realism, 111
Numbers, knowledge of, 64

Object formation, 43, 46, 49, 62, 66, 76, 125, 211, 214, 231, 251
Objectivity, constructed by the subject, 7, 19, 54, 76
Object permanency, see Object formation
Oléron, P., 129
Operation(al), 26, 55-58, 61, 76, 96, 125, 247-48
Operativity, 57, 85-86, 101, 134-35, 231, 249
Organization, biological related to intelligence, 12-21, 66, 169-70, 195-97, 244-45
Osgood, C. E., 74

Papert, S., 208
Percept-concept distinction, 20
Perception, 86, 134-40, 250
  studies of, 137, 139-40
Perceptual activity, 137-40
Philosophy, 4, 9-11, 181, 222-24, 226-27
  (see also Empiricism, Epistemology,

Philosophy (cont.)
  Innate intelligence, Knowledge, Logical positivism, Positivism, Representation, Subject)
Piaget's empirical method, 25, 172, 212, 228
Plato, 194
Play, symbolic, 90, 95-96, 212
Positivism, 184, 224, 226-27
Preoperational, 57-58, 63, 85, 95-97, 208, 212
Pribram, K. H., 59, 74

Regulations:
  and intelligence, 196-200
  organic, 18, 21, 168, 194, 207, 245
  in perception, 140, 211
Representation:
  distinct from knowing, 20, 77-80, 92-95, 126, 252
  in philosophy, 69-72
  in two senses, 79, 101, 252
Reversibility, 26, 32, 62, 208
  and conservation, 213-15, 247
Rey, A., 121
Rubin, E., 146

Saussure, F. de, 108
Scheme, 29, 44, 53, 56, 124, 156-59, 163, 178-79, 229-30, 234
  distinct from schema, 95, 102
  perceptual, 145-47
Semiotic function, 77, 86
Sensory-motor stage, 29-30, 43-54, 124-25
  substages, 45-59
Seriation, 13-14, 64, 125
Sign and Sign relations, 86-87
Simon, T., 127
Sinclair, H., 68, 99, 113, 130
Smock, E. D., 99
Social behavior, 16-17, 107, 187, 201, 207
Spatial knowledge, 7, 33-36, 48-50, 136, 185-92, 197-200
Stages, see Development
S-R theory, 22, 44, 74
Subject, in theory of knowledge, 16, 193
Sutton-Smith, B., 99, 101, 103
Symbol:
  behavior, 91-92, 251
  derivation, 49, 101-2, 156
  distinct from signal, 87-89, 126, 251-52
  operative and figurative aspect, 77, 94-96, 100, 104
Symbolic function, 77, 86, 89, 99, 102, 126, 251
  instruments, 100, 110

Tanner, W. P., 33, 219
Tarde, G., 201
Tarski, A., 123
Thinking, as action, 55-56, 59-60
Tinbergen, N., 239
Titchener, E. B., 80
Togeby, K., 128
Tolman, E. C., 74
Transformations:
    in conservation tasks, 213-14
    operative, 54, 56, 60-61, 101, 159, 247

Verbal thinking, 111-13, 119
Viaud, G., 199
Vienna Circle, 123
Vincent, M., 129
Vocabulary test, 112
Vygotsky, L. S., 117

Wallon, H., 126
Watson, J. B., 123
Wolff, C., 70
Wundt, W., 80